KEROUAC, THE WORD AND THE WAY

KEROUAC, THE WORD AND THE WAY

PROSE ARTIST AS SPIRITUAL QUESTER

Ben Giamo

SOUTHERN ILLINOIS UNIVERSITY PRESS
CARBONDALE AND EDWARDSVILLE

Selections from the unpublished works of Jack Kerouac are reprinted by permission of
Sterling Lord Literistic, Inc. Copyright by the estate of Stella Kerouac, John Sampas,
Literary Representative. By arrangement with Sterling Lord Literistic, Inc.

Library of Congress Cataloging-in-Publication Data
Giamo, Benedict.
    Kerouac, the word and the way : prose artist as spiritual quester / Ben Giamo.
        p. cm.
    Includes bibliographical references (p.) and index.
    1. Kerouac, Jack, 1922–1969—Criticism and interpretation.
2. Autobiographical fiction, American—History and criticism. 3. Quests (Expeditions)
in literature. 4. Beat generation in literature. 5. Spiritual life in literature. I. Title.
PS3521.E735 Z634 2000
813'.54—dc21   99-053205
ISBN 0-8093-2321-4 (alk. paper)

The paper used in this publication meets the minimum requirements of American
National Standard for Information Sciences—Permanence of Paper for Printed Library
Materials, ANSI Z39.48-1992. ⊗

FOR DANIEL F. KIRK—
GONE, GONE BEYOND, GONE ALTOGETHER BEYOND,
O WHAT AN AWAKENING.

Don't think of me as a simple character—A lecher, a ship-jumper, a loafer, a conner of older women, even of queers, an idiot, nay a drunken baby Indian when drinking. . . . In fact, I don't even know *what* I was—Some kind of fevered being different as a snowflake. . . . In any case, a wondrous mess of contradictions (good enough, said Whitman) but more fit for Holy Russia of 19th Century than for this modern America of crew cuts and sullen faces in Pontiacs.

—Jack Kerouac, *Desolation Angels*

Contents

Preface

"Out of your sleep arise and wake." This is all I clearly recall from a dream the other night starring Jack (Kerouac) Duluoz, an old desolate angel come to me in airy midnight with laughter on his dust lips. He was babbling to me like the brook in *Big Sur* did to him some enlightened but incomprehensible message about something vital—in fact the key to all of this existence and suffering and folly and ranging madly to and fro in this show. I bent my ear to it, a whispering voice coming either out of the bottoms of my mind or the tops of pure land heavens. Perhaps it was a voice halfway between kingdom hall and the demons in hell. Whatever the case, my sleep consciousness was not getting it. Sounds washed over me like the syllables in Kerouac's "Sea" poem:

> Parle, parle, boom the
> earth——Arree——Shaw,

Sho, Shoosh, flut,
  ravad, tapavada pow,
coof, loof, roof,——
    No,no,no,no,no,no——
    Oh ya, ya, ya, yo, yair——
    Shhh——

What does he want to tell me? I wondered. What could be on his breath of mind? What is it I need to know? What is that one perfect word? Then a boom wave hits and sends me over the top: "Out of your sleep arise. Wake up!"

He never came again. In the meantime I have been trying to make sense of the Duluoz Legend (the body of Jack Kerouac's personalist fiction) during my waking hours. No less frustrating and tortured, since I start at the end point—*Big Sur*—and a peaceful retreat at Monsanto's (Ferlinghetti's) cabin that turns quickly into one assault after another upon his peace of mind amid the "insane shivering canyon." The first sign that something is dead wrong is when Duluoz takes a deep "Yogic breath" at the seashore and, instead of that ecstatic swoon of contentment, even enlightenment, gets nothing but two lungfuls of iodine. He seems poisoned by the rushing rhythm of the waves' sudden crash and hissing recess back into the deep undertow, becoming faint: "It comes over me in the form of horror of an eternal condition of sick mortality in me——In me and in everyone——I felt completely nude of all poor protective devices like thoughts about life or meditations under trees and the 'ultimate' and all that shit, in fact the other pitiful devices of making supper or saying 'What I do now next?'" (*Big Sur*, 41). In the absence of such "devices" aimed toward human enterprise, man is reduced to a pitiful show of "mortal hopelessness." Duluoz's entire nervous system electrifies such bald facts of existence so that, when he recalls himself collecting sounds of Pacific waves from a sea cave, he understands that he's been playing a "happy game" with notebook, pencil, and words. "All those marvelous skeptical things you wrote about graves and sea death it's ALL TRUE YOU FOOL! Joyce is dead! The sea took him! it will take YOU!" (*Big Sur*, 182). It's all downcrashing from this point on—a descent into alcoholic sickness (brought on by too much sweet skid row wine), delirium tremens, the paranoic madness that goes with the territory, nightmares, and throughout a hastening of death—the signposts on the landscape everywhere. The stunning natural beauty of Big Sur and the peaceful solitude of the cabin in the canyon are all made horrific by the agonizing fact of death-in-life.

I begin with these incidents from *Big Sur* because therein Kerouac presents his idealized persona of Duluoz in its most vulnerable state throughout the entire legend, which comprises twelve "true-story novels," a book of dreams, and a collection of prose sketches. Stripped of those "protective devices," Duluoz lacks the wherewithal to fend off or deny death. Religious belief, whether Catholicism or Buddhism, is of little consolation—until the very end of the novel when the vision of the cross wins out—after much painful contention between those ancient forces. Writing can no longer magnify the aesthetic distance. Solitude does not offer transcendence, and the hedonistic routs in San Francisco don't bring much escape—only more pain and trouble. Completely undone, Duluoz carries on like one of those human vulture demons from his feverish cabin nightmare. All directions, both seaward and leeward, seem to echo the beat of a classic Western mantra: *timor mortis conturbat me* (the fear of death distresses me). To put it mildly.

Although horrific mortality plays a central role in the Duluoz Legend, there were always several "devices" that Kerouac used (believed in and relied on) to keep it from wreaking havoc with his central character's very being. The root of Kerouac's deeply felt sense of existence—both its comings and goings—can be traced back to the death of his brother Gerard from rheumatic fever at age nine (Jack was four). Both the sight and knowledge of his saintly brother's death at such a tender age had a lifelong affect on Kerouac. It was the first major rupture in his life, and one that imprinted upon him both a sense of idealism—to "'write in honor of his death'"—and an abiding feeling of flesh-frail life: vain, transitory, and sad. In *Visions of Gerard*, a novel written in 1956 about his brother's death in their hometown of Lowell, Massachusetts, Kerouac indeed pays tribute to the memory of Gerard and the legacy he passed on to his younger brother: "He left me his heart but not his tender countenance and sorrowful patience and kindly lights" (62). For the most part, a fair and honest assessment, since Duluoz was more sinner than saint; in short, one of us—flawed and shattered. But compassion and sympathetic understanding—aspects of both "beat" and *"beato"* (beatitude)—are provinces of the heart, and Kerouac never fails to show them in his writing. Gerard left his younger brother a reverence for life and a self-ideal that aspired to be in a state of beatitude—"trying to love all life, trying to be utterly sincere with everyone, practicing endurance, kindness, cultivating joy of the heart" (*Good Blonde & Others,* 51). Kerouac's lasting appeal to readers, young and old, corresponds with Merton's assessment of Pasternak's attraction: "it is the man himself, the truth that is in him, his simplicity, his direct contact with life, and the fact that he is full of the only revolutionary force that is capable of producing anything new: he is full of love."[1]

Such intimate knowledge about the end of things—and the transient factor in the nature of existence—led Kerouac on a search for artistic and literary forms that would take the beat of experience from the inside out. To honor Gerard, Kerouac would celebrate life with a reverent attention to the immediacy of the moment as it passes through and refracts the light of a particular place; and "since we all wander through flesh," he would take seriously the spiritual-intellectual beauty and mixture of joy and sorrow inherent in and made vivid by the condition of impermanence. Kerouac was, above all, a ragged priest of the word, a prose artist on a spiritual quest for the ultimate meaning of existence and suffering and the celebration of joy in the meantime— when you can get it, and by all means get IT, he would no doubt say, for his "mind whirl[ed] with life."

With Kerouac, such a quest, and the qualities of the man it embodied, was represented variously through a sustained and creative experiment in literary form. Except for his first novel, indebted to the lyrical style of Thomas Wolfe, Kerouac avoided any trace of literary affectation or imitative shaping in his prose art. He was a natural—a very intuitive writer, and arguably the most passionate, revealing, and underrated innovator of American literature in the twentieth century. Kerouac's original prose styles reflected the forms of his search for personal meaning and spiritual intensity. The styles varied from an exuberant brand of conventional narrative (e.g., *On the Road, The Dharma Bums,* and *Desolation Angels*) to spontaneous bop prosody (e.g., *Visions of Cody, Doctor Sax,* and *The Subterraneans*). About half of the novels in the Duluoz Legend were written in a spontaneous prose style, best characterized by its stream of consciousness that joined with the torrential flow of experience. This inventive prose style was also more suitable for writing that was confessional and pure, charged with excitement and feeling ("getting out [the] guts and heart the way it *felt* coming out," as Kerouac once put it).[2] But whether "conventional" or spontaneous, Kerouac's prose art—with its sheer energy and rushing enthusiasm, natural rhythm, musical phrasing (when spoken), richly detailed imagery, and sonic jazz improvisation—constitutes a level of writing that, according to John Clellon Holmes, fellow beat chronicler, "was the acme of brilliance—cadenced, powerful, cresting toward an imminent beach."[3] "His talent as a writer," Ann Charters rightly observed, "was not his inventiveness with new characters and plots, but rather his power to dramatize the spirit of his own life into romantic fantasy."[4]

To recreate the "spirit" of experience into artistic legend through forms of prose art became *the way* to proceed with a mystical quest that was at the same time literary and visionary. In *On the Road*, Sal Paradise, giving voice to Kerouac's position, confesses his belief in the sanctity of everyday life: "Life is holy and every moment is precious" (57). Kerouac goes even further in *Visions of Cody*, an experimental recasting of *Road*. It is clear that the writer/traveler's fervent mission has been appointed from a higher authority:

> At the junction of the state of Colorado, its arid western one, and the state line of poor Utah I saw in the clouds huge and massed above the fiery golden desert of eveningfall the great image of God with forefinger pointed straight at me through halos and rolls and gold folds that were like the existence of the gleaming spear in His right hand, and sayeth, Go thou across the ground; go moan for man; go moan; go groan; go groan alone go roll your bones, alone; go thou and be little beneath my sight; go thou, and be minute and as seed in the pod, but the pod the pit, world a Pod, universe a Pit; go thou, go thou, die hence; and of [this world] report you well and truly. (295)

The "image of God with forefinger pointed" is lifted right out of the Old Testament; it could also be an embellishment of Revelation ("I was in the spirit on the Lord's day, and I heard behind me a loud voice saying, 'Write in a book what you see,'" etc.) applied to an American, mid-twentieth-century cross-country necessity to undergo the sacred ordeal of earth-travel, nation-travel, to subject oneself to the terrific nothingness of experience, put oneself in jeopardy with the abysmal world, to humbly take upon oneself the burden of Christ's cross, and "die hence." But don't stop there: cry out, make utterance, for a complete, honest, and sincere accounting is required. So return in another form—*honnête homme*—and do justice. Such a calling implies anything but a facile sojourn. As Holmes remarked on Kerouac's sense of mission and commitment, "I shrank back from [his] books. I feared for his mind out there. . . . His eye was like a fine membrane vibrating between the intolerable pressure of two walls of water: the consciousness flowing outward to absorb everything in the drench of thought; and reality flooding inward to drown everything but the language to describe it."[5] Trying to sum it all up, especially as the religious vision got more complex in the mid-1950s, Ginsberg referred to Kerouac as the "American lonely Prose Trumpeter of drunken Buddha Sacred Heart"[6]—a fairly accurate reading of Kerouac's artistic identity, human floppings, and blended scope of his spiritual quest. For Kerouac was primarily a religious writer, thoroughly antinomian and personalist, hell-bent on testing experience to its profane depths and transcendent heights in order to "report . . . well and truly." His overall purpose in writing was to glorify life and offer comfort and sustenance to readers despite the antagonisms, hostilities, defilements, contentions, and sorrows weathered on the road and in town and city.

Although Kerouac was baptized a French-Canadian Catholic and raised and buried a Catholic, he was also deeply influenced by Buddhism, particularly from early 1954 to 1957 when traditional Eastern belief was integrated into several novels and formed the basis for poetry, scripture, musings, and a biography of the historical Buddha. In an interview one year before his death, Kerouac reinforced the place of both Buddhism and Catholicism in his literary art:

> What's really influenced my work is the Mahayana Buddhism, the original Buddhism of Gotama Sakyamuni, the Buddha himself, of the India of old. . . . Zen is what's left of his Buddhism, or Bodhi, after passing into China and then into Japan. The part of Zen that's influenced my writing is the Zen contained in the haiku. . . . But my serious Buddhism, that of ancient India, has influenced that part in my writing that you might call religious, or fervent, or pious, almost as much as Catholicism has. Original Buddhism referred to continual conscious compassion, brotherhood, the dana paramita meaning the perfection of charity.[7]

Kerouac's study and absorption of primary Buddhist material was a serious undertaking, and it was not solely in the service of his literary art. As he wrote in a letter to Malcolm Cowley (6 August 1954) soon after his discovery of Mahayana Buddhist teaching: "Since I saw you I took up the study of Buddhism and for me it's *the word* and *the way* I was looking for" (*Selected Letters, 1940–1956,* 430; emphasis mine). The combination of "the word" and "the way," and the overall Buddhist influence on the design of Kerouac's Duluoz Legend demands further attention. Kerouac's Buddhism may have been a "tangled and personal matter," as Charters comments in her biography; and, certainly, the juxtaposition of Buddhism and Catholicism occurs frequently (see, for example, *Tristessa* and *Visions of Gerard*). But it is also clear that Kerouac's expression of Buddhism and Catholic personalism in his work remains among the most powerful evocations and energetic expositions of traditional Eastern and Western belief in modern American literature. To put it all together into one codified yak phrase, Kerouac was a Canuck Catholic-Buddhist Beat Mystic. If you don't believe me, check his passport, right under the heading stamped Passing Through.

In a letter to Bob Lax (26 October 1954), Kerouac expressed his deep involvement with Buddhist teaching. The attainment of enlightenment and the "emancipation of all suffering," Kerouac wrote, ". . . can only be achieved in solitude, poverty, and contemplation—and in a gathering of homeless brothers." Kerouac wanted to match word with deed by living in a hut in the desert in order to "prove at last by example" (*Selected Letters,* 447–48).[8] He also divulged to Lax his aspiration to be a bodhisattva: "I intend to ascend by stages & self-control to the Vow to help all sentient beings find enlightenment and holy escape from the sin and stain of life-body itself." A notebook entry for that same year reveals Kerouac's short- and long-term plan for a "Modified Ascetic Life" and the consummation of incomparable enlightenment. Starting off with some immediate obstacles to leading the ascetic life, Kerouac would first beg off the sensual lifestyle—swearing off women-lust and drunken booze-binges. Not even "sipping" would be tolerated by the end of 1954. During 1955, he would work on his diet—moving from meat and potatoes to mostly vegetarian fare. Then, after completing a five-volume life work by 1956, Kerouac would embrace the Buddhist doctrine of *anatta* (no self) by doing "no more writing for communicating, . . . no more writing or I art-ego of any kind, finally no I-self, or Name." Thus divested of passions and the notion of a persisting self, in 1970 this man-with-no-name-no-title would become a homeless religious wanderer replete with wilderness robe. Finally, with a good sense for round numbers and the symbolism of the millennium, the year 2000 would witness "nirvana and willed death beyond death" (*Selected Letters,* 448n). When considering the raucous and troubled life that Kerouac led as the living embodiment of the Beat Generation, and his later drift into alcoholic home life, the notion of such a pilgrimage becomes even more endearing with time.

To see someone aim so high and land so low also tends to make one desperate. Desperate for what? Perhaps for some assurance that this cannot be, that this cannot happen to me. But there is no guarantee in life, and literature only makes the pain somewhat easier to bear. For Kerouac, as Richard Hill perceptively relates, "drinking was part of his pilgrimage": "He was a sensitive soul who'd set his sights on nothing less than enlightenment. When the booze failed to take him there, it at least numbed the disappointment. . . . And though he gave into his drinking, he never completely abandoned his search. His record of that search reminds us why we value him so much. It was a sacrifice from which most of us shrink, a gift for which he paid the highest price."[9] Such a sacrifice, although at heart personal, also speaks to a sense of vicarious atonement, for Kerouac's "perfect craving to believe" is a brilliant light snuffed out in the spiritual vacuum of American culture. In dying out of his time, he acted out his pain in the world, acted out the pain of the world. The insatiable craving was fed by the loss of the transcendent as a context in which truth, grace, and peace can be attained. In his review of *On the Road,* Gilbert Millstein, applying a passage from John Aldridge's *After the Lost Generation,* clarifies the relationship between literary figure and cultural setting: Kerouac embodies "the need for belief even though it is upon a background in which belief is impossible and in which the symbols are lacking for a genuine affirmation in genuine terms."[10] When combined with Kerouac's own mercurial personality and French-Canadian background, perhaps this absence of cultural reinforcement helps to explain why—in the end—he was much less the bodhisattva and much more the penitential martyr. Yet, who really knows? Perhaps he got to (pure land) heaven before they closed the door.

In light of this condition, the primary purpose of this book is to chronicle and clarify the various spiritual quests undertaken by Kerouac—as revealed by his novelistic writings. I realize that the persona in the fiction is a fervent self-ideal, but isn't this precisely what religious passion nurtures? *On the Road* is the real kick-start of the quest and so signals my actual point of departure, though I begin properly in the introduction with the first novel—*The Town and the City*—for an appreciation of important foundational themes, spiritual struggles, and stylistic shifts. *Big Sur* is the final turning point with respect to the course of Kerouac's search and so serves as my endpoint. Part one ("Road, Town, and City") deepens the discussion of Kerouac's Catholic mysticism and takes the beat of his bohemian impulses in the early novels written between 1951 and 1953, including *Visions of Cody, Doctor Sax,* and *The Subterraneans.* Part two ("The Noble Path") traces the infusion of Buddhist teaching in the progression of Kerouac's work. This involves a discussion of *Tristessa, Visions of Gerard,* and *The Dharma Bums,* all written between 1955 and 1957. Part three ("The Lifelong Vulture and the Little Man") examines the conflictual, uneven nature of the fervent quest that culminates in the completion of *Desolation Angels* and the writing of *Big Sur* in 1961. Although Kerouac wrote and published two more novels during the sixties (*Satori in Paris* and *Vanity of Duluoz*), these works, which I discuss briefly in the afterword, neither extend nor deepen the quest for a beatific vision of unified being. Rather, they remind us of Yeats's prophetic vision: "The painter's brush consumes his dreams."

Along the way, through an exploration of the defining novels in the Duluoz Legend, I undertake the search for IT—its various meanings, paths, and oscillations: from romantic lyricism to "the ragged and ecstatic joy of pure being," and from the void-pit of the Great World Snake to the joyous pain of amorous love, and, finally, from Catholic/Buddhist serenity to the onset of penitential martyrhood.[11] My approach to writing the book entails a combination of literary criticism (based on close readings of the novels) and modulation of perspective; the latter is meant to convey the meditative moment and my own emotional understanding of Jack Kerouac as prose artist. Despite the various orientations, styles, and thematic emphases of the works in question, each novel satisfies Kerouac's favorite definition of literature, that is, "the tale that's told for companionship and to teach something religious, of religious reverence, about real life, in this real world which literature should (and here does) reflect" (*Satori in Paris,* 10).[12] I can think of no better admonishment to the present state of the American novel and the critical discourse that aims to displace it into the warp of virtual unreality.

A recent issue of the *New Yorker* claims that "the cruelest thing you can do to Kerouac is reread him at thirty-eight."[13] Well, having read and reread all that Kerouac (and his estate) ever published after I turned forty-one, I don't feel like I've injured anyone, myself included. If anything, Kerouac should not be read (or reread) until one turns forty. The *New Yorker's* facile sentiment distorts the memory of Kerouac's achievement, recycling a popular myth that conceals the merits of his prose art and the beauty of a quest that reflects both exaltation and terror.

I am grateful to John Sampas, literary representative of the Kerouac estate, for permission to quote from Jack Kerouac's notebooks, journals, letters, and unpublished manuscripts housed in the Henry W. and Albert A. Berg Collection of English and American Literature, the New York Public Library. Rodney Phillips, curator of the collection, was most helpful in digging out all of the Kerouac material and making it available for my perusal. Also, special thanks is extended to Robert Cowley for permission to quote from the Malcolm Cowley papers at the Newberry Library in Chicago: copyright © by the Literary Estate of Malcolm Cowley. I want to express my appreciation to the Institute for Scholarship in the Liberal Arts, University of Notre Dame, for their help in defraying the cost of permission fees and indexing.

I owe special gratitude to the outstanding efforts of Ann Charters, Kerouac's first biographer and the editor of *The Portable Jack Kerouac Reader, The Portable Beat Reader,* and *Jack Kerouac: Selected Letters.* Quite frankly, my own understanding of Kerouac would have been hampered without such easy access to these invaluable letters.

Rev. Andre Leveille, C.S.C., was most generous with his time and helped me to grasp the important features of French-Canadian Catholic culture. The historical and theological context he provided had direct bearing on my understanding of the ethnic, regional, and religious forces that shaped Kerouac's outlook. I am also appreciative of the spirited support offered by Dori Clemens, Marty Moran, Ryan Smith, Sharon Wise, and Mark Yasenchack. A few very special people come to mind—Dan Kirk, Tim Labuda, and Jim Quirk. Without their good friendship, intelligent conversation, and inspiring wit, I might never have gotten IT.

Abbreviations

In this book, the following abbreviations are used for frequently cited works by Jack Kerouac:

BS	*Big Sur*
BB	*Book of Blues*
DA	*Desolation Angels*
DB	*The Dharma Bums*
DS	*Doctor Sax*
GB	*Good Blonde & Others*
MCB	*Mexico City Blues*
OTR	*On the Road*
SIP	*Satori in Paris*
SGE	*The Scripture of the Golden Eternity*
SL	*Selected Letters, 1940–1956*
SOD	*Some of the Dharma*
VOD	*Vanity of Duluoz*
VOC	*Visions of Cody*
VOG	*Visions of Gerard*

Introduction:
The Sorrows of Young Kerouac

"I have always wanted to write epics and sagas of great beauty and mystic meaning," Kerouac wrote to Bill Ryan in early 1943 (*SL*, 36). His first novel, *The Town and the City*, written between 1946 and 1948 and published in 1950 under the name John Kerouac, realizes this wish both in terms of the broad scope of subject matter—the saga of the Martin family in Depression and World War II America—and the full-bodied flowing lines borrowed from Thomas Wolfe in which the tale is rendered.[1] The novel is long and symphonic, divided into five major movements, and, yes, a river runs through it "continually fed and made to brim out of endless sources and unfathomable springs." The lyrical thaws of time and the river loosen a conventional form of ecstasy that feed Kerouac's youthful melancholy, nostalgia, warmth, and sense of the unknown, "and he ponders the wellsprings and sources of his own mysterious life" (3). The novel is Kerouac's first and last attempt to write deliberately in a standard fictionalized mode: third-person omniscient, with great attention to setting, plot, subplot, dramatic tension, multicharacter development, and romantic sensitivity to the mutability of nature. The result is a very muscular novel, profound and beatific, despite the rather conventional mold and derivative style—and not only the strong influence of Wolfe, but echoes of Stephen Crane, Theodore Dreiser, and F. Scott Fitzgerald can be heard as well.

Steeped in the tragic thaws of the Martin family and its eventual dissolution during World War II, when the "children were scattered like lights in the land," the novel initiates Kerouac's lifelong concern with dislocation and exile. In short, the pain of growing up, leaving the cocoon of small-town family life, and facing "what a strange sad adventure life might get to be." The Martin family is a much larger invention than Kerouac's own family of one brother and one sister.[2] Although the parents are based on Kerouac's own family, the Martin children—six sons and three daughters—are drawn from composites of relatives and friends; moreover, though Peter Martin is a projection of the young John Kerouac, the author also seems to split himself among brothers Joe, Francis, and Mickey. John Clellon Holmes, who was close to Kerouac at the time the novel was written—in fact read the work in manuscript form and praised it, wrote about the experience that underwrote *The Town and the City*: "I never fully understood the hunger that was gnawing in him then, and didn't realize the extent to which the breakup of his Lowell home, the chaos of the war years and the death of his father [in 1946], had left him disrupted, anchorless; a deeply traditional nature thrown out of kilter, and thus enormously sensitive to anything uprooted, bereft, helpless or persevering: a nature intent on righting itself through the creative act."[3]

The creative act pairs the vitality, absorption, and kinship of the Martin clan in Galloway (read Lowell, Massachusetts) with the impersonal, centrifugal forces that pull it apart. "Together there was never really cause for anything but rejoicing, the sheer force and joy of their numerous presence was in itself a surging enthusiasm, they looked at each other and knew each other well in that casual, powerful, silent way that brothers and sisters, parents and children have" (204–5). Throughout parts one and two of the novel, despite threats to familial unity, such as Joe's wanderlust, Peter's collegiate life and dreams of greatness, and the father's bankruptcy, the family still gathered round, members pitched in to stave off hard times, and together in communal bond they "roared with laughter." Eventually, however, the center does not hold, and the strong sense of community solidified in the town is undermined in parts three and four of the novel as war and life in New York City not only diffuse but distort the "lights." Part five concludes the novel with the death of the father, George Martin, and a brief reunion at his funeral. For Peter Martin, the main protagonist of the novel, the father's death is a major turning point in the direction of his life and convictions.

Throughout the novel, Kerouac presents the human condition in its physical, spiritual, and moral bearing. Behind such manifestations of life, one feels the expansive force of a mysterious presence tugging at the souls of the characters and spiritualizing their very existence. There is a Catholic religious aura that envelopes the story that is more personalist than official and hierarchical. While the mother teaches the "legend" of the Catholic faith, offering her children various degrees of formal involvement in the religion, the father argues with an old priest against the hypocrisy of the church, stating his preference for no earthly go-between: "I don't see how the church can come between a man and his God without somewheres breaking the direct contact" (42). Given such an influence, the triumphalist, hieratic forms of official religious belief become less important than the holy essence that underlies belief itself.

Though they may not understand it, none of the characters escape this spiritualization of existence. They are acted upon by IT, a vital force in the experience of living that takes one by surprise, suspending for the moment belief in the "real" concrete grey everyday facts of self and selfhood. As she's calling her children to supper, Marguerite Martin gets absorbed into the "otherworldly red light of late afternoon. . . . And she had paused, uneasy, standing there on the porch in that strange red light, and she had wondered who she really was, and who these children were who called back to her, and what this earth of the strange sad light could be" (25). Even the father, George, "a man of a hundred absorptions," true forerunner of Dean Moriarty in *On the Road*, enfolded in his own mad frenzy of running a printing business, playing the horses, visiting barbers, bars, and friends, supervising pool room and bowling alley, gambling at card games into the wee hours of the night, and raising a family to boot—"he wants to do everything, he does everything"—finds himself often lost in reverie. "There was something in Martin's heart that never ceased its wondering and sorrow. There were days when everything he saw seemed etched in fading light, when he felt like an old man standing motionless in the middle of this light and looking around him with regret and joy at all the people and things in his world." Stunned by the oddity and brevity of life, "he gazed brooding at his children, and wondered what it was that weaved and weaved and always begat mysteries, and would never end" (44–45).

What is it we do not know that is so true? Kerouac seems to ask this of his characters as they momentarily dematerialize into the claims of wonder, awe, mystery—their souls erupting to flash in the light of a bewildering fate that is not discounted nor limited to the conditioned knowledge of the political or social or psychological. As George Martin puts it when stunned by such thought, "This is it. . . . This is the way life is." Joe, the eldest son, racked by "a thousand raging enthusiasms," is also enfolded in his soul and wants something beyond the wild desires of his restless, brooding heart, though he cannot name it and doubts whether he can truly find it. "To all his friends and to his family he was just Joe—robust, happy-go-lucky, always up to something. But to himself he was just someone abandoned, lost, really forgotten by something, something majestic and beautiful that he saw in the world" (67). And Peter, the ambitious all-American football player, off to college on a scholarship, dreaming of "winning the awe of all," expresses Kerouac's strong personal identification with the "suffering and heroic, dark, dark Jesus and his cross, . . . he had wept at the spectacle of that heroic sorrow, and Jesus arisen triumphant, immortal, radiant and true" (121). While Francis, Peter's cynical slightly older brother, registers disbelief—"I don't believe in mysteries," Mickey, Peter's youngest brother, imagines himself as the Christ child in the manger at Christmas, with a growing awareness of the infant's fate and that "he [Mickey] too must suffer and be crucified like the Child Jesus" (178).

The heroic sorrows of young Kerouac are concentrated in the spiritual struggles of Peter Martin and his growing awareness of the cruel disruptions of history, the caprice of family members, the too-huge world beyond Galloway, the personal changes wrought by time and distance, the conflict between the values of town and city—old and young America, and of course the suffering associated with impermanence and death. In part three of the novel, the upheavals of the times begin to burst, slinging Peter and the other characters willy-nilly into the crooks and crannies of *terra incognita*. Because of a mixture of choice and necessity, decisive action propels the characters to move on: Peter's small-town friends are whisked away by the Army, his sister Liz elopes with a jazz musician and later divorces him to become an independent singer, another sister—Rosy—heads for a West Coast nursing school, the parents change dwellings with the younger children as the father jobs around, Joe joins up, and Francis enlists in the Navy after graduating from college (only to be discharged for feigned psychiatric reasons). Away at college, Peter, more interested in *life* than the lab or practice field, decides on an impulse to quit both football and school. In one stroke, he snuffs out all the hope and pride and great expectations his father had for him and instead finds work as a grease monkey near town. Caught up in the fervor of the war, he soon joins the merchant marine, which gives him the mobility and adventure his heart desires. But it also plays havoc with his sense of continuity and identity: "'Five weeks ago I was in Casablanca, four months ago I was in Liverpool, a year ago I was at the North Pole! Arctic Greenland; who ever heard of Arctic Greenland! And before that? I was a crazy kid, rushing back from scrimmage to eat big meals in my mother's kitchen at home. What a simple good little guy I used to be. What happened? Is it the war? Where am I going, the way I do things, why is everything so strange and far away now?'" (336). In New York City, where Peter repairs (to Manhattan), and where the Martins of Galloway now live (in Brooklyn), that strange feeling of discontinuity and fragmentation seeks complete evaporation: "Everything that he had ever done in his life, everything there was—was haunted now by a deep sense of loss, confusion, and strange neargrief. . . . —because it was no more" (359).

Such sorrows surrounding the ghostly void of lostness, however, give birth to the energized joy of new beginnings—new friends, loves, parents to know and meet again in the city. "What was all the excitement and mystery and sadness in his soul?" In looking into the enigmatic nature of human reality—the shifts and shakes of contingency—and into the varied nature of his own complex self, Peter plunges into a realization of a cosmic nature that might explain "the eyes of all human beings so . . . loathsome somehow, so wondrous and sweet." What creative force could both account and honor this life in all its varieties of experience and mood? "Something complete, and wise, and brutal too, had dreamed this world into existence, this world in which he wandered haunted. Something silent, beautiful, inscrutable had made all this for sure, and he was in the middle of it, among the children of the earth. And he was glad" (360–61).

Kerouac's vision of the divine resembles Pascal's Jansenistic-tinged view of the Christian god; "he is a God who fills the soul and heart of those whom he possesses; he is a God who makes them inwardly conscious of their wretchedness and of his infinite mercy; who unites himself with them in the depths of their soul; who fills it with humility, with joy, with trust, with love."[4] Kerouac suggests this traditional view of the divine (commensurate with the stable civic order of the town) and then proceeds to cleverly set it down in the drenching bohemian undersea world of New York City and Times Square. Peter Martin is drawn into this scene and the "great molecular comedown" of maddening Spenglerian visions offered by his friend Leon Levinsky (Allen Ginsberg). The energy behind the challenging social vision is wild and explosive, and the vision itself decadent and beat. It is all telescoped into the Nickel-O, an amusement center on Times Square where occur "'the final scenes of disintegrative decay: old drunks, whores, queers, all kinds of characters, hoods, junkies, all the castoffs of bourgeois society milling in there.'"

> "You see how bright the lights are?—they have those horrible bluish neons that illuminate every pore of your skin, your whole soul finally, and when you go in there among all the children of the sad American paradise, you can only stare at them, in a Benzedrine depression, . . . or with that sightless stare that comes with too much horror. All faces are blue and greenish and sickly livid. In the end, everyone looks like a Zombie, you realize that everyone is dead, locked up in the sad psychoses of themselves. It goes on all night, everyone . . . seeking each other . . . but so stultified by their upbringings somehow, or by the disease of the age, that they can only stumble about and stare indignantly at one another." (369)

Levinsky goes on to explain the atom-smashing physics underlying the sordid vision of the Nickel-O and the resulting "'feelings of spiritual geekishness: It's the great molecular comedown. . . . It's really an atomic disease, you see. . . . It's death finally reclaiming life, the scurvy of the soul at last, a kind of universal cancer. . . . Everybody is going to fall apart, disintegrate, all character-structures based on tradition and uprightness and so-called morality will slowly rot away. . . . Don't you see, it's just the beginning of the end of the Geneseean world'" (370–71). Peter, amused and skeptical and, for the moment, molecularly intact, admits to himself that Levinsky may be on to something: "For a moment he was almost afraid that there was some truth in Levinsky's insane idea, certainly he had never felt so useless and foolish and sorrowful before in his life."

As if to enact the vision, Levinsky and Martin take a subway ride uptown. During the ride, Levinsky, in an effort to expose the "paranoid persecution" madness latent in humanity, victimizes the underground passengers with his "magical newspaper performance," in which he singles out someone and stares intently through a hole in the paper. "There, with an awful shock, instead of headlines [one] saw a great living picture, the beady glittering eyes of a madman burning triumphantly." The prank has the intended effect on most passengers, and Peter realizes "the small pitiable truth in [Levinsky's] statement that everyone in the subway was somewhat insane." But the experiment was not a total success, and this grants Peter some levity and release, for there were those who enjoyed the performance, who "stared with delight at Levinsky's antics." A little boy actually joins in the performance, sticking his head in the other side of the hole in the newspaper, a funny face-off that Leon did not bargain for. This act breaks the spell of the mad magic, causing it to backfire, as now Levinsky becomes the one to fidget and blush. Leon rationalizes: children cannot recognize madness. But for Peter, and for Kerouac, the incident restores a primal belief in the innocent goodness of humanity, for Levinsky's predicted molecular comedown mutated into his comeuppance. The vision of the Nickel-O is thus suspended and absorbed into a more cosmic reality: "When he last saw him, Levinsky was standing there among the subway crowds, gaping around and musing darkly about the puzzle of himself and everybody else, as he would always do" (376–79).

Although Peter does not dismiss outright Levinsky's vision of the Nickel-O, his own sense of divine oneness in the order of the world leads him to accept the view from the bottom of the city without making invidious distinctions. Taking in the view of Times Square addicts, hoodlums, zoot-suiters, drifters, panhandlers, and assorted denizens, Peter reflects a Christ-like identification with the outcasts: "He knew all these things and they were impressed in his heart, they horrified him. These were only some of the lives of the world, yet all the lives of the world came from the single human soul, and his soul was like their souls. He could never turn away in disgust and judgment" (363–64). As Peter is drawn even further into the interesting and complex beat subculture, he lives out a bohemian version of the decadent vision. Will Dennison (William S. Burroughs), Junkey (Herbert Huncke), Kenneth Wood (Lucien Carr), Waldo Meister (David Kammerer), and others illuminate their unconventional urban underworld lives and "morbid demonisms" to him. The events that transpire document the first appearance of the "Beats" in literature—the spark that helped to ignite the cultural revolution of the 1960s. But for Kerouac, that spark was the light of revealed truth and the revolutionary thrust of Catholic tradition engulfing new cultural forms of being and expression. As Merton asserts, there is always this kind of revolutionary force inherent in the tradition, especially given its opposition to the egocentric desires and obsessions of humankind: money, prestige, possessions, power, knowledge, etc. If one is to follow Christ's example of poverty, humility, and suffering (a trinity that captivated Kerouac even as he moved into his Buddhist phase), one has no choice but to practice renunciation and wander in the ruins of materialistic American civilization. "'Be poor, go down into the far end of society, take the last place among men, live with those who are despised, love other men and serve them instead of making them serve you . . . and look for God in hunger and thirst and darkness.'"[5] Seen in this light, Peter's earlier decision to quit sport and college, a defining moment in his life that cut off the sure path to staid bourgeois comforts, can be viewed as his first true act of renunciation.

Peter's deepening involvement in the beat subculture, however, is not without its conflicts, and therein lies the tension between the town and the city, between traditional and modern social mores and values—all prophesied by Levinsky. This conflict creates a post–World War II generation gap ̇embodied in the growing rift between George and Peter Martin, father and son. George Martin, bewildered by the youth of the city, states his moral argument to his son: "Understand— this generation *knows* right and wrong, they sense it all right and that's probably why they do so many crazy things, like those friends of yours. It makes them jumpy and neurotic. But they don't *believe* in right and wrong. There's a big difference there—and what I'd like to know is how this all came about. . . . What are they teaching nowadays that's doing so much, *so much* to separate the children of this generation from their parents?" (408–9). In part, Mr. Martin attributes the lack of responsibility, concern, and hope among the young to the malaise caused by the war. And he accuses his son Peter of hanging around with "dope fiends and crooks and crackpots." "'Still sold on them, hey?'" Peter defends himself and his choice of friends, chalking it up to curiosity: "'they aren't exactly like the boys who used to hang around the barbershop with you in Galloway, you know. This is New York. . . . I only mean that these guys . . . have more on their minds— they're smarter in some ways—more interesting in some ways—you might say modern.'" Although the old man clearly doesn't buy it, the son rages on:

> "I don't swallow that stuff about curiosity, Peter. . . . I don't know what's happened to you, frankly. It all went wrong long ago, you're another victim . . ."
>
> "I do whatever I like! If I'm curious, I am! If I'm interested in certain people, I am! I'm not a victim of anything! I'm going to live in this world, I'm going to find out all about it, I'm not going to hide my eyes like a maiden in distress, or like an old Puritan either, or like a scared rabbit! I'm interested in life, any kind of life, all of it!. . . . Ever since I can remember you've been telling me what *not* to do, what *not* to do. But you never did tell me *what* to do!"
>
> "I'm not God, I can't tell you what to do, all I can tell you is what I *think* you should do—. . . . For all I know you'll end up a dope fiend yourself, a bum, a tramp, no better than the ones you hang around with. You threw away an education, you make a little money on ships and you spend it drinking and supporting a little slut—"
>
> "She's not that at all. . . . It's just another way of saying I'm a no-good bum, go ahead and admit it! So I drink, all right, I have my rea-

sons! What's the great thing we're supposed to be living for now anyway? What's the great faith, hope and charity of the age that's been dumped on our heads—" (418–22).

And so it goes, on into the early morning, but before the argument ends Mr. Martin gets the last thought in: "'Something *evil* and awful has happened, there's nothing but unhappiness everywhere. And the *coldness* of everybody!'" (423). The metropolitan stamp of indifference is a far cry from the innocence, closeness, warmth, and "*real* lives" of the working people of Galloway. The social distance is registered every time the Martins look up from their basement flat in Brooklyn and witness a huge advert laid out in crude design, revealing a man "holding his head in despair. Some indistinct writing beside him, blurred and dirtied by weathers and soot, proclaimed the indispensability of some forgotten medicine" (343). (The eyes of Fitzgerald's Dr. Eckleberg from *The Great Gatsby* get fleshed out by Kerouac two decades later.) In an attempt to reverse the familial temperature, Peter suddenly invites his parents out to dinner with him and his girlfriend. Mr. and Mrs. Martin are stunned into acceptance. As Peter leaves for Manhattan, he is in no way embittered by the heated discourse with his father. Catching sight of his father from the street, enshrouded in his literal subterranean Brooklyn gloom, lifts Peter back again to the transcendent level of existence. The son steps lively into a subway reverie, where thoughts float up and coalesce, binding all those moral questions and generational differences into an encompassing framework—the felt and intellectual experience of the divine in humankind. "'The most beautiful idea on the face of the earth . . . is the idea the child has that his father knows everything'":

> In the subway he brooded over the thought that *that* must be the idea men had always had of God. But he recalled sorrowfully that when the child grew up and sought advice he got only fumbling earnest human words, when the child sought a way of some sort he only found that his father's way was not enough, and the child was left cold with the realization that nobody, not even his father, really knew what to do. And yet, that children and fathers should have a notion in their souls that there must be a way, an authority, a great knowledge, a vision, a view of life, a proper manner, an order in all the disorder and sadness of the world—that alone must be God in men. (423–24)

The dialectical process—the friction of town and city—sharpens Peter's insight into a universal truth, a mystical understanding of a living God based on Catholic tradition, that he will pursue and absorb. Peter gives assent to such faith and to Merton's notion that "God himself is infinite actuality and therefore infinite Truth, Wisdom, Power and Providence, and can reveal Himself with absolute certitude in any manner."[6] First, however, the disorder and darkness must deepen before the individual and personal knowledge of *the way* reveals itself with any kind of clarity and definite purpose to Peter. In the novel, such disorder and darkness occur back-to-back. To begin with, Peter's involvement with the beat crowd eventually culminates in his being ensnared in a scandal—the suicide of Waldo Meister (in actuality, Waldo—David Kammerer—was killed by Lucien Carr in retaliation for his amorous harassments). Peter (as was Kerouac) is called in by police as a material witness and asked to identify the badly bruised and mashed body. The whole affair awakens Peter to the sordidness of his city life, and he longs for the sounds of an older and more earnest America: "voices without sarcasm and weariness and disgust, strong voices telling in a long way the chronicle of labor and belief and human joy" (432). However, the hope for the assured voices of the frontier and town weaken in the wake of his father's failing health. After a period of self-imposed exile, Peter finally returns to his family in Brooklyn so that he can be with his father who is dying. In the process, Peter makes a pivotal moral decision and resolves to nurture those values that he finds more aligned with his Catholic spiritual sensibility:

> A sharp knowledge had now come to him of the tragic aloneness of existence and the need of beating it off with love and devotion instead of surrendering to it with that perverse, cruel, unnecessary self-infliction that he saw everywhere around him, that he himself had nursed for so long.
>
> His father was dying—and his own life was dying, it had come to a dead end in the city, he had nowhere else to go. Peter did not know what to do with his own life but somehow he knew what to do about his father, who was now not only his father, but his brother and his mysterious son too. (468)

In going home, Peter establishes that sense of togetherness again, restoring familial unity. But such togetherness is no longer the occasion for rejoicing. Rather, an atmosphere of debilitation, pain, and loss pervades, along with the values of care and compassion, the poignant bond of our mortality. Living at home in Brooklyn, Peter takes on "a lonely dishrag of a night-time job that ticked away in the dreary midnights of city-time and city-blackness." Time itself and the ultimate all-unknowing blankness that it promises is now the antagonist, dissolving the opposition between town and city into eerie images of "gray dawns" and "pale flowers." George Martin, "wasting away throughout the Winter and into the Spring in the midst of dreadful wreckage," gives God a good talking-to during the odd, sleepless nights: "He raised his face mournfully to the poor cracked ceiling of midnight, he looked at heaven through the plaster-cracks of Brooklyn."

> He asked God why he had been made by Him, for what purpose, for what reason the flower of his own face and the fading of it from the earth forever; why life was so short, so hard, so furious with men, so impossibly mortal, so cruel, restless, sweet, so deadly. And he talked to the lone self that would die with him for always. . . . And when Peter came back in the mornings, the old man asked him what had happened all night in the cafeteria. . . . And then father and son looked at each other, and talked about the past, all the things in the million-shadowed blazing past, and about what they would like to do, what they might have done, what they should do now. . . . At these times they experienced moments of contentment talking to each other. This was the last life they would ever know each other in, and yet they wished they could live a hundred lives and do a thousand things and know each other forever in a million new ways, they wished this in the midst of their last life. (469–71)

Caring for his father and sharing their final moments together helps Peter to grow and recognize the fundamental virtues of living—what IT's all about. "He saw that it was love and work and true hope. He saw that all the love in the world, which was sweet and fine, was not love at all without its work, and that work could not exist without the kindness of hope." Together father and son attain an understanding about life's telos—including its troubles and difficulties and struggles—at times calling existence itself into question: "They did that every day, yet they did not hate life, they loved it. They saw that life was like a kind of work, a poor miserable disconnected fragment of something better, far greater, just a fragmentary isolated frightened sweating over a moment in the dripping faucet-time of the world, a tattered impurity leading from moment to moment towards the great pure forge-fires of workaday life and loving human comprehension" (472).

Until his father's death, the mood of the household alternates from black to white as if Kerouac wishes to remind the reader that dying is, after all, an intensified state of living, an acrobatic flight from the abyss to the veranda and back again. Life without end until the "miracle of everyday heartbeat" stops. Father to son on his death-chair: "That's right, my poor little boy," implying that this is what's in store for him in time. Son to father on the following page, after he discovers him dead: "You poor old man, you poor old man!"—the consolation for one extends pity to all (475–76).

It gets worse. Just before his father's plunge into sickness, Peter receives word that his close boyhood friend Alexander was killed in action in Italy. And shortly after his father's death his younger brother Charles is dug up from the rubble of an Okinawan battlefield. The literal "comedown" of "death reclaiming life" seems more and more justified with each passing day, and with it the "suffering awful knowledge and experience of hopelessness." During his father's funeral, held in New Hampshire, back to Mr. Martin's beginning near the old Martin farm, Peter begins to turn such knowledge into cold-blooded aquatic wisdom fit for "poor fish" as well as, in Holmes's words, uprooted, bereft, helpless, persevering humankind. During the long wake, brothers Joe, Peter, and Francis steal away to do some fishing, figuring the old man wouldn't begrudge them a brief respite from the satin mournfulness and eager throngs of consoling relatives and friends pouring into the small town of Nashua.

While Joe fishes, Peter, now even more sensitized to the pain and struggle existing in nature, is enmeshed in the web of an inescapable truth. It begins when Joe hooks a black bass and ends in compassionate comprehension of the sorrows he must bear. "Peter could not take his eyes off the struggling enchained fish. . . . He watched its gaping eyes almost with terror. Unaccountably he remembered something he had read a few days before, in the New Testament, something about Jesus and his fishermen casting their nets in the sea" (493). In his allusion to Matthew 4:18–22, Kerouac gives an interesting twist to the notion that following Jesus will make his disciples "fishers of men." For Peter, with one eye on the fish and the other on humankind, everything alive is eventually caught, torn, and "doomed for certain suffering." The only question that remains is when. The fishermen cast away only to reel in a cruel oscillation of nature: "'This is what happens to all of us, this is what happens to all of us! . . . Back and forth, back and forth, with a hook in his mouth.'" And, for Peter, there seems no other possible way for him to exist other than in pain and loss, "as though he himself had a hook torn through his mouth and was chained to the mystery of his own dumb incomprehension" (493–94).

Peter is swept away by his insight, and casts his own line, conveying the knowledge to Joe and Francis. Joe gets somewhat aggravated and Francis tries to joke playfully and evade the whole matter. But Peter, baiting and bobbing skillfully, persists with his passionate sermon. "'What the hell you want me to do,' called Joe, 'throw it back?'" Francis enters the fray: "'It's all right, he's only meddling in God's system.'" Peter and Francis go one-on-one in a dialogue between faith and disbelief:

> "I'm not God, I'm not supposed to meddle," cried Peter, staring at [Francis] worriedly, "and even if I could, say if I had the power of miracle, I couldn't alleviate the suffering without breaking up God's purpose in the whole thing.
>
> "There, perhaps, is the cream of the jest."
>
> "Ah! that's so easy to say! What are we supposed to do in a suffering world . . . suffer? That's not enough to satisfy the big feeling we might have of wanting everything and wanting to like everything. How can we be fair in an unfair situation like that?"
>
> "Why do you insist so much?" joked Francis again, to a degree grimly now.
>
> "Why is it that we can bear our own troubles and pain because we believe in . . . in fortitude—"
>
> "Soap opera talk, my dear boy. You should say 'quiet desperation.'"
>
> "—and we have to believe in fortitude," ignored Peter, "of course we have to, but we don't grant that fortitude to fellow creatures like the fish here."
>
> "How strange!" breathed Francis with sudden curiosity. It suddenly occurred to him that his brother Peter must be mad.
>
> Peter seemed to sense this. He pointed his finger, almost accusingly, but with a grin, rattling along: "Jesus warned against the sin of ac-

cusing any man of madness, Francis, he even said that no man was mad!" (495)

Still inspired, Peter leaps up to his feet to further engage Francis, speaking through him to their contemporaries as well, including Leon Levinsky and his notion of the great molecular comedown. First he quotes Jesus, "'Oh, faithless and perverse generation—it is because of your unbelief,'" and then offers his own interpretation: "'It was unbelief that created and aggravated the madness of the madman.'" Francis's comeback is a feeble remark about the tedium of original sin—"'the original slap in the face that everyone got'"—and its disappearance into the urbane secularism of modern society. "'Is that why *you* give up?' Peter looked up with sudden soft curiosity." Joe innocently breaks up the dialogue, and the fervent fishers of divine and human realities branch off to other things:

> talking warmly, enjoying each other's company with a kind of understanding they had never had among one another before. It was as though Peter had revealed their common situation, and their differences in it, their individual sorrows . . . by exposing himself like a child and agitating the drama of their secret and especial concerns, making them see one another with serious eyes. This was, after all, so much like the action of the man who had been their father. (496–97)

And this is also so much like the action of Kerouac the author in terms of both purpose and method—to reveal something universal in the human condition, and the uniqueness of individuals dancing variously to its beat beneath the stars, by displaying self in naive youthful exuberance. In the process, Kerouac turns up the volume to amplify the whispering rush of that water which feeds our "endless sources and unfathomable springs."

The brothers Martin return to the funeral and burial of their father, and the novel ends in a final chapter with Peter on the road, heading west, "going off to further and further years, alone by the waters of life, alone, looking towards the lights of the river's cape, towards tapers burning warmly in the towns, looking down along the shore in remembrance of the dearness of his father and of all life." In the end, Peter chooses neither town nor city, for he has died to both social forms. Instead, he moves on into open unknown territory— no doubt littered with the certainty of struggle and heroic sorrows.

One gets the feeling that the journey for Peter and Kerouac has really just begun. "When the railroad trains moaned, and river-winds blew, bringing echoes through the vale, it was as if a wild hum of voices, the dear voices of everybody he had known, were crying: 'Peter, Peter! Where are you going, Peter?' And a big soft gust of rain came down" (498–99). The answer, of course, is not given in the last line of the novel, but we can surmise that Peter deliberately casts himself away in the American night to go off to build his own cross in the world as it is—a no-good bum in search of *the way*—"God in men," sure to suffer each and every night yet rise again at the break of day. Following Christ as mediator entails both suffering and triumph—both the hook in the mouth and the mystical unity of the soul. Peter's belief and sense of fortitude—his courage to go on in adventurous hope and trust, bearing up for better times despite the knowledge of certain defeat—convey true lyrical grit. Is this not IT? "He put up the collar of his jacket, and bowed his head, and hurried along." With this final sentence, Peter Martin, who is simply *out there,* humbly vanishes from our sight, disappearing to found himself amid the rock-hard pavement and immense grace of the road. It is here, at this precise moment, that John Kerouac ceases to be (gone fishin') and the figure of Jack bursts onto the scene.

PART ONE

Road, Town, and City

Men grow rich, or take power,
ten thousand men want ten thousand things,
most see their hopes
go to ruin, a few see them all
come true—but the man whose life
    right now, this day
brings joy to his heart—
is happy beyond harm.
               —Euripides, *The Bakkhai*

I

What IT Is?

Kerouac wrote to his "Dear Ma" back in Ozone Park, Long Island, during the first leg of his journey across America in July 1947: "I've been eating apple pie & ice cream all over Iowa & Nebraska, where the food is so good. Will be in Colorado tonight—and I'll write you a letter from Denver. Everything fine, money holding out." He signed the note "Love, Jacky xxx" and included a postscript: "You ought to see the *Cowboys* out here."[1]

So did you ever read a book billed as the classic novel of the Beat Generation, in which the narrator and one of two protagonists in the novel makes his way cross-country eating apple pie and ice cream at every roadside diner simply because it's "nutritious and . . . delicious"? You won't find much rebellion in that homey Norman Rockwellian act. Yet it is part of being on the road, as integral to it as taking a spoonful of the "greatest laugh in the world" by an old-time Nebraska farmer and holding it to one's ear. Or hitching a ride on the back of a flatbed truck with an odd assembly of drifters linked by the crapshoot of time and motion and direction and by the hypnotic white lines of the highway's unwinding immensity. "This is a narrative of life among the wild bohemians of what Kerouac was the first to call 'the beat generation,'" Malcolm Cowley wrote in his acceptance report for *On the Road* to Viking Press in April 1957.[2] The report then goes on to highlight the juicy details that turn the story into a litany of mad adventures and kicks—the crazy antics of protracted juvenile delinquents "always on wheels." It would have been better to write merely what Sal Paradise states in the midst of his third trip back and forth across the continent—"the road is life."

What then is life? Life is suffering, the precepts of both Buddhist and Christian teaching. But in Kerouac's second novel, written in April 1951 and published in September 1957, the sorrows of young John do not stand alone; rather, for Jack, the road of life entails certain sadness paired with exuberant joy. The up and down scale of the novel is so exact that it brings Frank Sinatra's famous lyric to mind: "riding high in April, shot down in May"—"That's Life." And so it is, a most honest record of experience, especially from a writer "interested in life, any kind of life, all of it!" The oscillation between ecstasy and suffering—elation and dejection—appears to be the maxim of the novel. It simply goes with the territory, as if a physical law of motion—"our one and noble function of the time." This oscillation, in which characters and events both expand and contract, results in an uncanny state of equilibrium whereby the states of creation and annihilation balance out. Thus, for every IT one takes a HIT, and so on. Such a condition, especially when accelerated and telescoped as it is in the novel, generates rich insights into self and other, society in general, the stuff of human nature, and nature itself—its movement from high to low energy states and back again.

The proposition that the road is life, and life itself the equilibrist, demands a writing style that can respond to the movement between opposite emotive forces. In part, this is one reason why Kerouac turns away from the profound and ponderous lyricism of *The Town and the City*, that "Wolfean romantic posh," as Carlo Marx (Ginsberg) puts it from his Denver doldrums dungeon in *On the Road*, and toward a much more factualist narrative style. The style, though conventional and more objectively oriented, does contain a syncopated positive charge in order to heat up the novelistic system and capture that oscillation between the swells of excitement and the drain of despair. The proposition also leads Kerouac away from a strictly Christian form of ecstatic mystical union and towards an embrace of the aesthetic and hedonistic factors in the nature of existence, and their consequences. Though both Dean Moriarty and Sal Paradise refute the Nietzschean notion that God is dead—"God exists without qualms"—and although the pursuit of IT finally devolves to the biblical magic of Mexico, the frantic dynamism and will to power embodied in Dean Moriarty kick up the spectral dust of Nietzsche's ghost and conceal those highest values, anchored in the eternal and/or the enlightened one. These qualities do not necessarily make for an amoral novel. Rather, the altered morality expressed in *Road* descends, in part, from D. H. Lawrence's attribution of Whitman's achievement: "He was the first to smash the old moral conception, that the soul of man is something 'superior' and 'above' the flesh. . . . Whitman was the first heroic seer to seize the soul by the scruff of her neck and plant her down among the potsherds."[3] Such a passional soul, which finds its true home along the open road, naturally embeds the spiritual quest in the phenomenal world of sensation and, at times, in sensory indulgence.

In the Buddhist sense, however, to be unenlightened is to be simply ignorant. According to D. T. Suzuki, "so long as passions . . . were not subdued, and the mind still remained enshrouded in ignorance, no Buddhists could ever dream of obtaining a Moksha (deliverance) which is Nirvana, and this deliverance from Ignorance and passions was the work of Enlightenment."[4] Therefore, as viewed from his Buddhist phase of the mid-1950s, Kerouac's designation of *On the Road* as "'Pre-enlightenment' work" reveals the clarity with which he distinguished the spiritual dimensions and stages of his literary work. During this middle period, Kerouac often associated this Buddhist emphasis on deliverance with the Christian notion of self-denial and detachment from the spurious pleasures of the world so as to rest peacefully in the arms of God and/or heavenly Buddha. This direct relation led at times to Kerouac's superimposed perspective on Buddhism and Catholicism.

But for now, grinding through the gears of Kerouac's early phase, it is to that world of sensation we must return. The surface of *Road* is buzzing with frenetic activity, for the road provides the necessary link and life-line to the busy, restless, energetic multiplicities of the too-worn yet still-possible world. As Dean Moriarty puts it, "'Yes! You and I, Sal, we'd dig the whole world with a car like this because, man, the road must eventually lead to the whole world'" (230). It is all there for the taking, providing one has the wheels, the jack, and the knack: old highways, cars, hotels and flophouses, lunchcarts and diners, smokestacks, railyards, red-brick and gray-stone cityscapes, neon-glazed streets, insane bars and jazz clubs, cantinas and whorehouses. All stretched out *ad infinitum* along the road-world of the earth-bound eternal now, all madly and strangely and variously peopled with hepcats and musicians, Susquehanna ghosts, the phantom of Dean's lost father-bum, women, and the fellahin. However it is laid out, whether short or long, straight or curved, the road is the perfect vehicle for expressing all the "pure products of America go[ne] crazy," to borrow an apt poetic line from William Carlos Williams.

Think of Dean Moriarty, the hero of *Road,* lost western frontiersman turned urban cowboy—brakeman always on the make—a wild roaming being in perpetual motion. Gone, though not gone beyond. The character of Dean Moriarty (based on Neal Cassady) is the very personification of restlessness, "a wild yea-saying overburst of American joy" (10). Sal Paradise (alias Duluoz) catches the itch from him, going on the cross-country road by his own adventurous self and with his bosom buddy on several occasions—bosom because in Dean, with "suffering bony face," Sal sees his "long-lost brother" and lost bliss of boyhood among the rough trade of Paterson (another stand-in for Lowell). But whether or not Sal actually finds his "brother" and recovers that lost bliss is another question altogether. In the meantime, in between *time,* and all along the way, Sal "knew there'd be girls, visions, everything; somewhere along the line the pearl would be handed to me" (11).

Along the road, however, it seems as though the pearl of wisdom Sal desires has been exchanged for the ball bearings of cumbustive metallic flight in the form of a 1949 Hudson sedan. Paradise soon sees that Moriarty's soul is "wrapped up in a fast car, a coast to reach, and a woman at the end of the road" (230). As always, Sal goes along for the ride. On the one hand, Dean represents the perfervid Beat Gen-

eration chase for IT, which may be defined as the "ragged and ecstatic joy of pure being" (195). As a form of ecstasy, the search for IT
spins on the wheels of free, spontaneous, fleeting, hedonistic existence blurring the lines of our mortality. On the other hand, the tu-
mult of Moriarty's life conveys the "sorrowful sweats" that result from
crisscrossing the continent, driven by the mad rush of blind passion
and momentary whim of desire so that, by the end of the novel, Dean
has collected three wives, divorced two of them, spurted four kids,
and forsaken the East Coast to live once again with his second wife
on the West Coast. On his first solo trip cross-country, Sal makes
Denver and gets his initial glimpse into the organized chaos of Dean's
life from their mutual friend Carlo Marx. Sal asks Marx, "'What's the
schedule?'"

> "The schedule is this: I came off work a half-hour ago. In that time
> Dean is balling Marylou at the hotel and gives me time to change and
> dress. At one sharp he rushes from Marylou to Camille—of course
> neither one of them knows what's going on—and bangs her once, giv-
> ing me time to arrive at one-thirty. Then he comes out with me—first
> he has to beg with Camille, who's already started hating me—and we
> come here [Marx's apartment] to talk till six in the morning. We usu-
> ally spend more time than that, but it's getting awfully complicated
> and he's pressed for time. Then at six he goes back to Marylou—and
> he's going to spend all day tomorrow running around to get the nec-
> essary papers for their divorce." (42–43)

Both the road and Dean Moriarty are treated ambiguously by
Kerouac. Together they form the hard surface and romanticized subject for celebration as well as for registering sorrow—especially the
sadness bound up with suffering and the feeling of an impending
mortality. For the vehicle for joyous adventurous kicks is also the
agency for one's passing through, and the very nature of passing
through accentuates the fact that "time's running, running," as Dean
puts it on one occasion. Despite the frantic pace, despite the speed-
ing rush onward, Dean is still contained by chronological time; "''cause
now is the time and *we all know time!*'" he shouts (114). But does he
know or betray time? For to know time is to understand that it is
impossible to beat time—the "death-delivering ravages of time."[5]
"Where go? what do? what for?—sleep" (167). The road may be pref-

erable to the inn, as Cervantes wrote, but movement for the sake of movement on modern mid-twentieth-century American highways and byways is a sure path to pain—no pearl.

Even during Sal's first solo cross-country venture, where Dean is encountered only briefly in Denver, the force and counterforce of time tinged with desire are deeply felt. The false start from Bear Mountain is the first minor indication. Sal had wanted to follow the red line of Route 6 on the map because it spanned the continent, from Cape Cod to Los Angeles. But getting a ride proved impossible, and then the rains came to drench his idealism. He ends up hitching back to New York City and taking a bus to Chicago and picking up Route 6 in Illinois, a much more practical maneuver. By the end of chapter 9, while Sal is still in Denver, the oscillation between exuberant joy and certain sadness is already established. During a ribald night after the opera—which enlarges Sal's gloom—in the high altitude of Central City, he begins to reflect on the spectacle of man in nature:

> I wondered what the Spirit of the Mountain was thinking, and looked up and saw jackpines in the moon. . . . In the whole eastern dark wall of the Divide this night there was silence and the whisper of the wind, except in the ravine where we roared; and on the other side of the Divide was the great Western Slope, and the big plateau that went to Steamboat Springs, and dropped, and led you to the western Colorado desert and the Utah desert; all in darkness now as we fumed and screamed in our mountain nook, mad drunken Americans in the mighty land. We were on the roof of America and all we could do was yell, I guess—across the night, eastward over the Plains, where somewhere an old man with white hair was probably walking toward us with the Word, and would arrive any minute and make us silent. (55)

The old prophet appears several times throughout the novel, as if reminding readers to dig like miners for the meaning in experience, to ascertain the wisdom—if any—behind sheer sensual transient desire. This figure, so well positioned by Kerouac to question, at times ironically, the whole purpose of blurring thoughtless movement, first appears while Sal travels from Cheyenne to Denver: "I pictured myself in a Denver bar that night, with all the gang, and in their eyes I would be strange and ragged and like the Prophet who has walked across the land to bring the dark Word, and the only Word I had was 'Wow!'" (37). This is nothing but the hissing surface of the road shaped into three letters—the sound is all exclamation and no depth. Kerouac matches this amusing visceral high of experience with the sad stale low of the morning after in Central City: "Everything seemed to be collapsing." The following night, after the sigh of impatient sex, Sal and a girlfriend gaze up at the ceiling and wonder "what God had wrought when He made life so sad" (56–57). The only response is a reflexive one—move on to San Francisco.

Sal's itch to get on to the next destination and sign on board a ship to parts unknown numbs into a rather comical episode of entrapment in the land of everyday bourgeois domesticity. Not only does Sal live amid the incessant squabbles of his friend Remi Boncoeur (Henri Cru) and his cantankerous girlfriend Lee Ann in Mill City, California, but he signs on to work with Remi as a security guard in the barracks that temporarily quarters overseas construction workers. So thus far he has spent only about two weeks on the road before he is landlocked for a good two and a half months as he watches crew after crew ship out: "I was sworn in by the local police chief, given a badge, a club, and now I was a special policeman" (63). Sal is a somewhat inept and mildly subversive Chaplinesque cop as he makes his rounds, getting drunk with the dormers and accidently raising the American flag upside down on one occasion. But he hangs in there, sending most of his paycheck back home to his aunt and learning the difference between thieves and conformists, which isn't great, until the whole tedious affair overwhelms him. During a big night out with Lee Ann, Remi, and his stepparents, Sal lets loose: "I forgave everybody, I gave up, I got drunk. . . . Everything was falling apart. My stay in San Francisco was coming to an end. Remi would never talk to me again. . . . It would take years for him to get over it. How disastrous all this was compared to what I'd written him from Paterson, planning my red line Route 6 across America. Here I was at the end of America—no more land—and now there was nowhere to go but back" (77–78).

On the return, however, Sal finds someone and someplace to go before heading back—an amorous interlude with Terry, his Mexican girl whom he meets on a bus to LA. After a skittish start, the romance blossoms and Sal finds love in the midst of Mexican and Okie migrant farm worker communities. The combination of romance, ethnicity, and field-hand labor (at this time Sal alternately fashions himself an "old Negro cotton-picker" and a Mexican) unleashes his deep *sympatico* with the oppressed who live out the script of a premodern fellahin folk culture rooted to the land: "I looked up at the dark sky and prayed to God for a better break in life and a better chance to do something for the little people I loved. Nobody was paying any attention to me up there. I should have known better. It was Terry who brought my soul back" (96–97).

The expansive interlude proves tender and compassionate and also doomed to failure. Although vague plans are made to continue the affair in New York City, Sal and Terry both know deep down that this will never happen. "Everything was collapsing. . . . I told Terry I was leaving. She had been thinking about it all night and was resigned to it. Emotionlessly she kissed me in the vineyard and walked off down the row. We turned at a dozen paces, for love is a duel, and looked at each other for the last time" (99–101).

Tired, haggard, and weary, Sal begins to know the ravages of time by the end of his first trip across the country and back. As if to exaggerate his condition, Sal comes across the Ghost of the Susquehanna outside of Harrisburg, Pennsylvania—a misdirected "walking hobo of some kind who covered the entire Eastern Wilderness on foot. . . . poor forlorn man, poor lost sometimeboy, now broken ghost of the penniless wilds." Thrown out of a railroad station in Harrisburg at dawn, where he was sleeping on a bench, Sal Paradise begins to contemplate the cruel injustice of it all: "Isn't it true that you start your life a sweet child believing in everything under your father's roof? Then comes the day of the Laodiceans, when you know you are wretched and miserable and poor and blind and naked, and with the visage of a gruesome grieving ghost you go shuddering through nightmare life" (104–5). This feeling of disillusionment—"Gad, I was sick and tired of life"—is deepened even further by the time Sal returns to the swirl of Times Square with eight thousand miles under his belt. He takes in the futility of the "mad dream—grabbing, taking, giving, sighing, dying, just so they could be buried in those awful cemetery cities beyond Long Island City" (106). To make matters worse, the trip that launches Paradise on the road ends with a missed connection with Dean in New York City—Sal's "long-lost brother" lost again.

Thus awakened to the interplay of fervent dreams, suffering life, and drifting souls, Sal goes home to figure out what was lost and what was gained from the adventure. One thing, however, is for certain:

he now knows time—both its shifting ravages and its threads of continuity—for while he was gone his aunt "worked on a great rag rug
woven of all the clothes in [Sal's] family for years, which was now finished and spread on [his] bedroom floor, as complex and as rich as
the passage of time itself" (107). In this rough design, a certain equilibrium is stitched throughout the whole pattern: as time beats Sal
down it also restores him.

Throughout the remainder of the novel, however, after the beginning of the second trip—this time with Dean more than a year later—
there is no more mention of Sal's family (reduced to one brother,
Rocco, and his Southern relatives), save for his lone aunt whom he
lives with when off the road. What happened to the big joyous family togetherness of *The Town and the City*? Increasingly, the beats—
the "sordid hipsters of America that [Sal] was slowly joining" (Dean/
Cassady, Carlo/Ginsberg, Bull Lee/Burroughs, Remi/Cru, and so
on)—command more and more of Paradise's attention and energy as
the family recedes into near oblivion. In fact, all of the key members
of "the gang" appear to be orphanlike: Sal lives with his aunt; Dean's
mother died when he was a boy and his father—the "tinsmith" wino,
who raised his son on the Denver skid row—is now a gone hobo;
Carlo, who resides in his grotesque cave, the perfect placement for his
subterranean designs, never mentions family; and Remi, a real orphan,
was brought up by stepparents and, therefore, is "out to get back everything he'd lost; there was no end to his loss" (70). Such loss and
alienation are the driving forces behind "all this franticness and jump-
ing around" that the beats insist upon, revved up in their search for
freedom of spontaneous action, liberation of spirit, self-willed indi-
vidualism, and brotherhood. Therefore, as abundant American progress shifts into overdrive during the unprecedented military-indus-
trial state of the 1950s, the conformist ideal of social stability gets
exchanged for the careening, full-throttled seizure of mobility.

The second trip, which brings Dean and Sal into their first real
encounter, sees them shuttling back and forth between Testament,
Virginia, and New York City to move some furniture for Sal's aunt.
(Dean arrives out of the blue and so Sal's aunt finds something useful
for him to do.) The shuttle service is really a warm-up for a longer
cross-country trip to San Francisco by way of Texas and the Southwestern route. Now, even before embarking on the long road trip, Sal

wonders briefly whether it's better to race or rest his soul. Should he move or stay put? Which one is more beneficial to his well-being? Should they plan on finding a real destination somewhere—"go someplace, find something?" Or should they be magicians of the short stay, barely leaving their meaningless breath behind as they streak through the American night to the next place beyond the bend?

The answer: "The only thing to do was to go" (119). But not without some reservations, or at least a nagging absence of something vaguely felt left undone, incomplete, unattended. "Just about that time," Sal admits, "a strange thing began to haunt me. It was this: I had forgotten something. There was a decision that I was about to make before Dean showed up, and now it was driven clear out of my mind." The haunting decision had something to do with Sal's dream about the Shrouded Arabian Traveler chasing him across the desert, and who finally overtook Paradise just before he could reach the Protective City. In a moment of narrative calm and reflection, Sal considers the collective import of the dream:

> Naturally, now that I look back on it, this is only death: death will overtake us before heaven. The one thing that we yearn for in our living days, that makes us sigh and groan and undergo sweet nauseas of all kinds, is the remembrance of some lost bliss that was probably experienced in the womb and can only be reproduced (though we hate to admit it) in death. But who wants to die? In the rush of events I kept thinking about this in the back of my mind. I told it to Dean and he instantly recognized it as the mere simple longing for pure death; and because we're all of us never in life again, he, rightly, would have nothing to do with it, and I agreed with him then. (124)

The dream and its interpretation are soon left in the cloud kicked up by the red dust of the Hudson—"the too-huge world vaulting us, and it's good-by" (156). Ah, the protective device of escapism on the run. But at least for the duration of a rest stop, Sal managed to grip something fundamental about the *alpha* and *omega* of human existence—its mixture of bliss and mortality, joy and sorrow, and the beauty inherent in the appreciation of it all. Although Dean and Sal turn their backs on the spiritual significance of the dream, their minds "enshrouded in ignorance," Kerouac does not, for he lets the reader know that Sal Paradise "agreed with [Dean] *then*," as if to suggest that in time a different viewpoint might take hold, a perspective that would confront the realities of impermanence: the pain of birth, old age, sickness, and death.

But, for now, "we lean forward to the next crazy venture beneath the skies" (156). And merrily they go along, blurring time, which ends like the long stretch of the road itself, in death. The only reprieve from the terminus of chronological time is a high-octane mixture of speed and desire embodied in IT. IT, a transcendent state of pure excitement, stops the felt experience of linear time screeching in its tracks. It is first evoked by Dean when in the company of Rollo Greb, whose sense of excitement with life "blew out of his eyes in stabs of fiendish light." Dean tries to explain this strange suspension of being and time to Sal in a rush of hipster bop-isms: "'That's what I was trying to tell you— that's what I want to be. I want to be like him. He's never hung-up, he goes every direction, he lets it all out, he knows time, he has nothing to do but rock back and forth. Man, he's the end! You see, if you go like him all the time you'll finally get it.'" Sal seems perplexed: "'Get what?'" Dean exclaims: "'IT! IT! I'll tell you—now no time, we have no time now'" (127). Dean's utterance is really a double entendre, for he means not only later we'll discuss this matter, but also this is IT— "now no time, we have no time," or, in other words, we've beat the shroudy specter of time, and somehow sprung ourselves from the prison house of calendar and clock into an eternal now. The rush of IT blossoms at Birdland, where Dean and Sal immediately go after leaving Greb to hear George Shearing, a renowned jazz pianist, elevated by Dean to the stature of God. "And Shearing began to rock; a smile broke over his ecstatic face; he began to rock in the piano seat, back and forth, slowly at first, then the beat went up, and he began rocking fast, his left foot jumped up with every beat, his neck began to rock crookedly, he brought his face down to the keys, he pushed his hair back, his combed hair dissolved, he began to sweat" (128). Shearing, like Greb, rocks back and forth, not to a metronome, not to keep the cool beat of time's deterministic tick-tockery, but to escape it altogether. This is the intimate body language of IT—a hotly affirmative Dionysian gesture to "spastic ecstasy." Although "Dean was pop-eyed with awe," Sal registers skepticism, as if to take the rhythm of back and forth to another existential level—hot and cool, fast and slow, high and low, ecstatic and flat, IT and NOT: "This madness would lead nowhere. I didn't know what was happening to me, and I suddenly realized it was only the tea that we were smoking" (128–29). Though initially dismissive about IT, Sal continues to rock along for the ride through "old tumbledown holy America from mouth to mouth and tip to tip."

For the most part, the road keeps Paradise in the groove of time, but Sal does manage to slip away once in the story and experience that which had been scattered by the sparks of hedonistic activity, that which had been buried under the heap of unsubdued passion. This amounts to a countervailing sense of IT, and perhaps a glimpse into a spiritual form of ecstasy that will take root after the road trails off. After an amusing visit with Bull Lee, his wife Jane, and Carlo Marx in Texas, the ragged crew finally make San Francisco, where Dean abandons both Sal and Marylou, his first wife, in order to make amends with Camille, his second wife. "Where is Dean and why isn't he concerned about our welfare? I lost faith in him that year" (171). Sal, without food, money, or friends, growing delirious with hunger, picking up butts from the street near the Tenderloin, having the "beatest time of [his] life," is suddenly delivered from despair and the devastating jazz of time. Walking about, he seems to hear another note in the air—the long hollow breath of a bamboo flute signifying nothing.

IT begins to happen during an imaginary encounter with a proprietress of a fish-and-chips shop on Market Street, whom Sal takes to be his "strange Dickensian mother" from two centuries ago in England. He becomes unstuck in time, "now only in another life and in another body," unsure if he is in Frisco or N'Orleans or da city city city. In a projection of remorse, the mother lashes out at him and the son suffers the good Christian opprobrium for his inclination toward unbridled pleasure, the lush life of drunkenness and routs. "'O son! did you not ever go on your knees and pray for deliverance for all your sins and scoundrel's acts? Lost boy! Depart!'" And so he does, taking a leave of absence from the conditioned nature of things—from time itself:

> And for just a moment I had reached the point of ecstasy that I always wanted to reach, which was the complete step across chronological time into timeless shadows, and wonderment in the bleakness of the mortal realm, and the sensation of death kicking at my heels to move on, with a phantom dogging its own heels, and myself hurrying to a plank where all the angels dove off and flew into the holy void

of uncreated emptiness, the potent and inconceivable radiance shining in bright Mind Essence, innumerable lotus-lands falling open in the magic mothswarm of heaven. . . . I realized that I had died and been reborn numberless times but just didn't remember. . . . I felt sweet, swinging bliss. . . . I thought I was going to die the very next moment. (172–73)

This "step across chronological time," a wondrous adjustment to the fated dream of the Shrouded Traveler, is another form of ecstasy, an enlightened sense of IT, one that, though not a controlling principle in the novel, works momentarily to suggest what is missing from the first definition, that is, the "ragged and ecstatic joy of pure being." For Sal's shimmering glimpse of IT in the "timeless shadows" limns a form of Buddhist ecstasy (mixed with Catholic notions of angels and heaven) associated with liberation *from* being and not the more conventional liberation *of* being inherent in the original sense of IT. Such a liberation, in the former sense, is clearly present in Sal's vision, for he reaches the plank of the Protective City of his Shrouded Traveler dream, which is located much further east of the Arabian desert—the Far East. Springing from the plank of previous conceptions and cultural restraints, Sal dives deeply into the "holy void of uncreated emptiness." The Buddhist terms, concepts, and images that flash through the passage deliver Sal into a briefly felt state of nirvana or the All-At-One-Ment, as the Buddha puts it in the *Diamond Sutra,* and what F. S. C. Northrop refers to as the undifferentiated, all-embracing, indeterminate aesthetic continuum. Other arbitrary conceptions for this state of nonbeing include emptiness—void—ultimate escape; by any other name, it would feel like "sweet, swinging bliss."

In an instant, having tasted the fruits of nirvana, Sal is back in the realm of samsara—the born, created, shaped, differentiated. The normal gray quotidian is made fragrant by the fact that he is on the street starving. At this point, the narrator makes an interesting confession about the vision: "I was too young to know what had happened." It is a revealing remark that highlights the aesthetic distance between Kerouac and the character of Sal Paradise, while also taking the reader beyond the limits of this *Road* so as to suggest a sense of maturity and insight that have come in time/out of time. One assumes that such an admission, and the meaning that it packs, is the result of leading the examined life and the discovery of Buddhist teaching. In fact, given the pattern, tone, and dominant impulse of the novel, it seems as if the visionary passage is less a foreshadowing of Kerouac's keen interest in Buddhism and more of a retrofit once his self-study was underway in 1954, almost three years since he completed the *Road* manuscript, which was not published until 1957, thus allowing much time to play with various insertions and perform related editorial tasks.[6]

Be that as it may, snared by samsara, the youth resumes his lush course of desire through the here and now dreamworld of sensory delights. "In the window I smelled all the food of San Francisco"— bluefish, lobster, steamed clams, beef *au jus,* roast chicken, hamburger and coffee, chili beans, chow mein, pasta, soft-shelled crabs, ribs. How could this young man's dream of San Francisco be improved? Simply "add fog, hunger-making raw fog, and the throb of neons in the soft night, the clack of high-heeled beauties, white doves in a Chinese grocery window" (173–74). Clearly, Sal is back on track with the design of the novel, the thrust of the *Road,* especially after Dean arrives to rescue him from the plank of idle visions in strange shadows of butt-crusted San Francisco street emptiness. Then, as the second tour ends, the by-now predictable state of collapse ensues—back and forth, back and forth: "What I accomplished by coming to Frisco I don't know. Camille wanted me to leave; Dean didn't care one way or the other. . . . At dawn I got my New York bus and said good-by to Dean and Marylou. They wanted some of my sandwiches. I told them no. It was a sullen moment. We were all thinking we'd never see one another again and we didn't care" (177–78).

But only several months later, in the spring of 1949, Sal initiates the third trip—from New York City to San Francisco via Denver. In Denver, the rhythm of the road kicks in, and by now the reader understands the beginning point of the quest: movement from a state of rest to the early stirrings of desire. Walking around the African American quarters of Denver at "lilac evening," Sal feels uneasy in the low-lands of his soul. He realizes that he is simply a "'white man' disillusioned." Romanticizing the life of the "Negro" and Mexicans, Sal complains about the emptiness he feels at the very core of his existence, "feeling that the best the white world had offered was not enough ecstasy for me, not enough life, joy, kicks, darkness, music, not enough night. . . . It was the Denver Night; all I did was die" (180–81).

Sal's keen awareness of the nothingness within creates an insatiable hunger for life, an intense attachment to the "mad dream" envisioned from Times Square. When he hooks up with Dean in San Francisco, Sal's restless longing to affirm something passionate in every breath he takes is manifolded by Dean's "pious frenzy." Together, Sal and Dean find each other and see through each other; they meet again not only as companions of the road but as true friends in search of experience and meaning and togetherness. The sense of care that the two friends display, and the clarity of IT that occurs, gives the third trip a degree of tenderness and a growing depth of insight displayed by the narrator. Such development and maturation that Sal undergoes proves that Kerouac is no fool, no happy delinquent who, like a latter-day version of Peter Pan in zoot suit and chains, will never grow up. No, Kerouac is quite deliberate about IT all.

Shortly after Sal finds Dean in San Francisco, they both get thrown out of the house by Camille, quite deservedly I might add. Drawn and disoriented but still suffused with pointless excitement, Dean stumbles and circles around in a wild spin of pure blank random intensity. "Poor, poor Dean—the devil himself had never fallen further; in idiocy, with infected thumb, surrounded by the battered suitcases of his motherless feverish life across America and back numberless times, an undone bird" (188–89). In a pure moment of compassion and concern, Sal offers to pay his way to New York and then Italy—somehow he'll find the money. Dean, at first incredulous, giving Sal a look like the blinking sight of someone suddenly released from a dark closet, slowly adjusts himself to the fact that Sal is serious:

> Resolutely and firmly I repeated what I said. . . . I looked at him; my eyes were watering with embarrassment and tears. Still he stared at me. Now his eyes were blank and looking through me. It was probably the pivotal point of our friendship when he realized I had actually spent some hours thinking about him and his troubles, and he was trying to place that in his tremendously involved and tormented mental categories. Something clicked in both of us. . . .
> "Well," said Dean in a very shy and sweet voice, "shall we go."
> "Yes," I said, "let's go to Italy." (189–90)

Before they head out for the long impossible voyage, Sal defends Dean—"the HOLY GOOF"—to one of Camille's friends who has called him on the carpet. To Sal, Dean, in the face of this moral battering, appeared simply "Beat—the root, the soul of Beatific." "'Very

well, then,' I said, 'but . . . he's got the secret that we're all busting to
find and it's splitting his head wide open and if he goes mad don't
worry, it won't be your fault but the fault of God'" (195). The secret
Sal alludes to is the one bound up with further swayings into the ecstatic rhythm of IT. As with most things in life, first comes the direct
unmediated experience and only later the reflection and explanation.
So, once again, the novel turns to the sight and sound of jazz music
(led by a tenor sax man) to pick up the tempo and transport the audience into an exaltation of mind and feelings:

> The behatted tenor man was blowing at the peak of a wonderfully
> satisfactory free idea, a rising and falling riff that went from "EE-yah!"
> to a crazier "EE-de-lee-yah!" and blasted along to the rolling crash of
> butt-scarred drums hammered by a big brutal Negro with a bullneck
> who didn't give a damn about anything but punishing his busted tubs,
> crash, rattle-ti-boom, crash. Uproars of music and the tenor man *had
> it* and everybody knew he had it. Dean was clutching his head in the
> crowd, and it was a mad crowd. They were all urging that tenor man
> to hold it and keep it with cries and wild eyes, and he was raising him-
> self from a crouch and going down again with his horn, looping it up
> in a clear cry above the furor. . . .
> Everybody was rocking and roaring. (196–97)

The tenor man continues blowing and blasting and breathing be-
bop to his heart's content until the senses are aptly deranged and Dean
and the crowd curiously stand apart from themselves, outside of time,
which is the posture of ecstasy. "Dean was in a trance. The tenor man's
eyes were fixed straight on him; he had a madman who not only understood but cared and wanted to understand more and much more
than there was." Then a strange thing happens: the tenor man slows
IT down with a song from "this sad brown world"—"Close Your Eyes."
The juxtaposition of ecstasy and sorrow confirms Kerouac's belief in
paired emotive forces: the swoon of rapturous delight and frenzy will
soon give way to the placid tenderness of weary reflection, "because
here we were dealing with the pit and prunejuice of poor beat life itself in the god-awful streets of man." This is what it must mean to
know time truly, over and over again. Later, when Dean and Sal meet
the tenor man after his gig ends, Dean, still lit up, tells the musician
that he's looking for a ball. The tenor man tells it to him straight: "'Yah,
what good's a ball, life's too sad to be ballin all the time. . . . Shhee-

it!'" (198–99). In cooling down the orgiastic high of the human system, the tenor man hits those necessary flat notes that make life (and time) known in both its moments of emotional ferment and calm comprehension. In the meantime, Sal and Dean go back in the club for more. And so it goes.

On their way from San Francisco to Denver in a travel-bureau car, Dean and Sal, rocking the boat in the back seat, begin to draw from their own perceptions and recollections in order to enact the direct experience of IT. First, however, Sal wants to know what IT means, and Dean refers back to the previous night:

> "Now, man, that alto man last night had IT—he held it once he found it. . . . Up to him to put down what's on everybody's mind. He starts the first chorus, then lines up his ideas, . . . and then he rises to his fate and has to blow equal to it. All of a sudden somewhere in the middle of the chorus he *gets it*—everybody looks up and knows; they listen; he picks it up and carries. Time stops. He's filling empty space with the substance of our lives. . . . He has to blow across bridges and come and do it with such infinite feeling soul-exploratory for the tune of the moment that everybody knows it's not the tune that counts but IT—" (206)

The model seems clear enough: to know time is to escape its structure through improvisation, then the secret note is hit and the moment enlivened. But one begins from within the structure, some patterned chorus or thought that will, when deeply felt, sidestep itself and generate spontaneity. The moment then transports one out of the periodicity of time and into the fullness of being or pure spatial excitement. One only has to think of Coltrane's method and sound. There you have it, and—once you do—IT carries you away.

Once Dean and Sal begin their incessant yakking in the back seat, that which is normally concealed suddenly reveals itself, without plan or preparation. The thread of one recollection cross-stitches to another and "'NOW, I have IT,'" Dean exclaims, and proceeds to another patchwork in the story of his life—something that must be told, must be heard, some bright burning illumination that will make all the difference. "We were hot; we were going east; we were excited. . . . 'Yes! Yes! Yes!' breathed Dean ecstatically. . . . We had completely forgotten the people up front. . . . The car was swaying as Dean and I both swayed to the rhythm and the IT of our final excited joy in talking and living to the blank tranced end of all innumerable riotous angelic particulars that had been lurking in our soul all our lives" (207–8).

This is what it means, then, to experience IT and to know TIME—not only entering a momentary state of pure possibility, but, curiously, realizing the psychic equivalency of Einstein's inverse relationship between velocity and time (as stated in his special theory of relativity). Phenomenologically, the difference this makes to Sal and Dean is that space and time are released from their fixed trajectory of rational sequential stages. Likewise, the meaning of their high-tingled experience of being-in-time is perceived as not set in any absolute sense. Hence, for the moment, they are liberated, that is, they do not live in a state of consciousness in time, which is tantamount to betraying time, but rather bend time to consciousness. As Genevieve Lloyd explains: "The idea that consciousness is in time is the idea of self as determined. The idea that time is in consciousness is the idea of self as determining."[7] This relationship between IT and NOT helps to explain the oscillation from ecstatic joy to certain sadness that Kerouac projects into the novel. Dean perfectly expresses the notion of consciousness in time by making reference to the passengers up front: "'They have worries, they're counting the miles, they're thinking about where to sleep tonight, how much money for gas, the weather, how they'll get there—and all the time they'll get there anyway, you see. But they need to worry and betray time'" (208).

Once in Denver, while waiting to pick up another travel-bureau car to Chicago, Dean accelerates the momentum of IT into an energized state so charged that he seems to be a free electron, spinning out of control. He can only collide and bounce, stealing one car after another for random joy rides, but his fierce activity betrays the happiness: "All the bitterness and madness of his entire Denver life was blasting out of his system like daggers. His face was red and sweaty and mean." Sal stays free of the attraction and tries to put some ironic distance between himself and the "unbearable confusion" in the Denver night. In doing so, he draws a caricature of IT in a hillbilly roadhouse: "Everything was collapsing, and to make things inconceivably more frantic there was an ecstatic spastic fellow in the bar who threw his arms around Dean and moaned in his face, and Dean went mad again with sweats and insanity" (220–21). The irony is pointed and shows Kerouac's ability to stand apart from IT, in fact, to call IT into question, not only by veering toward the complementary pole of collapse, but by portraying how it can all go berserk. Extending this critical distance, as if to suggest a different vehicle for getting ecstasy—other than sheer speed raised to the nth power, Kerouac plants another Buddhist image while Sal tries to sleep: "At night in this part of the West the stars . . . are as big as roman candles and as lonely as the Prince of the Dharma who's lost his ancestral grove and journeys across the spaces between points in the handle of the Big Dipper, trying to find it again. So they slowly wheeled the night" (222). The view, which is so skyward, so altogether beyond, and such an overlooked complement to the oft quoted "mad ones" that "burn, burn, burn like fabulous yellow roman candles," temporarily takes Sal out of the dualistic oscillation and projects him onto a higher plane.

The road reclaims Sal in the morning and before long he is back into the grand rhythm of life. In the middle of the trip from Denver to Chicago, however, he feels the horrific hiss of the "senseless nightmare road," and hunkers down on the floor of the back seat to deliver his consciousness to time. No doubt, it's time to pay the piper for knowing IT: "Now I could feel the road some twenty inches beneath me, unfurling and flying and hissing at incredible speeds across the groaning continent with that mad Ahab [Dean] at the wheel. When I closed my eyes all I could see was the road unwinding into me. When I opened them I saw flashing shadows of trees vibrating on the floor of the car. There was no escaping it. I resigned myself to all" (234). Sal does not resist the rule of the road, for it has been laid down well in advance, and so gives himself up to the inevitable rushing rhythm of this human condition: knowing time and betraying time.

Once they make Detroit, the deterministic grip of consciousness in time is reinforced by the images of popular culture. Sleeping all night in a ramshackle movie-house, where the double feature plays and replays until dawn, Sal and Dean are entirely stuffed in their waking and sleeping hours with B movies, namely the "Gray Myth of the West"—"Singing Cowboy Eddie Dean"—and the "dark Myth of the East" set in Istanbul with George Raft and Peter Lorre. Sal comically comments on the awful effect of subjecting himself to the flicks: "All my actions since then have been dictated automatically to my subconscious by this horrible osmotic experience." In fact, at dawn Sal is almost swept up with the rubbish by the ushers—just another speck in the "come and gone" of the night: "Had they taken me with it, Dean would never had seen me again. He would have had to roam the entire United States and look in every garbage pail from coast to coast before he found me embryonically convoluted among the rubbishes of my life, his life, and the life of everybody concerned and not concerned" (244). This generalization extends the experience of entrapment, and its correlate of spiritual pollution, to all, for are we not all betrayed by time and its mindless reels of hegemonic culture remotely controlling us from afar?

This sense of consciousness in time, which subverts the ecstatic liberation of IT, is further heightened by virtue of repetition. As trip four winds down, along the way from Detroit to New York City, Sal starts to recognize the landscape. He'd been there before: "I realized I was beginning to cross and recross towns in America as though I were a traveling salesman—raggedy travelings, bad stock, rotten beans in the bottom of my bag of tricks, nobody buying. . . . The trip was over." Five days after they land in New York, at a party, Dean falls in lust with Inez; "he was kneeling on the floor with his chin on her belly and telling her and promising her everything and sweating." Not long after, Dean and Camille are discussing divorce on the telephone while she has his second baby, and a few months later Inez gets pregnant. What of Dean? Oh, he "was all troubles and ecstasy and speed as ever. So we didn't go to Italy" (245–47). Ah, rubbish—betrayed again! That's life.

Sufficiently rested and buoyant once again, Sal moves on during the following spring (1950) by himself to launch the final trip of the novel. The destination is Denver, but life has more surprises under its sleeve for Sal. By this time, Sal's uneasy feeling and deterministic dreamscape of an ultimate mortal reality rises to the surface again. This time the Shrouded Traveler combines with a vision of Dean storming toward Denver (unannounced and uninvited) to pick up Sal and a buddy and head down to Mexico—"the magic land at the end of the road," and the final place to attain IT in the novel. The vision describes a menacing image of Dean which is a view mostly submerged in the novel—subordinate to the hero's glamorization. Nonetheless, its force is great as it erupts into narrative consciousness. Even early on in the novel Sal sees the darker aspects of his friend and alter ego: "And Dean, ragged and dirty, prowling by himself in his preoccupied frenzy" (58). By the end of the novel, the sight has developed into a complete vision of Dean:

> a burning shuddering frightful Angel, palpitating toward me across the road, approaching like a cloud, with enormous speed, pursuing me like the Shrouded Traveler on the plain, bearing down on me. I saw his huge face over the plains with the mad, bony purpose and the gleaming eyes; I saw his wings; I saw his old jalopy chariot with thousands of sparking flames shooting out from it; I saw the path it burned over the road; it even made its own road and went over the corn, through cities, destroying bridges, drying rivers. It came like wrath to the West. (259)

The Shrouded Traveler, who reaps all consciousness and all time down the road—however they are equated, thickens with meaning and flares with intensity as Dean merges with this pursuer, making the figure notorious as well as perilous. Such a merger greets Sal with "bony purpose and gleaming eyes." Angel of death—like a clip of Groucho Marx hunched over, low to the earth, long strides, wings tucked, leering and muttering under cigar-breath while fluttering by uttering "hello I must be going." Time's despite. Is there no escape? Must there be no exit? Is that *it*?

Now it seems that only the route south of the border can restore sensations, intoxicate the emotions, and intensify the spirit of fellowship with humankind. Dropping down to Mexico is magical because it not only promises the new and unknown, but guarantees flight from the confines and "broken delusion" of corporate America and its aggressive technoid (and Cold War) civilization. Mexico's attraction for both Sal and Dean is that the road running through it unwinds time from present to past (the transition from advanced modern industrial state to a premodern folk society). They find in this devolution a chance to transcend both geographical and conceptual boundaries associated with the constraints of chronological time—its tireless goose steps toward the future and its progressive form of historic development that always insists—onward! Sal compares the road south of the border to

> driving across the world and into the places where we would finally learn ourselves among the Fellahin Indians of the world, the essential strain of the basic primitive, wailing humanity that stretches in a belt around the equatorial belly of the world. . . . These people were un-

mistakably Indians and were not at all like the Pedros and Panchos of silly civilized American lore—they had high cheekbones, and slanted eyes, and soft ways; they were not fools, they were not clowns; they were great, grave Indians and they were the source of mankind and the fathers of it. The waves are Chinese, but the earth is an Indian thing. As essential as rocks in the desert are they in the desert of "history." And they knew this when we passed, ostensibly self-important money-bag Americans on a lark in their land; they knew who was the father and who was the son of antique life on earth, and made no comment. (280–81)

These noble thoughts aside, the magic of Mexico is first experienced sensually in a whorehouse before the spiritual discovery of the land and its people fully emerges. Sal and Dean cannot escape that traditional masculine dualism of the virgin and the whore, and enter the latter before adoring the former. There does not seem to be any concrete mean in any part of the Americas for this duo. Listening to mambo amplified over loud speakers in the brothel, it seems to Sal that "the whole world was turned on. . . . It was like a long, spectral Arabian dream in the afternoon in another life—Ali Baba and the alleys and the courtesans" (289). After their mighty lust is quenched, they move on toward Mexico City, turning away from the pull of their loins and toward the push of more lofty images. On the way, they encounter some Mexican girls selling rock crystals: "Their great brown, innocent eyes looked into ours with such soulful intensity that not one of us had the slightest sexual thought about them. . . . 'Look at those eyes!' breathed Dean. They were like the eyes of the Virgin Mother when she was a child. We saw in them the tender and forgiving gaze of Jesus. . . . Their mouths rounded like the mouths of chorister children." The road finally spreads out into a holy vista—"the golden world that Jesus came from, . . . these vast and Biblical areas of the world." And in the midst of the sacred ancient site sits the profane City—"one vast Bohemian camp. . . . This was the great and final wild uninhibited Fellahin-childlike city that we knew we would find at the end of the road" (298–302).

But Sal speaks too soon, for the real end of the road typically results in disaster—this time terrible feverish sickness—which takes away all of his appetite for IT. To make matters worse in this foretaste of helpless mortality, Dean checks out of the picture and abandons Sal in Mexico City to go about his mad business of divorces, marriages, remarriages, and flings into the neon recesses of America, "dreaming in the immensity of it." Sal, recovered and heading back to New York City, at last crosses the prophet's path just over the Laredo border. It is the prophet's fourth and final appearance in the novel, the last chance to convey the word, and he does: "*Go moan for man*" (306). This strange but persistent figure thus gives Sal (and Kerouac) a way out of the endless oscillations between intense pleasure and devastating sorrow. It is no less than an admission that all life is suffering; this is where the road begins and ends, and the various detours around such a condition and first principle can only result in a peace that is hollow and restless. The mission of the writer is therefore discerned.

Kerouac jams the brakes on the novel in part five—a mere five pages—and skids to a stop. Actually, throughout the novel the road has been thinning out: part four (recounting the trip to Mexico) is only about half as long as the first trip of part one, which is the longest account; parts two and three, almost identical in length, each comprise two-thirds of the first part. Back in New York, Sal closes the novel with a farewell to Dean, who pops back up in his life once again. In perhaps much-too-facile a manner, Sal finds that concrete mean and falls in love with the woman of his dreams. So he seems to be settling down both to his life's work and to his heart's content. On the other hand, Dean, still traveling back and forth across the continent, a clanging caboose rattling through dawn and dusk, seems to have rocked himself off the proverbial rocker—derailed. He appears utterly senseless when Sal finds him unexpectedly with his girlfriend at their New York pad: "He hopped and laughed, he stuttered and fluttered his hands and said, 'Ah—ah—you must listen to hear.' We listened, all ears. But he forgot what he wanted to say. 'Really listen—ahem. Look, dear Sal—sweet Laura—I've come—I'm gone—but wait—ah yes. . . . Can't talk no more—do you understand that it is—or might be—But listen!'" (306–7).

Several days later, Sal says good-bye to Dean as he departs for the West Coast, "bent to it again." There is an unmistakable sadness in the air and this sets up the final paragraph of the novel—a sort of paean to the American dream and the passage of time, and to our home in the universe where we live it out, ending in a lone reflection on the ever transient nature of being-in-the-world. This closing reads like a final blessing, in which the author tucks in the story, characters, and reader, too, bidding all a fare-thee-well. One can tell that this is offered by someone who has finally reached a very deserved and knowing state of rest:

> So in America when the sun goes down and I sit on the old broken-down river pier watching the long, long skies over New Jersey and sense all that raw land that rolls in one unbelievable huge bulge over the West Coast, and all that road going, all the people dreaming in the immensity of it, and in Iowa I know by now the children must be crying in the land where they let the children cry, and tonight the stars'll be out, and don't you know that God is Pooh Bear? the evening star must be drooping and shedding her sparkler dims on the prairie, which is just before the coming of complete night that blesses the earth, darkens all rivers, cups the peaks and folds the final shore in, and nobody, nobody knows what's going to happen to anybody besides the forlorn rags of growing old, I think of Dean Moriarty, I even think of Old Dean Moriarty the father we never found, I think of Dean Moriarty. (309–10)

This elegiac note, which unites the panorama of space with the curvature of time, makes good on the prophet's message, for Kerouac, through Sal, expresses his mantric moan for humankind. The passage, both sad and joyful, as mixed as existence itself, achieves an equilibrium of sensibility, and thus provides solace and sustenance. Moreover, it works to disengage Sal and the reader from action in order to reflect and consider, to take in the immensity of it all: self, others, nation, world and universe. What remains to think on? Where is the meaning here—both hidden and overt? Now what? What of IT? In such a mood and in light of the legend's spiritual quest, one wonders about the pearl. Is it just now being handed to Sal and, in turn, to us?

The stillness and evocation of the passage—the sense of love, adoration, and wonder about the ultimate nature of existence—delivers the story from confusion and desire, from rocking back and forth and going up and down in ecstasy and sorrow. It also seems to invite calmness, self-possession, and contemplation. (Kerouac would later write in his biography of the Buddha, "Composure is the trap for getting ecstasy" ["Wake Up," episode two, 13].)[8] Dean may be hustling about at that very moment, but Sal sits on an old river pier, located squarely within linear time but still open to possibility, watching, summing up one phase of his life and opening the door to another. In doing so, he does not try to cross-step chronological time; a pier is not a plank. There is no springing into "the holy void of uncreated emptiness"— not yet. For the time being, Kerouac acknowledges our mortality— "the forlorn rags of growing old," but he also grants immeasurable freedom to us in the meantime, as if to ask each and every person somewhere along that road: What will happen? for "nobody, nobody knows." Taken in conjunction, this amounts to Kerouac's generous nod and wink to both states of existence: consciousness in time (self as determined) and time in consciousness (self as determining).

Without diminishing the joyful spontaneity of IT, the hedonistic lifestyle celebrated in *On the Road,* the novel also calls IT into question in the interstices of restless busy action and through the forms of unconscious dreamscapes and transcendent visions. Somewhere in the midst of all this earth-bound clutter an image emerges, momentarily flickering, of a finger pointed at the moon. That is all. But it is enough to challenge hedonism, not on the basis of morality, but simply in terms of the nature of things as they are. Northrop elaborates on the limitations inherent in treating IT as the ultimate mode of being in the world: "Hedonism as a complete philosophy of life is inadequate— not because it is naughty or because sensed things are not real, but merely because determinate things are transitory; and a philosophy which treats determinate pleasures as if they were a basis for living under all circumstances treats pleasure as an immortal law rather than the actual transitory thing which it is."[9] Therefore, the spiritual challenge facing Kerouac, or anyone on such a search for the divine or ultimate truth, is to reject what the senses perceive as the ontological be all and end all of this life. What the senses perceive is not unreal. It's just that, in the scheme of things, the frenzy of the phenomenal world must give way to an acceptance of the noumenal as the form of ultimate reality. How then to secure peace of mind and spiritual contentment? What are the conditions necessary for insights into the cross or the diamond of enlightenment? How shall one think of this fleeting world? Wherein lies the path (or device) to get beyond the *phenomenal* tricks of time:

> A star at dawn, a bubble in a stream;
> A flash of lightning in a summer cloud,
> A flickering lamp, a phantom, and a dream.[10]

2

Tearing Time Up

"I think of Dean Moriarty." The last words of *On the Road* provide the point of departure for Kerouac's next work, *Visions of Cody,* which, in his own words, marks the transition from a conventional "horizontal study of travels on the road" to an experimental and "vertical, metaphysical study" of Neal Cassady (*SL,* 327n). Even before writing the more conventional novel, Kerouac began to wonder about narrative form. In a letter to Cassady (8 January 1951), he raises and answers the following questions: "Who's laid down the laws of 'literary' form? Who says that a work must be chronological? . . . Let's tear time up. Let's rip the guts out of reality" (*SL,* 274). *Visions of Cody* is an attempt to do just that—to suspend and shred the temporal sequence of storytelling (linear narrative) by unleashing the style of sketching and spontaneous prose. Except for the last sixty pages, which retell the travel experiences of *Road* (but without the fictional framework), the study scatters the standard architecture of literary form into, as Kerouac perceived it, "a big multi-dimensional conscious and sub-conscious character invocation of Neal in his whirlwinds" (*SL*, 356).[1]

Kerouac came upon the vehicle of spontaneous prose in October 1951; in a letter to John Clellon Holmes (5 June 1952), he likened it to "revealed prose," "something beyond the novel and beyond the arbitrary confines of the story" (*SL*, 371). For Kerouac, this was much more than a literary technique: it was "the great moment of discovering my soul" (*VOC*, 93). Sketching, which is painterly, can be considered a method within the broader reaches of spontaneous prose, especially when the object actually exists before the writer. As Kerouac explained in a letter to Ginsberg (18 May 1952): "everything activates in front of you in myriad profusion, you just have to purify your mind and let it pour the words (. . . effortless angels of the vision fly when you stand in front of reality) and write with 100% personal honesty . . . and slap it all down shameless, willynilly, rapidly until sometimes I got so inspired I lost consciousness I was writing. Traditional source: Yeats's trance writing, of course. It's the *only way to write*" (*SL*, 356). Spontaneous prose in general aims to reveal the inner life of the author when provoked by either the externals of the world or the memories of times past. The spontaneous interaction between self and object results not in introspective writing but in a kind of mystical naturalism whereby consciousness and reality mutually absorb each other in the intuitive moment of apprehension.

Kerouac often likened the method to that of a jazz musician given to improvisation, with "no discipline other than rhythms of rhetorical exhalation and expostulated statement" ("Essentials of Spontaneous Prose," *GB*, 69). As Kerouac stated in a letter to Alfred Kazin (27 October 1954), writing spontaneous prose is like a saxophonist drawing breath and blowing phrases, then releasing from the phrase. The result is "jazzlike breathlessly swift spontaneous and unrevised floods . . . it comes out wild, at least it comes out pure, it comes out and reads like butter" (*SL*, 449). The style also claims to go at the material without preconceived notions, "from jewel center of interest in subject of image at *moment* of writing, and write outwards swimming in sea of language to peripheral release and exhaustion." Clearly, the energy that drives the style is orgiastic: "*Come* from within, out—to relaxed and said" ("Essentials of Spontaneous Prose," *GB,* 70–71). In short, spontaneous prose challenges an author to absorb the revelatory moment, the divine spark, writing freely and naturally and honestly and profusely, without literary affectation, and not only from the head, but from the heart and soul and through the body and blood, bones and bowels. At least in Kerouac's case, that is what it entailed. At its best, and in terms of sheer writing, Kerouac's spontaneous prose achieved a feral beauty, and a sense of fidelity, rhythm, and power that has been unparalleled in American literature.

The invocations of Cody/Cassady, and the various settings where he might roam, are spread across five discrete parts, each representing a different experiment with voice and vision. Part one, for instance, consists of brilliant descriptive sketchings of discrete scenes and events, mostly in and around New York City. In terms of social placement, Kerouac makes it clear just where he is writing from: the bottom of the world—old diners, B-movie houses, run-down employment agencies, El stations (and a john therein), a Bowery beanery, Hector's Cafeteria, subways, and the like. Favorite scene and lines: the bums in the Bowery beanery, "with all the cheap prices soaped-in on the plate glass windows. . . . I saw heaps of boiled potatoes alongside meat as those heartbreaking poor guys in their inconceivable clothes, World War I Army greatcoats, black baseball caps too small like Cody's father's with a witless peak, leaned elbows over their humble meals of grime—I saw the flash of their mouths, like the mouths of minstrels, as they ate" (6–7). The rapture that flashes in the onrush of prose is typical of Kerouac's sketching style; somewhere along the way, he will hit that mystical note in which the spirit of place, person, or type is exalted. As James Fisher rightly states: "To sanctify the world from the most 'profane' perspectives was a major part of Kerouac's artistic goal." *Visions of Cody* is an exemplary work in this regard. A visit to St. Patrick's Cathedral only reaffirms Kerouac's sense of mission: the priest "quotes MacArthur Old Soldier crap—mixing theological verities with today's headlines, blah, blah, I now go out, tired, into my own thoughts and have no place to go but find my road. . . . Everything belongs to me because I am poor" (31–33). Again, to quote Fisher, "Kerouac had done everything that Dorothy Day and Peter Maurin [founders of the Catholic Worker movement] could ever have asked of a fool for Christ.

. . . Kerouac's poverty earned him precisely the freedom they claimed would follow from a transcendence of materialism."[2] The sketching in part one ends in a letter written to Cody that mixes elements of the sacred and profane, juxtaposing wild sex with "sorrows of time and personality," and with compassion and love for another: "I'm completely your friend, your 'lover,'—he who loves you and digs your greatness completely—haunted in the mind by you" (39).

The intense affection for and identification with Cody, and his bottomless skid row background, extends the love for one to all those damaged and hurt and punished underneath the glaring neons of Great America. In part two, while presenting Cody's early life and times around Denver pool halls and flophouses, Kerouac paints a dark vision of America, lightened only by his deep religious feeling for lost, homeless, drifting souls relegated to a state of social death. A view of Cody broadens to take in others sharing a similar fate in the hostile land:

> America, the word, the sound is the sound of my unhappiness, the pronunciation of my beat and stupid grief—. . . . America is being wanted by the police, pursued across Kentucky and Ohio, sleeping with the stockyard rats and howling tin shingles of gloomy hideaway silos. . . . It is where Cody Pomeray learned that people aren't good, they want to be bad—. . . . America made bones of a young boy's face and took dark paints and made hollows around his eyes, and made his cheeks sink in pallid paste and grew furrows on a marble front and transformed the eager wishfulness into the thicklipped silent wisdom of saying nothing, not even to yourself in the middle of the goddamn night—. . . . America's a lonely crockashit. (90–91)

Kerouac sees evidence for this conclusion all around him: in the beaten face of a corner newsstand midget, in the blank look of "ferret-faced hipsters," among poor married couples and "Negroes" asleep on benches, and where a young night-shift worker also sleeps "head down at the trolley stop with his right hand palm-up as if to receive from the night— . . . as though on the tip of his tongue he's about to say in sleep and with that gesture what he couldn't say awake 'Why have you taken this away from me, that I can't draw my breath in the peace and sweetness of my own bed but here in these dull and nameless rags on this humbling shelf I have to sit waiting for the wheels to roll' and further. . . ." All of the lost ones in America are symbolized by this figure, who asks for the good citizens of the republic not only to hear but to see their plea as well:

> "I'm alone, I'm sick, I'm dying. . . . see my hand uptipped, learn the secret of my heart, give me the thing, give me your hand, take me to the safe place, be kind, be nice, smile; I'm too tired now of everything else, I've had enough, I give up, I quit, I want to go home, take me home O brother in the night, take me home, lock me in safe— . . . all is peace and amity, . . . to the family of life—. . . . take me to the family which is not—but no hope, no hope, no hope, I wake up and I'd give a million dollars to be in my bed, O Lord save me." (91–92)

In seeing through Cody and into others who have been hollowed out, Kerouac unlocks and learns the secret in their collective heart. The procedure he follows in doing this is both simple and instructive. First of all, he bothers to look their way. Second, he does not turn away. Third, his sensitivity and empathy draw him further into their very misery. Fourth, he humanizes this misery by giving it both presence and voice. And, finally, he cares enough to put their hands into ours so that we might see and know them as well. The question, however, remains: What are we prepared to give?

Part three of *Cody*—"Frisco: The Tape"—is the longest and most experimental attempt in the work to "tear time up" and "rip the guts out of reality." The deliberate aim to represent discontinuity and create a sense of simultaneous multidimensionality is raised to a new level—the experiential high and its "utter contempt for ordinary connectives" (89). While stoned on tea, pumped by bennies, and sweetened by wine, Kerouac tape-records conversations between Cody and himself (and, at times, others who join the fray) over several nights of reel-to-reel "whirlwinds." Part three, then, consists of the unedited transcripts of these nights of diversion and departure from the burdensome workaday motion of chronological time. Cut to the tape:

> Jack. Who me?
> Cody. —that's the prop, man, that's the prop—well who's gonna handle the prop?—go ahead, take it, I don't care . . . it's yours. . . . You come in without a prop, you got a prop *(Jack laughs) (because Cody imitating an Italian)*
> Jack. You're the Italian, see, who's selling the coconuts

Cody. Well if I'm not gonna smoke any Prisno beach I shall return
... to my shoes—Phew! I was missin you round Akron, trying to catch
a glimpse of your eyes. Some as big as your head, Jimmy!
Jimmy. Yeah?
Jack. Where's me wine? . . . oh there it is! *(Evelyn has it)*
Cody. He's drunk. . . . The wine of contention has become the wine
of mellowment and merriness
Jack. Oh the wine of mellowment! And *what?* . . .
Cody. And merriment! No I said melliment, mellimist-
Pat. —I thought you said merriness—
Cody. . . . . sepurious . . .
Pat. What, su*perf*luous
Cody. Superflous, that's it . . . wine has become superflous
Pat. Superious
Cody. Sup*ee*rious, that's the word
Everybody. What word?
Cody. Spoorious . . . spurious
    (Party continues on other side of reel)
    (Stan Kenton band playing "Artistry in Boogie") (very loud) (169–70)

A rather spoorious derangement of the senses, to say the least. In
reading through the entire transcript, one cannot help but chuckle
along, but with this conviction: for the most part, you could do as well
if not better in your own living room with your own microcassette
player or camcorder. The Fourth Night is the best one, that is, the most
substantive, because of the interesting reminiscences and stories told
by both Jack and Cody of their lives and relationships. Kerouac's early
impressions of Burroughs, Ginsberg, Herbert Huncke, Lucien Carr,
David Kammerer, Edie Parker, and others are recounted here, and the
recent whereabouts and condition of Cody's homeless father and other
family members are discussed. Despite the memorable reconstructions
of people, dates, and events, time appears to be spliced together here
in a curious way, reeling out of the mildly hallucinatory mind that tears
and repastes reality—the guts of it—like one of Burroughs cut-ups.

Part four—"Imitation of the Tape"—accelerates the rupture of time
and coherency through a mixture of dream, memory, and images from
popular culture that unwind in a surreal B movie of the imagination.
This is a conscious/subconscious attempt to write as if in a drug-induced state, often joining Kerouac's voice with the excited rambling

sudden shifts of Cassady's style—the "Cody I" experiment in merger. The usual connectives, sequences, and transitions have been dismissed as Kerouac abruptly alternates between the fantastic and incongruous recollections of boyhood and young adulthood experiences. The eccentricities of the free, random style in this brief part make "The Tape" seem like a stuffy panel discussion at an annual academic conference. In this sense, like all art, it is an improvement on life.

The final part—"Joan Rawshanks in the Fog"—begins with an observation of a Hollywood film crew shooting a scene from a Joan Crawford movie set in San Francisco before a crowd of craning onlookers. Kerouac joins the anonymous crowd and describes, frame by frame, the illusory spectacle, grotesque materialism, and undeserved fame of Hollywood in action. Upon seeing Rawshanks in the midst of the painstakingly contrived nature of the set, Jack cannot hold it in any more: "I said to her 'Blow, baby, blow!' when I saw that thousands' eyes were fixed on her and in the huge embarrassment of that . . . all these people are going to see you muster up a falsehood for money, you'll have to whimper tears you yourself probably never had any intention of using; on some gray morning in your past what was your real tear, Joan, your real sorrows, in the terrible day" (281). This contrast between false image and genuine reality speaks to our discontent in fashioning our own lives in accordance with the role of protagonist. The result is a general cultural malaise as we, like dull planets, depend on Hollywood to project its starburst of glamorous lights onto the movie screen so that our lives may flicker and move with dramatic action. "Joan Rawshanks in the fog, could it be the terrible dolors we all felt when we saw her suddenly alone in the silence, standing by the litup fence making ready to emote to millions, to erupt, vomit and obhurt to others; we are so decadent with our moues" (286). For Kerouac, Hollywood must be seen as serving our own combustible source of starlight: the only possible role for Hollywood, and its glut of social dreams, is to enrich "our own wild dreams."

And so it does, as Kerouac gets on with further unveilings of his own bright complicated visions, leaving Hollywood behind in the dim dustbin of its own cultural production. Several pages later, in his masterful section depicting a vision of Cody and the Three Stooges, a blend of spoof and hymn, Kerouac proves that one can use the materials of popular culture to create a wild, astounding, and ingenious dream of one's own invention. The numerous shifts from the lightning-swift narrative line in this brief sketch are lush and effective in combining free association stream of consciousness with literary merit. The sketch—which richly blends burlesque, slapstick, reverie, observations of city districts, biography, personal memories, classical allusions, and God—marks the acme of Kerouac's spontaneous prose in the study.

The remainder of the final part completes the "vertical, metaphysical study" of Cody by using a variety of formats that keep the reader guessing—up until the retelling of travel experiences that comprised *On the Road.* From that point on, the connective tissue is reestablished in the writing. The ending of the study manifests Kerouac's vision of loss and futility and love and pity all in the midst of a departure that leaves one facing "the necessary natural blankness of men—and Cody is blank at last."

> I not only accept loss forever, I am made of loss—I am made of Cody, too—he who rode a boxcar from New Mexico to L.A. at the age of ten with a bread underarm, (hanging from the grabiron) (over the couplings), he who lost his mother at nine, his father was a bum, a wino alcoholic, his brother ignored him. . . .
>
> GoodbyeCody—your lips in your moments of self-possessed thought and new found responsible goodness are as silent, make as least a noise, and mystify with sense in nature, . . . as silent and all this, as a bird crossing the dawn in search of the mountain cross and the sea beyond the city at the end of the land.
>
> Adios, you who watched the sun go down, at the rail, by my side, smiling—
>
> Adios, King. (397–98)

When Ginsberg first read the manuscript of *Cody* in 1952 (the book was not published in its entirety until 1972), he wrote a letter to Kerouac critiquing the work: "Sounds like you were just blowing and tacking things together, personally unrelating them, just for madness sake, or despair" (*SL,* 373).[3] Less than a month later, he wrote to Cassady: "Jack's book arrived and it is a holy mess—. . . . It appears to objective eye so diffuse and disorganized—which it is, on purpose—that it just *don't make.* Jack knows that too, I'll bet—why is he tempting rejection and fate?"[4] During the early 1950s, Kerouac's sensibility of rupture and discontinuity in the service of tearing up time and ripping reality apart to expose its very guts was anathema even to a figure like Ginsberg in his pre-*Howl* phase of poetics. Later, in his introduction to the published work, Ginsberg rehabilitated his opinion of *Cody*. In the meantime, he came to appreciate it as containing "the most sincere and holy writing I know of our age. . . . It's a consistent panegyric to heroism of mind, to the American Person that Whitman sought to adore. . . . 'Adios King!' a farewell to all the promises of America, an explanation and prayer for innocence, . . . a humility in the face of . . . hopeless America, hopeless World, in hopeless wheel of Heaven, a compassionate farewell to Love & the Companion" (x–xii). Ginsberg was right, absolutely right in *both* early and later assessments of the work. But the question still remains: why was Kerouac tempting fate? The answer lies in his very reason for writing *Cody* in the first place: "I'm writing this book because we're all going to die . . . my heart broke in the general despair and opened up inwards to the Lord, I made a supplication in this dream" (368). This is perhaps the best reason for writing anything that just "don't make" along the sensible and insistent trajectory of time.

3

The Revelation to Ti Jean

In a letter to Neal Cassady written at the end of 1950, Kerouac professed his faith in the Christian myth and its premise of original sin in a manner that would later be developed and refined in his fourth novel, *Doctor Sax:*

> Neal, this minute, I believe that Christ is the son of God, I do so believe tonight and probably now for the rest of my life, and I hope so. So I'm not "jealous of Jesus to the point of madness" like Mr. Nietzsche. . . . I'd say "ha-ha!" when I said it wasn't a STAR sought ME out, but a WORLD SNAKE; . . . I believed from early infancy, or sensed, in late-afternoon dreamy ways, that a SNAKE was coming after me. . . . I now know, the SNAKE came for all of us and caught us all, but Christ is the son of God & died for our sakes truly. . . . And to grow to be a man, however unfortunate and covered with sin and self-disgrace, and be foolish. For God intended it. (*SL,* 250–51)

It seems that, rather than hitching his wagon to Emerson's star, Kerouac grounded his soul in the ancient soil of the Great World Snake—Satan in steady pursuit, gaining on us, inch by inch. The only salvation from being claimed entirely by such evil resides, of course, in another mighty (and greater) force: God and his mediator-redeemer, Christ. Kerouac's belief suggests the Jansenistic influence that crept into the extreme piety and rigor of his French-Canadian Catholicism.

Jansenism, a seventeenth-century Catholic sect, stressed the corruption of human nature by original sin (see Genesis 3) and the power of divine grace. Rooted in Augustine and his teachings on grace, which insisted on the consequences of the original fall and the need for redemption, and also colored by the Reformation, the sect looked very selectively upon the dissemination of such grace. It embraced the doctrine of predestination that had been expressed by the Council of Trent: "though [Christ] died for all, yet all do not receive the benefit of his death, but only those to whom the merit of his passion is communicated."[1] Jansenism exaggerated the Augustinian view of human nature, stressing the guilt, depravity, and helplessness of humankind. Pascal, though never a strict Jansenist, absorbed much of this attitude and orientation, referring to man as a "slave of delectation." In one of his *pensées,* Pascal clarifies an oddity of Christianity: "It bids man recognise that he is base, even abominable; it also bids him desire to be like God. Without such a counterweight, his elevation would make him vain, or his abasement would reduce him to a terrible state of abjection."[2] This speaks directly to the imprint of French-Canadian Catholicism on Kerouac's sensibility. In another one of his *pensées,* Pascal raises the ante: "True conversion consists of self-annihilation before the universal Being whom we have often angered, and who may legitimately damn us at any moment; in recognising that we can accomplish nothing without him, and that we deserve nothing of him but disfavour."[3]

In *Doctor Sax: Faust Part Three,* Kerouac, writing from the perspective of a man-child, attempts to stand Jansenistic Catholicism on its head while at the same time registering its holy terrors. In the process, he also conveys a liberating vision of Revelation that reverses the direction of wrath and destruction; rather than instigated from on high (those seven angels trumpeting destruction) it is unleashed from below (the bottomless pit of the Great World Snake). Kerouac's mastery over the use of solecisms and greater control over his spontaneous prose, now placed in the service of storytelling, and his interest in both exposing and challenging his Catholic heritage, make *Sax* not only his most imaginative work, but his most hopeful one (and his personal favorite).

The novel, written in 1952 when Kerouac was thirty years old, is in turn frightening, amusing, serious, macabre, adventurous, mysterious, and wondrously joyful. A mixture of dream, memory, and fantasy, the story seeks to resurrect time, to keep it from becoming extinct or assuming "that rigid post or posture death-like denoting the cessation of its operation in my memory and therefore the world's" (75). Once again, Kerouac evokes the state of time in consciousness as a viable way to keep ourselves and our lives free of unbearable constraint—to stay alive to our own being-in-time rather than deadened to conditioned result. The novel, set in Lowell and spanning Kerouac's young boyhood years, captures a child's personal experience of religion as it merges with a whole realm of supersensible reality—an entire pantheon of sacred and secular ghosts. The sense of being haunted was acutely felt when Ti Jean was very young:

> Doctor Sax I first saw in his earlier lineaments in the early Catholic childhood of Centralville—deaths, funerals, the shroud of that. . . . Figures of coffinbearers emerging from a house on a rainy night bearing a box with dead old Mr. Yipe inside. . . . We had a statue of Ste. Therese in my house—on West Street I saw it turn its head at me— in the dark. Earlier, too, horrors of the Jesus Christ of passion plays in his shrouds and vestments of saddest doom mankind in the Cross Weep for Thieves and Poverty—he was at the foot of my bed pushing it one dark Saturday night . . . —either He or the Virgin Mary stooped with phosphorescent profile and horror pushing my bed. That same night an elfin, more cheery ghost of some Santa Claus kind rushed up and slammed my door. (4)

If memory and dream "are intermixed in this mad universe," as Kerouac claims at the end of the first chapter, then so too are the elements of the spiritual and supernatural, for they are drawn and blended into a child's impressionable mind from a variety of sources: Catholic images, French-Canadian ritual, primitive myth, folklore legend, and the phantoms of popular culture, including "The Shadow," "Doc Savage," and "Phantom Detective." In an era of increasing secularization, amply funded by rationalist ideologies, Kerouac worked against the grain, reinvesting the entire setting of Lowell, and his young consciousness, with the tremulous experience of the supersensible, as if to affirm the existence of a Hidden Sphere of Being.

Though at first they come to haunt the boy willy-nilly, in time the phantoms—both traditional and modern—order themselves in coherent fashion on either side of an ancient theme: the contention between good and evil. Such opposition occurs in the very midst of boyhood innocence, an appropriate precondition for revelation. In fact, Kerouac seems to pair the innocence of birth with the evil ever-present in Lowell and the world at large, "the moon glinting in a rat's eye" (11), as if to argue both for and against the Jansenistic notion that human nature is purely base and negative. In a fanciful memory of his birth, Kerouac recalls: "I remember the afternoon, I perceived it through beads hanging in a door and through lace curtains and glass of a universal sad lost redness of mortal damnation . . . the snow was melting. The snake was coiled in the hill not my heart" (17). Though born of ambivalence, that last sentence of the passage wants to reinforce a sense of innate purity, displacing evil to an external location—Snake Hill Castle, where the Satanic cult is holed up.

The whole purpose of Doctor Sax, whose methods in battling evil are Faustian but aim divine, becomes the challenge of Ti Jean as well: the development of "moral nerves" and the ability to "recognize good and evil and intelligence" (32). Of course, the premise for such ability is the fall itself and the state of original sin: "But the serpent said to the woman, 'You will not die; for God knows that when you eat of it your eyes will be opened, and you will be like God, knowing good and evil'" (Gen. 3:4–5). Therefore, we come round to "mortal damnation" and its attendant states of shame, enmity, pain, toil, and expulsion from immortality. This, Kerouac seems to say, is our starting point in the heroic struggle that remains to be won. So given this ragged inheritance, prophetic Sax, propelled to huge labors of mastery and conquest over evil, in earnest reclamation of a power robbed him, is duly enlisted in the battle set in time from the very beginning.

"Mwee hee ha ha ha," echoes Doctor Sax's refrain, a black-caped

LaMonte Cranston Shadow-like figure; and, like the popular crime fighter, Sax is naturally given to ambiguity, though he always fights for right in the end. Actually, Sax makes the Shadow appear rather pedestrian and out-phantoms him in style and appearance, sporting a black slouch hat (that conceals a rubber boat) and a visage of putrid-green night face, fiery red hair, brows and eyes that look malevolent, menacing, mocking in the midst of mystical endeavor, "a mad fool of power, a Faustian man" (43), and an alchemist by necessity in his efforts to protect the innocent. No doubt, this is quite an improvement upon popular culture and upon the Faustian legend, particularly given Sax's alignment with fervent religious engagement. He is indeed a strange figure, one who seems to rise up out of the industrial waste of Lowell, someone who deftly melds mysticism with the crazy antics of a holy stooge. Our first glimpse of him in the novel is when, after "a maniacal laugh [that] rises from the marshes, Doctor Sax comes striding with his stick, blowing snot out of his nose, casting gleeful crazy glances at frogs in mud puddles . . . old Doctor Sax here he comes. Rain glints on his nose as well as on the black slouch hat. . . ." His prophetic mission becomes immediately apparent: "'The end of the world,' he says, 'is coming . . .' He writes it on the walls of his underground house. . . . —he was a big fool forever looking for the golden perfect solution, . . . —for the boiling point of evil . . . —in South America, in North America, Doctor Sax had labored [for twenty years] to find the enigma of the New World—the snake of evil [a.k.a. the Great World Snake]" (27–28).

Doctor Sax's long and immaculate search for the ultimate mixture of powderous poisons to poof the snake of evil lead him to scour both North and South America. "'Palalakonuh beware!' is written on his wall. . . . Palalakonuh is merely the Aztec or Toltec name (or possibly Chihuahuan in origin) for the World Sun Snake of the ancient Indians of North America" (31–32). Kerouac thus joins Christian and primitive myth. Finally, in a further attempt to universalize the quest, Sax is also aided by Italian doves, *pippiones*, who travel to Tibet to secure invaluable herbs from Buddhist monks. Prophetic Sax prepares for the impending catastrophe, and rails against complacency: "'The snake is Rising Inch an Hour to destroy us—yet you sit, you sit, you sit'" (77). Looking up to the castle just outside of town, the modern embodiment of fallen Babylon—"a dwelling place of demons, / a haunt of every foul spirit," Sax broods on his Faustian mission in the service of divine salvation:

> "Ah—will my cloak ever flare and flutter in the darkness and great wind of Satan rearing from the earth with his—ugh! Therefore *meet* . . . that I have dedicated my life to the search and study of the Snake . . . for no—these mortals who here com-*bat* the hour of their sleep with traditional wings of angels . . . and moo their caps, or flaps—these Lowell, these mortality-rates—the children, the brown shroud of night—*meet* that I protect them from horrors they can not know. . . . I'll simply jump into the pit.
>
> "They think a pit exists not?" (151)

The pit yawns underneath the Castle of Snake Hill, upon which the other side gathers, that is, the rangy forces of evil embodied by the gruesome figures of Slavic folk legend gone tilt: vampires, vamps, wizards, gnomes, bats, and apostate Cardinals, all of whom prey ruthlessly on the good and unsuspecting citizens of Lowell. This Satanic cult is led by Count Condu and the Wizard: Condu, the vampire, "was sibilant, sharp-tongued, aristocratic, snappy, mawk-mouthed like a bloodless simp, mowurpy with his mush-lips swelled inbent." His theology is simple and reductive, if not a bit self-serving: "'I like my religion practical—blood is good, blood is life'" (23, 26). As for the Wizard, he is the real Faustus in this story, for he has joined with the devil: "He still bears the horrible marks of his strangulation and occupation by the Devil in the 13th century" (52). Together, the Count and the Wizard, and a host of other swarmy notables, supervise the gnomes' mean operation beneath the castle: the construction of numerous underground levels in order to build a redoubt somewhere down in the depths of the mine, which will greatly facilitate the sighing Snake's rise to the surface—heretofore only an inch an hour.

Therein lies the grisly business. And therein lies the need for Sax, who was everywhere in Lowell: "his glee supported us and made us run and jump and grab leaves and roll in the grass when we went home—Doctor Sax gets into the blood of children by his cape . . . the glee of night in kids is a message from the dark, there is a telepathic shadow in this void bowl slant" (57–58). Yet despite the glee that Sax provides amidst dark forebodings under castle walls, an important question pops into Ti Jean's mind: "what great difference was there between Count Condu and Doctor Sax in my childhood?" (46). This is simply another way of stating the former question: how does one distinguish between good and evil so that one truly knows which end is (*should* be) up and, conversely, down? For Ti Jean, it all comes down to a simple matter of scruples, which are temporarily abandoned when, in imitation of Sax, whom he has only seen in the shadows of Lowell (not yet understanding his real import), he takes on the persona of the Black Thief. Donning a slouch hat and cloaked by a Mephistophelean cape, Ti Jean terrorizes the neighborhood. "'Beware, To-night the Black Thief will Strike Again'. . . . I let go my 'Mwee hee hee ha ha' in the dark of purple violet bushes, . . . meditating the mysteries . . . and the triumph of my night, the glee and huge fury of my night, mwee hee hee ha ha." After stealing his friend Dicky Hampshire's bathing trunks, hoop, pole vault, wagon, and sundry other items, Ti Jean is finally caught and snapped out of his dark illusion. As he is apprehended, the difference quickly becomes apparent, and he fesses up without delay or pretense: "Mrs. Hampshire . . . said to me gravely in the eye, 'Jack, are *you* the Black Thief?' 'Yes' . . . I replied immediately. . . . 'Then bring back Dicky's things and tell him you're sorry.' Which I did, and Dicky was wiping his red wet eyes with a handkerchief." The mad drive toward deception, mastery, conquest, and possession—all Faustian qualities that can easily transform into mookish Condu-isms with a malign flick of the wrist—is seen in the broken face of another and instantly recognized. "'What foolish power had I discovered and been possessed by?' I asts meself" (47–49). Popeyed out of his hurtful prank, Ti Jean begins to know the color of evil, albeit *petit mal.* Nonetheless, it is a significant distinction, especially for the confrontation to come.

In the meantime, life goes on. So while Count Condu and the Black Cardinal, Amadeus Baroque, dismiss the heretical leftist movement of the Satanic cult—the Dovists, misguided idealists who believe the Snake will prove merely a husk of doves at the final hour—Ti Jean is pictured wrapped in the protective gloom of his home and town. The mundane level of existence and sensible texture of life—the scenes of boyhood fantasy play, the sounds of the Victrola, the smell of supper on the stove, the taste of freshly baked cupcakes—are seen by the reader as innocent designs set against the eerie rumblings of Snake Castle Hill. In the face of such horrible fantastic happenings, how long can such meek designs last? There is no other choice; Kerouac knows they must give way: "God bless the children of this picture, this bookmovie. I'm going on into the Shade" (97).

The shadow is cast when Ti Jean witnesses the sudden collapse and death of a man crossing the Moody Street Bridge at night. This event brings to mind other people and scenes that heighten the fact of suffering and the original "sin of life"—death. Like the sight of the funeral parlor perceived from the orphanage grotto—the Twelve Stations of the Cross arranged in separate glass kiosks with life-size statues, "everything there was to remind of Death, and nothing in praise of life" (125). Especially with Sax flitting from the back of one station to another, the grotto spooked and haunted, "culminating . . . [in] the gigantic pyramid of steps upon which the Cross itself poked phallically up with its Poor Burden the Son of Man all skewered across it in his Agony and Fright" (123). Uncle Mike, "the saddest Duluoz in the world," dying these past ten years, amplifies the meaning of the sorrowful visions: "'O the poor Duluozes are all dying!—chained by God to pain—maybe to hell! Oh my poor Ti Jean if you know all the trouble and all the tears and all the sendings of the head to the breast, for sadness, big sadness, impossible this life where we find ourselves doomed for death—why why why—just to suffer . . . for nothing— my child poor Ti Jean, do you know my dear that you are destined to be a man of big sadness and talent—it'll never help to live or die, you'll suffer like the others, *more*'" (118–20).

Every visit to Uncle Mike at any doomsday hour of the day or night drenches the spirit in fear and trembling: all reminds of death. Given the near totality of suffering and death in and around Lowell, Kerouac begs the question: where is something in praise of life to be found? For the time being, the only answer seems to lie in the "unconscious arrangement" of a flu epidemic, that is, the comfort Ti Jean feels at his mother's side as they are both driven to bed for a week by sickness: "so secure did I become that death vanished into fantasies of life, the last few days were blissful contemplations of the Heaven in the ceiling." Well again, the shade seems to recede for a while (until the floods commence), and Ti Jean now feels that he has "conquered death and stored up new life." Kerouac also gets in on the action here, as the adult emerges in the following line to invoke the tumultuous spirit of life to topple the solemn state of death: "Beautiful music, regale me not in my bier heaps—please knock my coffin over in a fist fight beer dance bust, God" (148). And though Ti Jean does not yet know it, Doctor Sax is also working in the service of life, concocting potions and flitting about in the night, in an effort to restore the lost bliss of goodness and innocence.

Before any such restoration can occur, however, the flooding of the Merrimac River, as prophesied by Sax, must pour out nature's wrath and destruction. The floods, a foretaste of the demoniacal strife to follow, are not "flowing from the throne of God," as pictured in Revelation, but from a more diabolical source. That "river of the water of life" turns into a "huge mountain of ugly sinister water lunging around Lowell like a beast dragon. . . . The river was Drowning Itself" (165–67). Ti Jean's initial excitement in the face of nature's wild spectacle gradually turns to grave symbolic concern about what this "unforgettable flow of evil . . . and of Satan barging through my home town" might portend. Of course, Sax, "King of Anti-Evil, . . . Enemy of the Snake" (168–70), is on hand to witness the disaster with one eye floating out to the flooded town and the other one fixed on the serpentine sludge beneath the castle. When the river swallows the town clock, the balance between nature and culture is upset, creating an unsettling sense of distortion: "time and the river were out of joint." A sense of loss pervades the marshy atmosphere of the town, "the gloom of the unaccomplished mudheap civilization when it gets caught with its pants down from a source it long lost contact with." Although the river eventually reaches its crest and begins to go down, "the damage has been done" (180). The stage is thus set for another long forgotten source to rear its ugly head again and rage through the land.

And so, after a lull before the darkest hour, during which the simple joys of everyday life in Lowell glow like hearthstones smoldering in mundane satisfaction, Doctor Sax and Ti Jean finally team up to examine and know the *difference*. Sax, with his protege clinging to his cape, brings the lessons—"the understanding of the mysteries"—on home to the youth. "'Moo-hoo-hoo-ha-ha-ha,' came the long, hollow, sepulchral sound of triumphant Doctor Sax's profound and hidden laughter. I made my own cackle-laugh, with hands cupped, in the excruciatingly exciting dark shadows of Saturday Night. . . . Gliding together . . . Doctor Sax and I knew . . . everything about Lowell" (199). The drift through the Lowell night precedes the adventure to the castle, because the lessons of life in this natural realm are to be learned before the supernatural is encountered. These are blunt and harsh lessons in horrific humility concerning life's own mysterious course through the here and now, there and later phenomena of living in time and through the welter of experience. As they look in on little Gene Plouffe through the window, ensconced in his bed covers reading a "Star Western," Doctor Sax explains to Ti Jean the facts of life in his own inimitable style:

> "You'll come to when you lean your face over the nose will fall with it—that is known as death. You'll come to angular rages and lonely romages among Beast of Day in hot glary circumstances made grit by the hour of the clock—that is known as Civilization. You'll roll your feet together in the tense befuddles of ten thousand evenings in company in the parlor, in the pad—that is known as, ah, socializing. You'll grow numb all over from inner paralytic thoughts, and bad chairs,—that is known as Solitude. You'll inch along the ground on the day of your death and be pursued by the Editorial Cartoon Russian Bear with a knife, and in his bear hug he will poignard you in the reddy blood back to gleam in the pale Siberian sun—that is known as nightmares. You'll look at a wall of blank flesh and fritter to explain yourself—that is known as Love. The flesh of your head will recede from the bone, leaving the bulldog Determination pointing thru the pique-jaw tremulo jaw bone point—in other words, you'll slobber over your morning egg cup—that is known as old age, for which they have benefits. Bye and bye you'll rise to the sun and propel your mean bones hard and sure to huge labors, and great steaming dinners, and spit your pits out, aching cocklove nights in cobweb moons, the mist of tired dust at evening, . . . —that is known as Maturity—but you'll never be as happy as you are now in your quiltish innocent book-devouring boyhood immortal night." (202–3)

Not altogether morose, Sax follows such knowledge about life and disillusionment with some rather sage counsel: "'FEAR NOT THE GREEN LOSS—every twig in your cerebular tree is aching to return to you *now*. No particular loss is there in the use of the loss— . . . all and every moment is yearning to stay grown to you even as the peerade passes it'" (204). Once again, when seen in conjunction, these two passages present another example of the competing states: consciousness in time, and time in consciousness. Nevertheless, however illuminating and profound, Sax cannot linger over these relatively mundane matters. They are simply stated and understood, spoken on the fly, if you will, gloom-shroud of disemboweled knowledge measured out the hard way, by slop and by drop, under sweat-drip of sun and ice-freeze of moon,—that is known as wisdom.

So on to the magical and supernatural realm they fly—to the destruction of the Great World Snake, stopping first at the forge-works located in Sax's subterranean shack to pick up the incredible mixture of deadly herb powders—a virtual "Ikon for the Void." The frenzied Faustian magician, seeking to transcend ordinary human ability, craving the ultimate power over evil, prepares for Armageddon: "'Anoint thee, son . . . we're going into Homeric battles of the morn. . . . The Blue Era!' cried Doctor Sax, dashing to his kiln—His shroud flew after him, he stood like a Goethe witch before his furn-forge, tall, emasculated, Nietzschean, gaunt" (211–12). Despite his enervated superhuman inflation, Doctor Sax is not without normal concerns and doubts. After ranging madly across the Americas for two decades to find the perfect solution, and just when the decisive conflict is at hand, Sax is momentarily seized by paralysis: "'The Snake's not real, tsa husk of doves. . . . I've waited 20 years for this night and now I don't want it. . . . Somehow it seems the evil thing should take a care itself, or be rectified in organic tree of things.'" Without much delay, Sax mumbles his way through these second thoughts and strengthens the resolve that remains—"'I go and make my mention, I go and seek my tremble'" (218–19).

Now it's on to Snake Castle Hill. Evading monsters, gnomes, Mayan spiders, huge scorpions, and garter snakes, our dynamic duo manage their way through beastly caves and, finally, to the decrepit dungeon and parapet of the infamous pit of the Great World Snake. On the parapet, Doctor Sax confronts the Wizard: "Sax stood proudly, whitely, before all of them; his grandeur was in the weariness and immovability of his position." The Wizard cajoles Sax into taking a peek at his lifelong enemy. There is a momentous pause in the action as Sax takes this opportunity to acquaint Ti Jean with the proportions and scale of evil. It is merely another facet of seeing and knowing the distinction between snake and dove. As Sax and Ti Jean look down from the Parapet of the Pit (like "looking down through a telescope at a planet"), the poor unknowing youth spies two lakes, a thin river running below them, and a rocky mountain. Realizing that the boy knows not what he sees, Sax comes to the rescue, ranting and raving in a peda-gogical style only appropriate to the convulsive and disturbing revelation at hand:

> "The lakes, the lakes!" screamed Sax leaping to the parapet and pointing down and cruelly grabbing me by the neck and shoving my head down to see and all the spectators primming their lips in approval—*those be his eyes!*"
>
> "Hah?"
>
> "The river, the river!"—pushing me further till my feet began to leave the ground—*that be his mouth!*"
>
> "Howk?"
>
> "The face of Satan stares you back, a huge and mookish thing, fool!—"
>
> "The mountain! The mountain!" I began to cry.
>
> "That—*his head.*" (224–26)

Kerouac seems to have a good sense of proportion, though it tends to pale compared with Revelation (12:3–4), which stresses the Great Red Dragon's enormous size (with seven heads and ten horns) and power: "His [Satan's] tail swept down a third of the stars of heaven, and cast them to the earth." Nonetheless, the effect on the lad is just as devastating, especially when the revealed sight of the Great World Snake is paired with its consequence—the Pilgrimage, led, of course, by the Wizard, who embellishes the notion of the "beast that comes up from the bottomless pit . . . [to] make war on them and conquer them and kill them" (Rev. 11:7). The Wizard, co-leader of the "black mass ecclesiasts," thus boasts:

> "I'll lead him through all the land, a hundred feet ahead, bearing my burden torch, till we reach the alkalis of Hebron. . . . We will darken the very sun in our march. . . . Fires shall eat your Lowells—the Snake'll make the subways his feeding-place—with one coy flick he'll snop up whole Directories and lists of the census, liberals and reactionaries will be washed down by the rivers of his drink, the Left and the Right will form a single silent tapeworm in his indestructible tube . . . the earth's returned to fire, the western wrath is done." (227–28)

The time for Judgment Day is now, and the good doctor, climbing the wall of the parapet with suction cups, begins his impossible magical feat with an incoherent invocation: "'Ah priests of the hidden Gethsemane. . . . Oh molten world of jaw-fires drooling lead—

Pittsburgh Steelworks of Paradise—heaven on earth, earth till you die
. . . but these old Doctor Sax eyes do see a horrid mess of snapdragon
shit and pistolwagon blood floating in that wild element where the
Snake's made his being and drink for all nigh on ta—Savior in the
Heaven! Come and lift me up'" (233). As Sax releases the vial of powders down into the pit, they burst and explode into awesome colors;
but the entire castle shudders and rocks in shocking earthquake, not
as a result of the magic but in response to the snake rising to the surface on his redoubt. Ti Jean, aghast, peers down into the pit, and discovers a primal source for his torment: "I began to look at its two great
lakes of eyes [and] I found myself looking into the horror, into the
void, I found myself looking into the Dark, I found myself looking
into IT, I found myself compelled to fall. *The Snake was coming for
me!!"* (238).

Kerouac's recurring sense of IT has now turned into a frightening
insight into the ancient form of evil; and, for once, in this framework,
IT becomes a felt experience that he does not exalt but decries, for
the man-child does not want to face the wrath and destruction of
Judgment Day, especially when unleashed from the bottomless pit.
Who knows what havoc those mighty forces in contention—the Snake
and the Golden Being of Immortality—might wreak upon the helpless inhabitants of earth once they get going? How will Ti Jean fare in
eternity? Will he land on his feet amid fleecy clouds or end up in the
ulcerated belly of the beast? IT is simply too much to contemplate.

As the Snake rises, the castle collapses, skewering, upending, and
pitting the Satanic cult. No mercy for this crew. But what of Sax and
his potions? Looking like an ordinary American schmo without his
vestments on, Doctor Sax faces the facts of his enormous aspirations
and the deflation of his Faustian-Sax-Superman-beyond-good-and-evil
ego: "'Goddam, it didn't work. . . . The herb didn't work . . . nothing
works in the end, . . . there's just absolutely nothing—nobody cares
what happens to you, the universe doesn't care what happens to mankind'" (240–41). Powerless beneath the Hidden Sphere of Being, old
Sax reverts to nihilism to account for his massive failure.

But suddenly, just when the Jansenists would be nodding their heads
and looking askance at the spectacle of the horrible beast rising from
its bottomless pit, saying, Read my lips, "It was and is not and is to
come" (Rev. 17:8), just then a huge majestic bird, with a wing span

ten to fifteen miles wide, appears out of the heavens to spoil the original design. "It was the Bird of Paradise coming to save mankind as the Snake upward protruded. . . . Tortured earth, tortured snake, tortured evil, but this Implacable Bird. . . . This could not be Judgment Day! There was still hope!"

> And just as the Snake had wound itself out to coil once around the rim of the Parapet and was trying to ease his ass out a hundred miles of hugeness and slime. . . . Just as this happened—the Great Black Bird came down and picked it up with one mighty jaw movement of the Beak, and lifted it with a *Crack* that sounded like distant thunder, as all the Snake was snapped and drawn, feebly struggling, splashing sweat—
>
> Lifted it in one gigantic movement that was slow as Eternity—
>
> Heaved skyward with its ugly burthen—Rollypolly mass of snake, curlicue, thrashing in every way upon the imprint heavens of poor life—how could anything take it in its beak—
>
> And raised up into the bedazzling blue hole of heaven in the clouds. (242–44)

In this benign vision of Revelation, in which Judgment is forestalled, no scrolls need be opened, no seals broken, no bowls of God's wrath poured onto earth. No one is condemned, and no one thrown into the lake of fire. Kerouac has essentially rewritten the account of the beast ascending from the pit to devour humankind (Rev. 17:8) to read as follows: It was and is not and never will be. For the fierce Bird of Paradise has plucked out the very heart of evil and hauled its dreary carcass away: "Off—up———up the bird rises farther. . . . The sailing objects in that distant Up are peaceful and very far—they are leaving the earth—and going into the ethereal blue—aerial heavens wait for them. . . . The sky is too bright, the sun is too mad, the eye can't follow the grand ecstatic flight of the Bird and Serpent into the Unknown—And I tell you I looked as long as I could and it was gone—absolutely gone" (244–45). Doctor Sax, "made a fool of," looks on in astonishment. His terse conclusion is the final purchase on this version of Revelation: "'I'll be damned. . . . The Universe disposes of its own evil'" (245). Such a benevolent vision, in which something convulsive and disturbing is made visible and then eliminated, not only restores hope but a sense of universal harmony as well. It is as if Kerouac wants to affirm a homogeneous universe that, contrary to the second law of thermodynamics, functions in a state of *dis*equilibrium, dispelling entropy (disorder) rather than conserving it. This altered state of physics has a theological thrust, in which the cosmos is tilted toward goodness and innocence, and where God's mercy is stretched to the limit. In the process, the self-destructive Jansenism in Kerouac's Catholic background has been released as well (though not permanently). Sketching in his notebook during the time *Sax* was composed, Kerouac wrote the following: "Evil dies, but good lives forever. . . . The greatest & only final form of 'good' is human—pray to God for the great reality (on yr. knees in Italian railyards near spectral tenements). . . . The true work is our belief; true belief in immortal good; the continual human struggle against linguistic abstraction; recognition of the soul beneath everything, & humor. . . . This is the return of the will." (ellipses in original).[4]

As for Doctor Sax, Kerouac's message to him appears rather clear: there is no need to be so exercised about it all and so inflated above and beyond the ordinary; given such a benevolent universe, all is blessed from on high; so throw your powers away and nurture your charms. "I have seen Doctor Sax several times since, at dusk, in autumn, when the kids jump up and down and scream—he only deals in glee now" (245). Kerouac's vision of Revelation is a simple and innocent and pure argument against nihilism; for power is the only value left when God is truly dead and done with, and Kerouac stakes a claim that this is not our fate, nor should it be. On the contrary, it is the whole realm of supersensible reality (and order) that, through a child's eyes, Kerouac brings to vivid life again, prevailing not only over disorder but over the deadened state of our loaded-down secular lives as well—given wholly to the pursuit of positivism and materialism. Kerouac seems to say that such a condition has dulled and limited our vision, casting our eyes at best toward the distant horizon, but never downward to the pit nor upward to the eternal pendulum of the Great Unknown.

Kerouac's revelation in *Sax* is pointed: one does not have to bear up without any religious or metaphysical consolation. He confirms this in the conclusion of the novel, as if to prove that death need not rule—that there is always something here in praise of life. As the Snake is raised up to the heavens, Ti Jean, hearing the bell ringing from the belfry, knows the town and himself have been spared the terror of an unspeakable abomination. The serene and tranquil picture that replaces such evil designs is evident everywhere. Ti Jean knows this difference as well as he now knows the distinction between good and evil, Sax and Condu, God and Satan. The sense of renewal is total:

> . . . the Lord rose on Easter morning, daisies rejoiced in fields beyond the churches, almighty peaces settled in the clover—up rose the huge monstrosities that have left our Spring! Our Spring is free to fallow and grow wild in its own green juices. . . .
>
> I went along home by the ding dong bells and daisies, I put a rose in my hair. I passed the Grotto again and saw the cross on top of that hump of rocks, saw some old French Canadian ladies praying step by step on their knees. I found another rose, and put another rose in my hair, and went home.
>
> By God. (244–45)

"By God"—the last two words of the novel—means for Kerouac that only by His grace have we won the "almighty peaces settled in the clover" and in every nook and corner of the universe. And he reminds the reader that such peace has not been won without an acknowledgment of both Christ's sacrificial cross and glorious resurrection. This too is offered in praise of life, and as given in Revelation (2:10): "Be faithful until death, and I will give you the crown of life." Perhaps this is why Ti Jean sports his own decorative crown and walks about with a carefree, joyful, even celebratory air; for, no doubt, in this story everything comes up roses.

4

The Track of Glory

"Once I was young and had so much more orientation," opens Kerouac's sixth novel, *The Subterraneans.* In reading on, one soon realizes that the author sets out to confirm this statement with hundreds of literary proofs. If anything is clear in this novel, then it must be the overwhelming sense of disorientation that suffuses the narrator's soul. The confident, triumphant youth of the town, who was both crowned and blessed with good-boy hope, has by now—as an adult—lost his bearings in the undertow of the cityscape. He is simply swept away.

The novel, written in three nights during October 1953, offers an explicit account of a brief but intense interracial romance embedded in the beat scene of San Francisco.[1] As with most of Kerouac's prose, it is remarkable how fresh and lively the work seems today—forty-five years after the fact. The novel still holds up these many mornings after mainly because Kerouac's prose style is infected with a relentless Dionysian spirit that collapses the rational mind in favor of the frenzies that "make shrill barbarian joy flare up."[2] It is as if Kerouac has gone electric, for the spontaneous prose in *The Subterraneans* seems like the charged currents of contagious excitement powered by the mind's many-leveled free associations. The style also amplifies the raw energy and tribal impulses of the bohemian subculture of the early 1950s and its unconventional modes of being. Finally, the spontaneous prose is very well suited to Kerouac's confessional approach to self-limitation, romance, beat behavior, and the attendant antagonisms, doubts, and conflicts that emerge.

During the first part of *The Subterraneans,* for a good fifth of the novel's length, the prose is very agitated and contains no fixed narrative line. For example, there are thirteen departures from the vanishing narrative line in the opening two paragraphs of the novel. The syntax within a given sentence is rather conventional in its structure; it is the synaptic juncture among sentences that electrifies: all those cross fires, nervous jumps, leaps and bounds, soaring flights, and unpredictable circuitries reverberating. After reaching a decisive point (see pages 19–21), a more-or-less stable form of narration begins to take hold. Nonetheless, an abiding sense of disjuncture remains intact throughout, as if Kerouac were claiming that this is how the pre-reflective mind actually operates before the editing, shaping, and revision occur (read "craft"). But the motivation for the novel is more complex than merely affirming Kerouac's essentials of spontaneous prose in practice. Moreover, the design and execution of the novel betray a mysterious trinity of factors: one part Benzedrine yak-talk; one part Dionysian-inspired madness; and one part pure Catholic confession. What we get in the bargain, aside from everything happening all at once, is a narrator who remains brutally honest about his own faults, refusing to give the reader a sympathetic view of himself or his situation. We also get some valuable insights into the fury of the moment, the essence of love, the construction of glory, and the traditional Catholic vision that resolves three into one.

What is ironic in the opening pages of the novel is the distance Kerouac puts between himself and the subterraneans. One immediately senses an uneasy relationship between the narrator—Leo Percepied—and the beat subculture which he observes and participates in. It appears as though Kerouac wants to disavow early on the role of spokesman for the beats, let alone king or father. This stance, a curious form of approach/avoidance, is often supported with self-lacerating remarks, in which the narrator feels disliked and cast off by the new bohemians from the very beginning in 1943. He refers to himself as a "big gleeful hood," (13) and imagines that Mardou, the love interest, is more drawn to "thin ascetic strange intellectuals of San Francisco and Berkeley and not . . . [to] big paranoiac bums of ships and railroads and novels and all that hatefulness which in myself is to myself so evident and so to others too" (6). Moreover, the narrator openly identifies himself as "an unself-confident man" and an "ego-maniac" who is rather crude in matters sexual (1). In the words of an elder subterranean, the narrator is quite simply "'the craziest piece of rough trade that ever walked'" (62).

This strained involvement with the subterraneans, and the unflat-tering portrait that is drawn of the narrator, continues in edgy prose for about the first twenty pages of the novel. Then something curi-ous happens: love settles a restless soul—for a spell. In meeting Mar-dou, the narrator enters the relationship in lust and loathing, but soon finds intimacy and love on the other side, moving swiftly from sexual conquest to shared story and deep affection: "Quick to plunge, bite, put the light out, hide my face in shame, make love to her tremen-dously because of lack of love for a year almost and the need pushing me down—our little agreements in the dark, the really should-not-be-tolds—. . . she began to tell her story . . . and thus began our true love—" (16–19). Oddly, Mardou's story of her flips and fugues brings a certain coherence to the novel. The narrator begins to calm down and weave a thread as he envisions her black Cherokee background and her half-breed hobo father: "sitting . . . with sweet Mardou I think, 'And this is your father I saw in the gray waste, swallowed by night—from his juices came your lips, your eyes full of suffering and sorrow, and we're not to know his name or name his destiny?'" (21). Reflect-ing on Mardou's father, and the vanished race that he represents, the narrator's compassion for his lover and "founder of her flesh" extends to a whole people as well:

> I saw the vision of her father, he's standing straight up, proudly, hand-some, in the bleak dim red light of America on a corner, nobody knows his name, nobody cares—. . . . "But they were the inhabitors of this

land and under these huge skies they were the worriers and keeners and protectors of wives in whole nations gathered around tents—now the rail that runs over their forefathers' bones leads them onward pointing into infinity, wraiths of humanity treading lightly the surface of the ground so deeply suppurated with the stock of their suffering you only have to dig a foot down to find a baby's hand." (19–21)

True love enters through the word. As he listens sympathetically to Mardou, the narrator absorbs, retells, and imagines; in the process, he incorporates her story heart and soul. This is how it starts, with talk and secrets, the rapture of being engulfed in each other confirmed by sound: "We begin our romance on the deeper level of love and histories of respect and shame" (21). As Mardou and the narrator express this deeper, confessional level of being, the lovers are united in mutual understanding and tenderness. For the time being, the narrator's egotism, mania, and self-consciousness are laid to rest by eros.

This is how love works, Kerouac seems to be saying, for the reader witnesses the heightened intersubjectivity between the lovers as expressed in both Mardou's and the narrator's voices, at times distinctive, at other times joined. As Mardou relates her mad tale of flipping out early one Easter morning, the reader hears her own peculiar language and style of narration. This alternates with the narrator's retelling or explanation of events in the broader and submerged context of Mardou's life among the subterraneans. These forms of narration are given even more variation with the use of intermittent dialogue (to advance the story) and interior monologue (to reveal unspoken reaction, or the thoughts of that secretive self withheld from the lover). The story itself has to do with Mardou stepping out naked onto the predawn streets of San Francisco, waiting alone on a fence in an alleyway for some sense of direction. The narrator places this innocent and indecisive figure of Mardou on a much larger canvas so that, once again, his concern about her vulnerability extends to the nobility and conquest of a once-proud and distinguished people:

> —the song of the Asia hunting gang clanking down the final Alaskan rib of earth to New World Howls (in their eyes and Mardou's eyes now the eventual Kingdom of Inca Maya and vast Azteca shining of gold snake and temples as noble as Greek [sic], Egypt, the long sleek crack jaws and flattened noses of Mongolian geniuses creating arts in temple rooms and the leap of their jaws to speak, till the Cortez Spaniards,

the Pizarro weary old-world sissified pantalooned Dutch bums came smashing canebrake in savannahs to find shining cities of Indian Eyes high, landscaped, boulevarded, ritualled, heralded, beflagged in that selfsame New World Sun the beating heart held up to it)—her heart beating in the Frisco rain, on the fence, facing last facts, ready to go run down the land now and go back and fold in again where she was and where was all— (25–26)

In ennobling Mardou, along with her racial and ethnic heritage, the narrators of this story within a story set the stage for a wondrous regression from the stain of culture to a purifying state of nature, thus clearing the slate for new beginnings. This image of being reborn, both to oneself and to another, is most apt for an Easter morning. "'I'd made up my mind,'" Mardou recounts, "'I'd erected some structure, it was like, but I can't—.'" Kerouac completes the thought: "Making a new start, starting from flesh in the rain. . . ." Stripping it down and then building back up on her own terms, Mardou begins to reestablish her world. She moves naked from the alley to a stranger's door, knocks, and is christened with a first blanket and then some "first clothes" from an Italian woman. (In Mardou's own words: "'Here is a woman, a soul in my rain, she looks at me, she is frightened.'") Then she borrows money from a friend to purchase a brooch she'd seen before in a handicraft shop at North Beach—"'it was the first symbol I was going to allow myself.'" The narrator sums up the spiritual progression: "Out of the naked rain to a robe, to innocence shrouding in, then the decoration of God and religious sweetness" (26–27).

In absorbing Mardou's story, by truly taking it to heart, the narrator displays his sympathy for her, his ability to feel strongly with her as she feels with herself. In a step that moves beyond sympathy to merger with the lover, Kerouac transforms Mardou's words into his own, alternating a point of view conveying fragility with the narrator's counsel. This lover's discourse, a testament to Kerouac's receptivity and a projection of his sensibility, is simply another, more imaginative form of call and response. It begins as Mardou comes down the fence and moves on tiptoe through the alleyway:

"Why should anyone want to harm my little heart, my feet, my little hands, my skin that I'm wrapt in because God wants me warm and Inside, my toes—why did God make all this all so decayable and dieable and harmable and want to make me realize and scream— . . .

I quaked when the giver creamed, when my father screamed, my mother dreamed—I started small and ballooned up and now I'm big and a naked child again and only to cry and fear. —Ah—Protect yourself, angel of no harm, you who've never and could never harm and crack another innocent its shell and thin veiled pain—wrap a robe around you, honey lamb—protect yourself from rain and wait, till Daddy comes again, and Mama throws you warm inside her valley of the moon, loom at the loom of patient time, be happy in the mornings." (26)

The final way in which Kerouac reflects the transformation wrought by love, and its shared discourse, is by letting Mardou and her story swirl around inside his imagination. After establishing her presence inside of him, the narrator now takes off in lyrical "lostpurity" flourishes that appear in parentheses (see pp. 31–33). It is Kerouac's way of reemerging in sync with Easter morning as he finds it—on the workaday sidewalks of San Francisco, relating his own poetic version of events commensurate with "'that great confidence and gold of the morning'" Mardou refers to (34). The strength of this mystical unity eventually cracks up and the story finally ends with Mardou locked up in the nuthouse for forty-eight hours. All wrapped up in Mardou's Easter passion, the narrator admits that

no girl had ever moved [him] with a story of spiritual suffering and so beautifully her soul showing out radiant as an angel wandering in hell and the hell the selfsame streets I'd roamed in watching, watching for someone just like her and never dreaming the darkness and the mystery and eventuality of our meeting in eternity. . . . We hugged, we held close—it was like love now, I was amazed—we made it in the livingroom, gladly, in chairs, on the bed, slept entwined, satisfied—. . . . Our stories told, our love solidified. (36–37)

At this point in the novel, the portentous elements of the story coalesce and the narration solidifies as well. Just prior to the second part of the novel, the reader is given a précis of what will happen. We glimpse the narrator's many goofs, which include "drinkings and downcrashings and times I ran out on her," as well as the final desertion that results in Mardou's betrayal (38). But drunken folly, an inherent part of the Dionysian ritual of intoxication, whereby the benefits of ecstatic celebration blend with the dangers of chaotic madness, is but one of several elements that define the narrator's constructive-destructive tendencies. The other elements consist of conflicts that pair doubt with desire and the sexuality of love with the asexuality of work. Such conflicts lead to the ultimate resolution, a kind of Faustian bargain in which the narrator exchanges essence for construction.

The tension between the narrator's love for Mardou and his general sense of well-being begins to surface soon after the storytelling episode ends. Whereas love seeks its territory in the essence of sexuality, well-being marks its progress in the daily construction of moral duty. The latter, which embodies the reality-seeking principle of sobriety, guides productive action and, in this instance, literary creation. Combining traditional and feminist perspectives, Mardou expresses the hypostatic notion of woman (epitomizing essence) and pairs this with man's basic preoccupation and penchant toward objectification. "'Men are so crazy, they want the essence, the woman is the essence, there it is right in their hands but they rush off erecting big abstract constructions. . . . They rush off and have big wars and consider women as prizes instead of human beings, well man I may be in the middle of all this shit but I certainly don't want any part of it'" (16). Although the narrator agrees in principle with Mardou, he cannot bring himself to quit the track of glory and deconstruct his own grand erections. He finds her essentialism so compelling that he can't stop himself from being himself, that is, from assuming his male-scripted, masculine role: "And so having had the essence of her love now I erect big word constructions and thereby betray it really. . . . I have to rush off and construct construct—for nothing" (17). For nothing short of glory, that is, the furious race to the attainment of praise, honor, distinction, and renown.

This engendered conflict between essence and construction is accompanied by numerous doubts about Mardou and her racial background, daily habits, and sanity. At first, the narrator is tongue-and-cheek about how Mardou might undermine his southern self-image, "like in that Faulknerian pillar homestead in the Old Granddad moonlight." Taking a good gulp from that image, he wonders: "What would they say if my mansion lady wife was a black Cherokee, it would cut my life in half, and all such sundry awful American . . . white ambition thoughts or white daydreams." He is more serious, however, concerning the impact of his confessions upon Mardou, especially those that contain a racial component. After relating one rather intimate detail to her, he thinks to himself: "It must have stabbed her heart to hear, it seemed to me I felt some kind of shock in her being at my side as she walked" (45). Another doubt with respect to the racial factor is actually more of a fear that "she was really a thief of some sort and therefore was out to steal my heart, my white man heart, a Negress sneaking . . . the holy white men for sacrificial rituals" (49).

A final doubt, one that threatens to derail the romance, involves the narrator's own homosexual interests and flirtations. On two occasions, the narrator's ultramasculine pose is subverted, and he willingly subjects himself to public humiliation by fawning over the gay writer Alva Lavalina (Gore Vidal) and the red faun boy. He actually stands Mardou up for Lavalina; however, the reader is given the distinct impression that nothing untoward occurred at the latter's place, save for the fact that Leo fell asleep on the couch and was several hours late in meeting up with Mardou. Much like Pentheus in Euripides' *Bakkhai,* Kerouac's narrator displays an alter ego wherein lies a feminine narcissism, softness, and play of submission. While the narrator explains that such behavior was simply part of putting Mardou to the test, one wonders about his (and Kerouac's) fear of being dominated and overwhelmed by Mardou's sexual power. After paying tribute to the feel of her French quarter, the narrator admits a "final lingering physiological doubt." But this physical doubt belies a more primal psychological fear related to the active force concealed within essence: "the pull and force of [Mardou's vaginal] muscles being so powerful she unknowing often vice-like closes over and makes a dam-up and hurt. . . . this contraction and greatstrength of womb." The narrator thinks back to when he heard of a friend's first sexual encounter with Mardou, in which he "experienced piercing unsupportable screaming-sudden pain, so he had to go to a doctor and have himself bandaged and all . . . I now wonder and suspect if our little chick didn't really intend to bust us in half" (76).

Taken as a whole, however, these aforementioned doubts—whether superficial or deep-seated—alternate with certain desires and affirmations regarding the loved one. As previously mentioned, the narrator is drawn to her spiritual struggle. He also admires her beauty and finds himself attracted to her hip, modern style of new-generation panache and enjoys cutting around the city with her and being seen. Of course, there are also the good times—like sending love letters or sharing a fifth of Tokay on the perch of Nob Hill, the infinite pleasures of the boudoir, terms of endearment or reassurance, plans for the future, and the infectious silliness and telepathies of lovers who begin to feel utterly at home with each other. Together, the doubts and desires weave the skeins of joy, passion, ambivalence, and anguish—that taut web where lovers typically find themselves enmeshed.

It is not simply the bad times that doom this relationship. Though the drunken goofs, repeated lateness, irritations, temper tantrums, and constant flights back to the sober world of novelistic solitude tend to gain the upper hand on the good times, in fact, "to make [them] sick," ultimately the affair is sabotaged by the narrator's own dream that rapidly turns into a self-fulfilling prophecy. The dream involves Mardou's betrayal of the narrator with one of his rivals, Yuri Gilgoric (Gregory Corso), a young poet who recently descended into the subterranean scene intent on breaking up the established trinity of Adam, Carmody, and Leo (namely, Ginsberg, Burroughs, and Kerouac—the ur-beats). Of course, in the spirit of confession, the narrator tells all to both Mardou and Yuri, thus planting the idea in their heads. Before long, the dream begins to alter life, which in turn reinforces the prophecy of the dream. The dream's surge into reality starts when the narrator inadvertently spies Mardou and Yuri flirting. Then, although still aroused by eros and clearly agitated with jealousy, the narrator begins to plan and act in ways that he does not fully endorse. In other words, he begins to ditch Mardou and, in doing so, dig his own grave:

> I saw for the first time their youthful playfulness which I in my scowlingness and writer-ness had not participated in and my old man-ness about which I kept telling myself "You're old you old sonofabitch you're lucky to have such a sweet thing" (while nevertheless at the same time plotting . . . to get rid of Mardou, without her being hurt, even if possible "without her noticing" so as to get back to more comfortable modes of life, like say, stay at home all week and write and work on the three novels to make a lot of money and come in to town only for good times if not to see Mardou then any other chick will do . . .). (81)

Unable to reconcile the many conflicts that fracture his love for Mardou, the narrator, letting up a good deal of the thread himself, simply lets matters unravel. As Mardou and Yuri get close to "making it," the narrator's heart sinks. But he seems to take masochistic pleasure in such an eventuality: "my heart sank deep—it sank so I gloated to hear it [a possible tryst between Mardou and Yuri] for the first time and the confirmation of it crowned me and blessed me. . . . 'Well boy here's your chance to get rid of her' . . . but the sound of this in my own ears sounded awfully false" (85). Finally, in a drunken binge, the narrator takes the final step that triggers Mardou's betrayal:

> The final shocker being when in a cab together she's insisting I take her home (to sleep) and I can go see Sam alone (in bar) but I jump out of cab, madly . . . and run into another cab and zoom off, leaving her in the night—so when Yuri bangs on her door the following night, and I'm not around, and he's drunk and insists, and jumps on her as he'd been doing, she gave in, she gave in—she gave up. . . . the pain, why should "the sweet ram of their lunge in love" which has really nothing to do with me in time or space, be like a dagger in my throat? (38–39)

The prophecy fulfilled, Mardou's light on "Heavenly Lane" no longer shines for the narrator. Love dies—a signal of a more universal truth: "'But some day, dear Leo, that light will not shine for you'— this a prophecy irrespective of all your Yuris and attenuations in the snake of time. . . . And at home I wandered around . . . as if I could smell the flowers of death in the air, and I went in the South San Francisco railyard and cried. Cried . . . sitting on an old piece of iron under the new moon" (102–03). The loss and sorrow that accompany the separation from Mardou soon give way, once again, to more fundamental matters, such as "'discharg[ing] the debt / of penitence that's paid when tears are shed.'"[3] Though staked to the iron-bound yard (the ten-block-long "BETHLEHEM WEST COAST STEEL" neon sign before him), Leo's vision is cast upward, like an ancient stargazer registering the distance from earthly to divine. He is focused on the expanse of the heavens beyond the transient city "Lane," noxious industrial misappropriation, and waxing celestial body. And what he sees there is the face of his mother and a vision of her protective, angelic love for him: "that expressionless-because-so-profound face bend-ing over me . . . as if to say *'Pauvre Ti Leo, pauvre Ti Leo, tu souffri, les hommes souffri tant, j'ainque toi dans le monde j'va't prendre soin, j'aim'ra beaucoup t'prendre soin tous tes jours mon ange.'*—'Poor Little Leo, poor Little Leo, you suffer, men suffer so, you're all alone in the world I'll take care of you, I would very much like to take care of you all your days my angel'" (103–4).

No doubt by now a few questions must come to mind: Is the narrator's failure to love Mardou simply an expression of spiritual impoverishment and bondage to self? Where does the track of glory end— in the South Frisco railyard? Is that it? And what kind of soul-sickness is this that would turn a man into a drunkard, a drunkard into a lover, and a lover into a child? Inflicting yet another lash on himself, the narrator actually improves on his mother's consoling lines: "poor *stupid* Ti Leo" (emphasis mine).

In defense of Kerouac, and Ti Leo, there is something else at work here, something perhaps alien to those socialized into the American pop culture Church in the aftermath of Vatican II, during the mellowing period of creamy Catholicism. Kerouac ingested his immigrant Catholicism the hard way, scourging himself for being a penitent sinner, stretching himself on the rack of time, and subjecting himself to the guilt, suffering, and self-abasement of a subterranean martyr who, though seeking peace and well-being, could not control the holy terror of his passions. In short, he believed; and because he believed in the classic teachings of Catholicism, he found himself lacking and longing for spiritual purification in the midst of certain human folly. If he were, say, a lapsed Unitarian then there would be nothing left to write about. But a lapsed Catholic pre–Vatican II figure with pagan impulses and a medieval load on his conscience, let loose amid the secular strife of the modernist era—now there we have at least a basis for spiritual struggle. Such struggle not only gives credence to the traditional Catholic cycle of sin, guilt, and redemption, but offers new meaning to being cast off and sunk beneath the tracks of glory as well:

> Something fell loose in me—O blood of my soul I thought and the Good Lord or whatever's put me here to suffer and groan and on top of that be guilty and gives me the flesh and blood that is so painful the—women all mean well—this I knew—women love, bend over you—you'd as soon betray a woman's love as spit on your own feet,

clay—. . . . "deep in the dark pit of night under the stars of the world you are lost, poor, no one cares, and now you threw away a little woman's love because you wanted another drink with a rowdy fiend from the other side of your insanity." (104–5)

In light of this abject condition and posture of humility, Leo's vision of his mother-love should not be reduced to mere neurosis or infantile fantasy. Rather, similar to Dante's Beatrice, the narrator's return to the angelic demeanor and protective consolation of his mother reveals a higher spiritual purpose—it is an intermediate step to God's own love and solace.[4] In part, this helps to explain why the narrator abandons the narrow confines of "Heavenly Lane" (eros) for the hope of reaching the greater platonic expanse (agape). Also, we must keep in mind that to be childlike and pitiable—ignorant, helpless, and dependent—constitute the necessary preconditions for crying out and opening oneself to receiving grace and true glory. For Kerouac, it is the ache of living and the pain of losing that jump-starts that cycle which begins in grief and ends in hope. In the words of the narrator, the pain that compels him to write the novel "won't be eased by the writing of this but heightened, but . . . [it] will be redeemed" (18). Given this emphasis, one realizes that Kerouac is playing the hard way and that a necessary sacrifice transcends the continuum on which he slides, back and forth, from Dionysian intoxication to the well-being of sobriety. His deeply felt sense of self-laceration and need for spiritual purity is a modern example of *Contemptus Mundi,* a traditional Christian theme reinforced by classical thought, which does not view the world as something to be enjoyed; rather, it is a place of sorrows and trials that prepare one for a better, otherworldly destiny amid "the love that moves the sun and the other stars."[5]

Kerouac's vacillation between hedonism and asceticism warped the grooves of the real track he was on. The lesson this continual back and forth brought home to him was that sweetness and happiness were always vulnerable to fury and pain, "and if only it were a dignified pain and could be placed somewhere other than in this black gutter of shame and loss and noisemaking folly in the night and poor sweat on my brow" (18). For Kerouac, the plight of the subterraneans was equivalent to the futility inherent in the human condition itself; the beats simply exaggerated this in their own inimitable way. Moreover, only a transcendent vision that stressed a view of the temporal world as one promising suffering and tribulation could still the frenzied motion of that figure on the (t)rack of time and lift him out of the "black gutter" of existence.

By the end of the novel, the narrator begins to raise himself out of turmoil by seeking some sense of levity. As if wearing a holy smile that says, *look, all this madness is merely an illusion of embodiment,* he finds the spiritual release that perhaps justifies all those messy carnal realities. Although clearly pierced—"stabbed by Yuri—by Mardou . . . forsaken and shamed"—Leo resolves to turn his hurt into a halo, forgiving all, and seeing events as part and parcel of a deflated divine comedy (or farce). Conjuring an image of Yuri in a daydream, Leo sees "suddenly the glare of a jester angel who made his presence on earth all a joke and I realize that this too with Mardou was a joke and I think, 'Funny Angel, elevated amongst the subterraneans'" (109–11).

So there you have IT. Perhaps this entire chapter is a roundabout way to answer one basic question: Is a Kerouac novel worth his grief? Mardou would probably respond in the negative, for she felt that "Baudelaire's poem [was] not worth his grief": "'I would have preferred the happy man to the unhappy poems he's left us'" (10). Kerouac is Baudelaire, for he ends *The Subterraneans* with these final two lines: "And I go home having lost her love. And write this book" (111). This is the real motive behind the dream-prophecy fulfilled in the novel; it is one intent on the construction of glory, both secular and sacred.

Although part of me agrees with Mardou, I am inclined to think that Kerouac's work was worth his grief on at least two counts: one, his sacrifice on the altar of literature produced some astonishing and enduring results that cultures throughout the world will appreciate and benefit from for a long time to come; and two, such work was an autobiographical necessity. That is, Kerouac's general sense of well-being (and sustained moments of sobriety and disciplined action) depended on writing as a way of bringing order to life's destructive elements (the shadow of Dionysian intoxication). Without writing and the construction of glory, Kerouac would have drowned in those turbulent subterranean waters before his time. On the other hand, and as Kerouac well knew, greatness can also be "a big chill in the wind" (9). And how many more years did it really give him? So, after the narrator checks out of the novel, one afterimage remains. I imagine Mardou joining the female chorus of *The Bakkhai,* adding her voice to the essence of that collective:

> Life passes so fast—
> knowing that, who would chase
> greatness, and lose the sweet life
> already in our hands?
> Men die on the track of such glory—but I call
> what they do madness.[6]

PART TWO

The Noble Path

The road that's followed goes forever;
in half a minute crossed and left behind.
—Gary Snyder, "Night Highway 99"

5

Gone Beyond

One day in early January 1951, several months before composing the roll manuscript of *On the Road,* Kerouac ducked into St. Patrick's Cathedral on Fifth Avenue. At this time, when his spirituality sought religious form, it still rested in the Gothic architecture of Christianity. This coming together of spiritual content and religious form was not necessarily a smooth marriage; it had been arranged by his immigrant Catholic heritage. Once inside, initially rebellious toward the authority of the Church, Kerouac found a pew and "sneered as all the commonplace 'renegade Catholic' thoughts came to [him] in regimental order." But before long, the aura of the Cathedral softened his attitude, and he was "lost in real sweet contemplation of what was going on." For the moment, Kerouac evaded the undignified materialism of the modern and managed to dodge the cascading shadows of skyscrapers. Was it Manhattan in 1951 or Stuttgart in 1450? He couldn't be sure. The young priest's sermon about poverty, humiliation, and suffering connected the "invisible world" of these two eras, that is, "the advantages of humility and piety in the invisible world that will surmount the pride and decadence of the visible." Kerouac could not help but agree. As if to test the dignity of this rock of ages, Kerouac spies two "old W.C. Fields absentminded stumble" priests making a novena

> like any other two old guys, like seeing your father and my father in priest vestments, burly, red-faced, harassed, hurrying at their tasks, and such gently lovely tasks, the reading of words they had read a thousand times before, all about angels and the Lord and the Lamb and the Virgin Mother, over and over again, till it really becomes interesting and mysterious. . . . They looked like they were making a living. God knows I'm not being facetious here—or funny, or sarcastic. (*SL*, 286–88)

The collapse of the sacred and profane into "gently lovely tasks" is quintessential Kerouac. Under one roof, religious form and spiritual content (not to mention an image from popular culture) meet in harmony. Perhaps inspired by the Cathedral's vaulted ceilings and rose windows, Kerouac sets his sights even higher. The transcendent vision that emerges, rooted in simple virtues and embodied in the devotions of the two old stumble priests, expresses a gnostic and universal longing that ultimately rejects materialism and the corporeal in exchange for the attainment of "pure souls":

> I wished that the church was not only a sanctuary but a refuge for the poor, the humiliated, and the suffering; and I would gladly join in prayer. . . . I wished all mankind could gather in one immense church of the world, among the arcades of the angels, & when it came time to take of bread, I wished Jesus would reach out his hand to a single loaf and make of it two billion loaves for every single soul in the world. What else would we need besides God and the bread for our poor unfortunate bodies? And then someday we could all become pure souls—not animals and not even mortal men, but angels of heaven—and spend all our time, like the old priests, scanning the words of God over and over again till they become our only concern, our only language, our only imagery, our only wish and our only life, eternal life. (SL, 286–92)

Three years after this incident, Kerouac would make good on his claim that "all things are different forms that the same holy essence takes" (*SL*, 525). By this time, Kerouac would fashion himself as a kind of Buddhist desert father, proclaiming: "THE WHOLE WORLD A MONASTERY, ASCETICISM, CHASTITY. . . . self-realization or highest perfect wisdom, ecstasy of transcendental insight, . . . the emancipation of all suffering sentience from the unbroken chain of suffering's causation can only be achieved in solitude, poverty, and contemplation—and in a gathering of homeless brothers" (*SL*, 447). Though the religious worldviews have become vastly different, it is remarkable that the underlying "holy essence" remains virtually the same as that manifested in the sanctuary and refuge of the church—poverty, humiliation, and suffering.

From kneeling in a Gothic cathedral to sitting in a Buddhist monastery measures the distance covered by Kerouac's leap of religious form. About one year before his discovery and immersion in Buddhism, while working on the railroad in San Francisco, Kerouac's spiritual urgency clearly made itself known: "All I want to do is love—God will come into me like a golden light & make areas of washing gold above my eyes, & penetrate my sleep with His Balm—Jesus, his Son, is in my Heart constantly."[1] Not until after his failed love affair with Alene Lee (Mardou from *The Subterraneans*) would such spiritual intensity reconfigure itself to fit an Eastern form. Kerouac stumbled upon Buddhism in October 1953, after a "wild summer, ending in despair and sadness, . . . and then, miracle of miracles, . . . sadly walking across the railyards by the full sad yellow moon, I went to the library to pick up books on Oriental Philosophy and came up, idly, with Asvhaghosha's Career of Buddha, or Buddha-Charita, which I read with heavy heart getting lighter every hour, rushing back to the library for more Buddhism" (*SL*, 525–26).

By early May 1954, Kerouac was *on the way* with his Buddhist studies, writing to Ginsberg that, "generally speaking, I have crossed the ocean of suffering and found the path at last" (*SL*, 410). In this letter, Kerouac included a bibliography of Buddhist materials, including Samuel Beal's translation of the *Dhammapada* (texts from the Buddhist canon), Dwight Goddard's *A Buddhist Bible,* and Henry Clarke Warren's *Buddhism in Translation* in order to inspire and direct Ginsberg toward the diamond of enlightenment, "which I advise and in fact insist on with all my heart heat and argument and brotherliness" (*SL*, 416).[2] Kerouac also informed Ginsberg that he was preparing an account of Buddhism from his own "private memorial notes," meditations, poems, blues choruses, prayers, and sketches (recently published as *Some of the Dharma*), which was meant to serve as a guide, a sort of handbook, for both himself and others. Later in that same month (17 May), Jack wrote to Carolyn Cassady that he was now leading a "quiet meditative life in my room and in the sunny yard where I have planted a vegetable garden, and turning down requests from beautiful girls over the telephone" (*SL*, 419).

Kerouac's immersion in Buddhist self-study and meditation from December 1953 (when he began *Some of the Dharma*) to March 1956 (when he wrote his last entry) found form in seven books written in an intensive two-year period (1955–1957). If he was practicing Non-Ado and diminishing with one hand, "discard[ing] such definite imaginations of phenomena as your own self" (*SGE*, 34), he was scribbling furiously and accumulating with the other that supported some notion of an ego entity, a persistent literary self seeking "Fame Immortal" ("Daydreams For Ginsberg," in *Scattered Poems*, 12). Of the seven books written during this time, Buddhism plays a dominant role in five (*Wake Up*, a biography of the Buddha; *Mexico City Blues*; *The Scripture of the Golden Eternity*; book one of *Desolation Angels*; and *The Dharma Bums*) and a present though more balanced role in the remaining two (*Tristessa* and *Visions of Gerard*), not to mention "San Francisco Blues." This is an astonishing creative outpouring of work for any writer. In fact, it was the most productive period of Kerouac's career, surpassing in sheer volume the five novels he had written between 1951 and 1953, demonstrating that the discovery of Buddhism was both an inspiration for the ongoing spiritual-literary-artistic quest as well as a very useful "protective device."

Both inspiration and device blended into an undifferentiated whole as Kerouac sought a form of original Mahayana Buddhist ecstasy that would not only offer consolation for disappointment, suffering, and loss, but provide the means and conditions necessary for delivering one from the trepidations of "mortal hopelessness." No doubt his conversion to Buddhism soothed Kerouac's grief and anxiety that centered on his professional writing career. By January 1954, Kerouac had written five unpublished novels plus sketches and poetry. In fact, the first break into print since *The Town and the City* (1950) had not come until the summer of 1954, when *New World Writing* accepted an excerpt from Kerouac's *Road* novel—"Jazz of the Beat Generation," mainly due to the efforts of Malcolm Cowley. (*Paris Review* accepted another excerpt the following summer—"Mexican Girl.") Buddhism provided Kerouac with the fortitude he needed to bear up; actually, near the end of his immersion Kerouac began to see the neglect of his work, which required "humility and patient suffering," as being "intended as a path [to] Buddhahood" (*SOD*, 411).

Neither difficulties in love nor work, however, fully explain the depth of Kerouac's involvement with an Eastern way of life that promised emancipation of the body, enlightenment of the mind, and tranquility of the spirit. Consolation, justification, and substitution all explain away his attraction to Buddhism, which was at once deeply personal, intellectual, and spiritual. The conversion did what any conversion would do—it gave his spirit new life, another huge house to inhabit and roam within for a good while, and it endowed him with a seemingly unlimitable reservoir of concepts, images, and practices to draw upon for the writing trade. In sum, the infusion of Buddhist teachings combined the word and the way in a transcendental form of belief that would take Kerouac's spiritual quest beyond, altogether beyond, into unforeseen awakenings and struggles.

The conversion to Buddhism was driven by unresolved conflicts that created confusion and turmoil. In *Some of the Dharma*, Kerouac reflected his growing awareness that hedonistic coddling of the senses ensnared one in opposite emotive forces. By scaling the heights of Buddhist meditation, Kerouac realized he could transcend the rigid dualisms that ailed him throughout his life, thereby attaining equanimity of mind or, as he commented parenthetically, the "zero point between joy and sorrow" (*SOD*, 10). Soon after his introduction to Buddhism, Kerouac knew that the only way to resolve the conflict inherent in *On the Road*, and prevent those ecstatic highs and abysmal lows, was to stay even. This then became the primary aim of his spiritual liberation during his Buddhist phase, to get off that roller coaster of transient desire (the "tormented state") and aspire to a new form and vehicle for rapture—Buddhist bliss. As if having both *Road* and *Subterraneans* in mind, Kerouac limns a fundamental truth associated with attachment to the world: "If torment is love then love is torment and all sentient life is in a tormented state which it calls joy and sorrow and which, when removed from before the Mirror of Emptiness, vanishes. Unwind the thread of the world to unborn ecstasy, for the soul is dead" (*SOD,* 21). Or, in a subsequent codification, "SENSATION equals CRAVING equals GRIEF" (*SOD,* 27).

On an even more fundamental level, the overriding appeal of Buddhism to Kerouac was that it offered him a fruitful illusion that alleviated the unbearable "burden of time" and the discord bred of time, which haunted and dogged him throughout his life. For Kerouac, this burden was interchangeable with mortal hopelessness (the drag factor of death-in-life) and, thinking back to the ending of *The Town and the City,* with that ripping hook-in-mouth disease symbolizing a universal truth: we are all "doomed for certain suffering." All of this simply goes with the delineated territory of chronological time, a determinant condition made vivid and somewhat illusory by fluctuation, extinction, and the pervading feeling of impermanence. If we bundle this all together, we see that this is an old theme for Kerouac. In fact, one is reminded of the Shrouded Traveler from *On the Road,* that mysterious figure who embodies the burden of time and its final clutches. Recall that the road is life—fleeting, linear, finite—and, all along the way, time's running, running, just like Sal in his recurrent dream, staying just one step ahead of the Shrouded Traveler, who is the spirit of death in hot pursuit. Finally, and before Sal reaches the Protective City, the Traveler nabs his victim. As an ethical way of life, philosophy, and transcendent belief system, Buddhism would help Kerouac meet such an endemic burden, one that weighed so heavily upon him throughout his life. And although his search for Buddhist enlightenment would prove arduous and disturbing, often working against the grain of his temperament, it offered Kerouac a grand new vision and order, a fantastical though proven way, and a reliable device to guide his step across chronological time "into the holy void":

> So that the Shrouded
>   Traveller
> Behind us
> Makes tracks in the dust
>   that don't exist. . . .
>   The Reward
>   To the Victor

Then Goes.
The Victor is Not Self

(*MCB*, 129th chorus)

In widening the appeal of Buddhism from personal to intellectual and spiritual concerns as well, Kerouac was swayed by the all-embracing, unifying vision of the "freedom of eternity," as he would put it in both *The Dharma Bums* and *Desolation Angels,* a freedom attained in the very interstices of the transient. Surely this was a religiously legitimized way to know time and to restore a feeling of lost bliss by locating eternity in the very midst of the here and now. Kerouac's adoption of Buddhism helped him to temporarily side-step previously ingrained conceptions of a personal God—the Immovable Mover who "dreamed this world into existence," and take a detour around the wretched self-abasement and soul-sickness nurtured by a morbid-minded Jansenism. Buddhism provided him with a means beyond rupture and discontinuity (see *Visions of Cody*) with which to spring himself from the prison house of chronological time, thus opening up a whole new cosmos that he could loaf within and invite his Buddha not-self. Kerouac's conversion to Buddhism (never categorical) was prompted by nothing less than his quest to dissolve the sin of life itself: death, and the stain of original sin thereby implicated in that Occidental bargain of belief.

The leap of faith in such an unconventional spiritual journey (for an American in the 1950s) was propelled by acknowledging the precepts of Buddhism and practicing the Four Noble Truths. Kerouac's Catholicism, childhood losses, and dislocations during and after World War II enabled him to embrace fully the First Noble Truth that all life is suffering. This includes both the ordinary sense of the term associated with the pain of growing old, falling sick, and dying as well as the suffering bound up with experiencing change—the flux of time—that makes this life, with all of our attachments to it, seem so impermanent and insubstantial. In regards to the latter sense of suffering, Neruda's lines come to mind from one of his love sonnets:

It's today: all of yesterday dropped away
among the fingers of the light and the sleeping eyes.
Tomorrow will come on its green footsteps;
no one can stop the river of the dawn.[3]

The Second Noble Truth is the arising and origin of suffering, attributed to the desire for sense pleasures (the material, social, and sensual goods of this world) and clinging to fruits of the mind-self, to the cycle of continuity and becoming. As it is inseparable from the First, the Second Truth also implies the Third, the cessation of suffering and the extinction of desire by cultivating detachment and wisdom. This is tantamount to liberation *from* being whereby form is emptiness and emptiness form. The Fourth Noble Truth entails the way leading to cessation of suffering—the concrete mean between hedonistic self-indulgence and self-mortification related to extreme asceticism. This final Truth opens the door to the Eightfold Noble Path which emphasizes the three essential categories of Buddhist training: ethical conduct, mental discipline (aided by meditation), and perfecting wisdom.[4] According to Buddhist thought, following the precepts and embracing these Four Noble Truths will bring personal insight into the ultimate nature of things—an enlightened sense of spiritual ecstasy born of stillness and peaceful calm.

This experiential and intuitive sensibility of Buddhism must have appealed strongly to Kerouac, as well as the emphasis, hypnotically expressed in the Buddha's *Diamond Sutra,* on the "Consummation of Incomparable Enlightenment."[5] For Kerouac, this sutra—which was his favorite—distilled a pure form of transcendence raised to the nth power, making the heights scaled by Emerson, Thoreau, and Whitman seem like gracefully terraced hills in comparison to the rugged, ethereal reaches of Mount Sumeru. Also, the cultivation of detachment and withdrawal from the world espoused by Buddha in this sutra dovetailed with Kerouac's recurring longing to renounce both town and city and live in a hut (at times envisioning a hermitage) somewhere in the desert of the southwestern United States or Mexico. In 1952, about the time *Sax* was completed, Kerouac jotted down this pre-Buddhist conviction in his sketch notebook: "Won't be free to be what I want till I've renounced everybody and everything but solitude—& am alone in Eternity with my Work—It is for me to do . . . like Blake—Believe & rely in no one! Live alone! Love alone!—Like Balzac—alone—don't even talk to nobody—become an angel."[6] Such isolation was a romantic notion that Kerouac absorbed and applied to those conditions he felt necessary in his own effort to create and, by virtue of creating, to touch and manifest the divine. Actually, this hankering for complete and utter renunciation marked every phase of Kerouac's quest, but it was most suitable to the fundamental orientation of Buddhist thought and practice, especially given this worldview's nihilism (i.e., an admission of the unreality of the world) and pessimism regarding one's intense attachments to the world as we find it. The other conditions essential to the "incomparable" quest for enlightenment, all inscribed in *The Diamond Sutra,* include the following: abandoning the notion of an ego-personality or cherishing a separated individuality; being mindful of arbitrary conceptions, notably language, as inherently problematic and given to illusion and deception (therefore, trust only Essential Mind, or as Kerouac put it, "True Mind itself, Universal and One, . . . mind is IT itself, the IT");[7] and relinquishing all phenomenal distinctions, that is, being dead to the appearance of things so that one does not depend upon notions evoked by the sensible world.

It is obvious that both in his life and art Kerouac's adherence to the word and the way of pure Buddhist teaching, including its Five Precepts, Four Noble Truths, Eightfold Noble Path, Six Paramitas (spiritual ideals), Four Jnanas (holy states), and Ten Perfections, was rough and fluctuating and, at times, irreconcilable with other competing perspectives and modes of being. However, as *Some of the Dharma* attests, Kerouac was a serious and devout student of Buddhism. He was also painfully honest with himself concerning his spiritual progress (or lack thereof) with the dharma. After one year of intense reading, study, meditation, and writing, Kerouac took stock and provided the following accounting:

> I am at the lowest beatest ebb of my life [. . .] full of alcoholic sorrow and dragged down by the obligations of others, considered a criminal and insane and a sinner and an imbecile, myself self-disappointed & endlessly sad because I'm not doing what I knew should be done a whole year ago when the Buddha's printed words showed me the path . . . a year's delay, a deepening of the sea of troubles, sickness, old age creeping around my tired eyes, decrepitude and dismay, loss of solitude & purity—I must exert my intelligence now to secure the release of this Bodhisattva from the chains of the City. (SOD, 185)

After lashing himself thus, Kerouac begins to exert his intelligence. First he gives himself a good talking-to in order to shore up his sense of resolve. He advises himself regarding the requisites of a bodhisattva (a Buddhist saint who, though attaining enlightenment and nirvana, vows to help liberate all sentient beings): cast off all attachments to the world; "all contacts, reputations, attainments, responsibilities, connections and hindrances of all kinds that fumigate his Mind Essence with the defiling smoke of ignorance. . . . The Bodhisattva must truly cast off his chains himself, then the Buddha shall come and lead him to the Pure Land. Radiant and effortless activity of the mind, instead of the stained and hysterical activities of the self" (*SOD*, 185).

Throughout *Some of the Dharma,* and despite the impressive, thorough, and insightful understanding of Buddhism Kerouac demonstrates, one is frequently reminded of this fact: Kerouac could not cast off his chains from either those "hysterical activities" of the self-in-the-world nor from those "printed words" that kept his devotion locked away from the key of transforming practice. For the word far exceeded the way in Kerouac's relationship to Buddhism. About halfway through *Some of the Dharma,* Kerouac complained, "All I know is words." What he had perfected in terms of enlightenment was the intellectual undertaking of "Right Study." As Kerouac candidly put it, "I was not yet *awake to what I knew*—Which explains why I still compartmentalize my Dharma, no Awakened Intuition Constant, just Rational Words so far—" (*SOD,* 227, 260). Kerouac was very perceptive about his own failings; he concluded his first year accounting with the dharma by making the following observation, which reveals the limitations of "Right Study": "My mistake has been assuming that I can dwell inside mind essence as in sitting inside a bright room; but all I can do is look at it, perceive it" (*SOD,* 185). Although study and devotion finally give way to a satori by the end of *Some of the Dharma,* most of Kerouac's time with the *Dharma* is spent peering into that radiant room and recording the view with astonishing discernment and verve, as if he were a "writing Buddha," or, more accurately, a writing bhikku (disciple).

Shortly after Kerouac's Buddhist study was bearing fruit,[8] Gary Snyder encouraged Kerouac to write a sutra of his own. The result was *The Scripture of the Golden Eternity,* which, according to Rick Fields, historian of American Buddhism, is "one of the most successful attempts yet to catch emptiness, nonattainment and egolessness in the net of American poetic language."[9] Of a total of sixty-six sections, only three combine Buddhism with Catholicism; therefore, this scripture reads much more like a sutra both in content and style, incorporating, as Anne Waldman writes in her introduction, the "magical language" and "illogical syllogisms" at the heart of paradoxical Buddhist discourse (*SGE,* 2). Like the ending of *Some of the Dharma, The Scripture* reveals a more unified Kerouac in command of his restless mindself. In fact, Kerouac distills the insights, convictions, and progress documented in the *Dharma* throughout his *Scripture.* For example, in section 46 of *The Scripture* Kerouac poses the same question that he asks after experiencing one of his samadhis near the end of *Some of the Dharma*: "What does it mean that I am in this endless universe thinking I'm a man sitting under the stars on the terrace of earth, but actually empty and awake throughout the emptiness and awakedness of everything?" (*SGE,* 47).

At the end of *The Scripture,* Kerouac relates his satori-like vision of blownout nirvana-hood, which gives the reader a sense of what the experience might be like. After smelling flowers in his yard, Kerouac stood up too abruptly, breathing deeply. All the blood rushed to his head and he passed out on the grass: "I had apparently fainted, or died, for about sixty seconds."

> During that timeless moment of unconsciousness I saw the golden eternity. I saw heaven. In it nothing had ever happened, the events of a million years ago were just as phantom and ungraspable as the events of now or of a million years from now, or the events of the next ten minutes. It was perfect, . . . the golden emptiness. . . . There was no question of being alive or not being alive, of likes and dislikes, of near or far, no question of giving or gratitude, no question of mercy or judgment, or of suffering or its opposite or anything. It was . . . the joyful mysterious essence of Arrangement. . . . The "golden" came from the sun in my eyelids, and the "eternity" from my sudden instant realization as I woke up that I had just been where it all came from and where it was all returning. (SGE, 59–60)

Nine months before the *Scripture* was written, Kerouac foreshadowed the "golden eternity" in the 232nd chorus of *Mexico City Blues,* clearly distinguishing between Christian theism and Buddhist indeterminacy:

> There is no Universal Salvation Self,
> The Tathagata of Thusness has understood
> His own Luvaic Emanations

As being empty, himself and his womb
Included—No Self God Heaven
Where we all meet and make it,
But the Meltingplace of the Bone Entire
In One Light of Mahayana Gold.

(MCB, 234)

Together both chorus and scripture flush out the essential emptiness
of Buddhist "emanations"; they also attest to Kerouac's notable departure from the "Pre-enlightenment" phase of his outward journey
on the road.

Mexico City Blues and *The Scripture of the Golden Eternity* brightly
reflect Kerouac's deep draft of Buddhist concepts and images, particularly those related to selflessness, ignorance and enlightenment,
samsara and nirvana, karma and rebirth, detachment, and the playful paradoxes that make one skeptical of arbitrary conceptions, such
as the following from the 190th chorus:

In seeking to attain the Dharma
    I failed, attaining nothing,
And so I succeeded the goal,
Which was, pure happy
        nothing.
No matter how you cut it
        it's empty delightful boloney

(MCB, 190)

Perhaps the most resonant sounds of *Mexico City Blues* are contained
in Kerouac's Buddhist hymn that appears in the 228th chorus. In this
buttery expression of the holy, Kerouac's preoccupations that mark
many of the choruses melt away. What the reader is left with is an
attentive and compassionate "earth-man" who seems to be blowing
from the mezzanine of the planet. The chorus is worth quoting in full:

Praised be man, he is existing in milk
        and living in lillies—
And his violin music takes place in milk
        and creamy emptiness—
Praised be the unfolded inside petal
        flesh of tend'rest thought—
        (petrels on the follying

wave-valleys idly
 sing themselves asleep)—
Praised be delusion, the ripple—
Praised the Holy Ocean of Eternity—
Praised be I, writing, dead already &
 dead again—
 Dipped in ancid inkl
  the flamd
  of T i m
 the Anglo Oglo Saxon Maneuvers
Of Old Poet-o's—
 Praised be wood, it is milk—
 Praised be Honey at the Source—
Praised be the embrace of soft sleep
—the valor of angels in valleys
 of hell on earth below—
Praised be the Non ending—
Praised be the lights of earth-man—
Praised be the watchers—
 Praised be my fellow man
 For dwelling in milk

(MCB, 230)

Having represented Buddhism directly in biography, poetic jazz choruses, and sutra, Kerouac would also turn to the novel in order to advance the word and the way, writing *Tristessa, Visions of Gerard,* and his Buddha-shrine: *The Dharma Bums.* The form of the novel itself, given to descriptions of the phenomenal, and Kerouac's own penchant for concrete expressionism created special challenges for a writing bhikku whose real genius rested in his ability to relate the multifaceted reality of individual experience and the legitimacy of day-to-day relationships of individuals to one another. As an experiential novelist, Kerouac was primarily concerned with those very concrete, aesthetically immediate, emotional, and fleeting sense-perceptions that attach us to the discriminating mind-world of the novel. Given such sensuous conditions and natural predilections, viewed as real and good for their own sake, the novels Kerouac wrote to express his Buddhism were far more integrated with his personality, Catholic heritage, and identity as a prose artist than any other writing that he produced during his Buddhist phase, which could afford to be more experimental in conveying the eternal, abstract, and formless qualities of the Essential Mind. Because Kerouac's prose art was primarily a means to relate to the reader through the sensorium of felt experience, and by uniting knower and object, his novels combine the concrete and the elusive (or intangible) in vivid, unique, and, at times, bewildering ways. In short, to use Isaiah Berlin's heuristic classification, Kerouac was an ingenuous fox, by nature drawn to multiplicity, who wanted to be a hedgehog, yearning for *a* solution, *the* answer—a unifying explanatory framework for suffering and spiritual liberation. As fate would have it, Kerouac's karma mixed the two creatures together and came up with a shaggy hybrid that was neither/nor and then some.

6

Icon for the Void

In 1952, when Kerouac was visiting Bill Garver in Mexico City, he sketched in his notebook a piece entitled "Benzedrine Vision—Mexico Thieves Market—Memoirs of a Bebopper."[1] The sketch, which moves from Garver's apartment to being alone on the fellahin street looking for a hotel, details Kerouac's growing feeling of rejection and aimlessness. While walking the streets, he begins to lose his sense of reality, soon becoming a pitiable homeless figure in the Mexican night. In this state, he has a vision of his mother, offering consolation and help. The bebopper, overcome with weariness and exhaustion, eventually finds his lair and, with a flimsy roof over his head, the rain of disturbing thoughts turns into two visions. The first vision is of heaven, in which "everyone was simply a level higher than they are on earth," and the second is one of madness, which he witnesses when looking at his reflection in the mirror. The bebopper then considers three options:

(a) "give myself up to a madhouse, to the VA hospital for mental treatment"; (b) "go on as before"; or (c) gain immediate relief from "the burden of time—just a good big overdose of morphine." The sketch concludes with the bebopper taking the final option: "Get a needle and works in a drugstore, a supply of M. from D., get in bed, heat spoon over alcohol flame, melt tablet or powders. Therein, suck up in dropper, put on needle, then aim for big blue Ti Jean athletic muscle, and puncture, till blood comes up in dropper, then slowly push down to ecstasy of death—no more possible worries of any kind."

Several years later, in 1955, about the same time Kerouac was writing *Tristessa,* he wrote in verse just how the needle felt going in—"like shovin a nail in me," and in another sketch notebook he jotted down the following: "Life is suffering. You're done up at birth only to be done in at death."[2] Sketch, verse, and note remind us just how integral Mexico City was to Kerouac's "immense triangular arc" that also included New York and San Francisco. More often than not, when Kerouac passed through Mexico City to complete this necessary triangulation he was not turning the wheel of the dharma, but rather rotating on the axis of his own samsara. Back again in Mexico City during August and September of 1955, where he was working on *Mexico City Blues* and *Tristessa,* Kerouac wrote to Ginsberg from Bill Garver's place at 212 Orizaba Street in early August: "Feel aimless, ephemeral, inconceivably sad, don't know where I'm going, or why———. . . . All I want as far as life-plans are concerned from here on out, is compassionate, contented solitude———Bhikkuhood is so hard to make in the West" (*SL,* 505–6).

One result of such bottomed-out feelings and best-laid plans was the "long short story" that comprised part one of *Tristessa.* (The novella was completed a year later when Kerouac was again visiting Mexico City.) Taken as a whole, the novella seems to be Kerouac's attempt to place himself and readers face-to-face with the "truth of their present personal horrors."[3] Tristessa, in real life known as Esperanza Villanueva, was the widow of Burroughs's former Mexican connection—Dave Tercerero, "D." in the conclusion to "Benzedrine Vision." Half Indian and half Spanish (her fictionalized name means sadness), and very poor and emaciated, she was a morphine addict with whom Kerouac fell in love. In actuality, although he likened her to "High Priestess Billy Holiday," he fell for her "sacrificial sick body" and the glory of her icon that shone forth from the void of addiction. Near and dear to Kerouac's "drunken Buddha Sacred Heart," this icon curiously combined the verities of the invisible world (humility and piety) along with the afflictions of the visible world (poverty and suffering). Moreover, throughout the novella, there exists no refuge, no sanctuary for Tristessa and her kith and kin. In fact, much of the action in the story takes place on the street itself and in the gutter at the very bottom of Kerouac's world south of the border.

The living icon of Tristessa making her ritualistic rounds through Mexico City partially defines the horror. But it is made present and personal by virtue of Kerouac's compassionate love for her, which, in keeping with his Buddhist undertaking (and so unlike his relationship with Mardou in *The Subterraneans*), is marked by detachment from sensual desire and its consummation. Since Tristessa, and Kerouac's relationship to her, is the subject and concern of this novella, her image radiates an exquisite torment of pain and love, one Kerouac simply cannot resist. Although this American bhikku tries mightily to restrain himself from unwrapping "the bundle of death and beauty" that is Tristessa, the struggle to cast off his chains and quit the tormented state of attachment—"the racks and tortures of sexual beauty"—appears to lengthen rather than diminish the shadow of his suffering (52). (Ellis Amburn's recent claim that Kerouac had sexual relations with Esperanza fifty-six times over a forty-two–day period is simply false. In his research at the Kerouac archive in Lowell, Amburn mistakenly took the year '56, which Kerouac had written down next to Esperanza's name, for the frequency of sexual encounters. So much for the rigors of contemporary biography.)[4]

Curiously, Tristessa represents the aimlessness, ephemeral qualities, and long sadness Kerouac himself felt at this time. Kerouac is not simply projecting his angst and sorrow onto the icon in the void; rather, he and the image just happen to blend naturally into an extended North American setting that reflects the experience of extreme marginality. Both could not have drifted further from the conventional notion of the good life. Given the sordid realities of addiction and affliction amid the dismal atmosphere of the relentless Pan-American rain, the novel appears to embody the First Noble Truth—all life is sorrowful. In fact, sorrow and suffering form that precise point upon which both the Catholic culture of Mexico and Kerouac's transported Buddhism pivot. "Morphine is for pain" and to endure the night; this speaks existentially for both Tristessa and Old Bull Gaines (Garver). The following, however, speaks for the spiritual lesson that Kerouac is attempting to draw out from the experience as a whole: "Tristessa says 'How is Jack,—?—' She always asks: 'Why are you so sad??—*Muy dolorosa*' and as though to mean 'You are very full of pain,' for pain means *dolor*—'I am sad because all la vida es dolorosa,' I keep replying, hoping to teach her Number One of the Four Great Truths,— Besides, what could be truer?" (14, 18). Only this, the pivotal *fons et origo* of Christian belief: "All of us trembling in our mortality boots, born to die, BORN TO DIE I could write it on the wall and on Walls all over America—" (32).

If death is born of life, then sorrow and suffering become the chronic labor pains we must bear along the way. This really defines the natural sickness that overcomes Jack in the novella—"the sickness of the poison in my heart" (41)—a pervasive malaise that morphine cannot undo. For Kerouac, the synthetic poison that is supposed to ease or erase the endemic poison in the human heart is ineffectual. The natural poison he is infected with remains, coursing and thumping through his veins and arteries. Simply put, it is a condition of despair, the utter loss of hope, an admission of defeat spiked clean through the grand trunk railway of the main aorta. "All of us trembling in our mortality boots." For addicts like Gaines and Tristessa, however, morphine works to numb the pain of living and dying. In fact, it is so effective that, over time, "Madame Poppy" becomes the preferred substitute for human love and experience. Gaines explains to Jack: "'When you got morphine, you don't need anything else, me boy. . . . When you've got Opium you've got all you need.—All that good *O* goes down in your veins and you feel like singing Hallelujah!' And he laughs. 'Bring me Grace Kelly on this chair, Morphine on that chair, I'll take Morphine'" (48–49).

Although Jack tries and dislikes morphine, preferring Juarez Bourbon whiskey as his medicine of choice, his real method for calming his trembling nine-holed frame rests in taking the Buddhist vow of celibacy. Hence the title for part one of *Tristessa*: "Trembling and Chaste." Along with the vows of solitude and meditation, celibacy completes the kind of Buddhist detachment that Kerouac was aiming for at this time—nearly ten months after embarking on the ancient Eastern way. About a quarter of the way into the novella, he writes: "I have sworn off lust with women,—sworn off lust for lust's sake,—sworn off sexuality. . . . I want to enter the Holy Stream and be safe on my way to the other shore. . . . She knows I admire and love her with all my heart and that I'm holding myself back" (22). In trying to extinguish the fires of lust and infatuation from his own huge charnel house of desire, Kerouac takes a major step in attempting to bypass the pleasure/pain dualism inherent in attachment to the sensual world. How does one pull it off? Kerouac suggests that it's done with a shrug of the shoulders amid the sweet spin of the senses. Just imagine yourself superannuated, an octogenarian, and the rest takes care of itself:

> Like Goethe at 80, you know the futility of love and you shrug—You shrug away the warm kiss, the tongue and lips, the tug at the thin waist, the whole warm floating thing against you held tight—the little woman—for which rivers flow and men fall down stepladders—The thin cold long brown fingers of Tristessa, slow, and casual and lazy, like the meeting of lips—The Tristessa Spanish Night of her deep love hole, the bullfights in her dreams of you, the lazy rainy rose against the idle cheek—And all the concomitant loveliness of a lovely woman a young man in a far-off country should yearn to stay for—I was traveling around in circles in North America in many a gray tragedy. (52)

As a young man, Jack knows that he ought to yearn for her and, of course, in a way he does; however, such passionate feelings get sublimated. As Kerouac wrote in a letter to Ginsberg in early September (after *Tristessa* was underway), "Didn't come 'to Mexico to cultivate sex,'" as Cassady probably had assumed or advised (*SL,* 512). Rather, the wandering bhikku from the East Coast headed south of the border in order to cultivate detachment—an entirely new habit that would prove difficult to cement in the pavement of the *Paseo de la Reforma.* Nonetheless, such cultivation demanded that Kerouac turn over the lovely dark skin of Tristessa Spanish Night until it revealed the beatific virtues of "Sympaticus Tristessa." Once accomplished, he could then generously extend sympathy, mercy, and kindness, giving due "Adoration to Tathagata, Sugata, Buddha, perfect in Wisdom and Compassion who has accomplished, and is accomplishing, and will accomplish, all these words of mystery" (14). Jack's strong sense of compassion for "holy Tristessa" also turns her into an archetype, a saintly Meso-American Indian Madonna with "long sad eyelids, and Virgin Mary resignation" (8). And his compassionate response to this icon in the void causes him to sanctify her world from the profane perspectives of abject poverty, drug addiction, and junk-sickness-unto-death.

As indicated previously, both Buddhism and Catholicism tend to pivot around the compassion that arises from Tristessa's vulnerability, at times circling separately, at other times arcing in combination. Ensconced within her "tenement cell-house" deep in the labyrinth of Mexico City, Kerouac suggests both his marginal social position in the world as well as his syncretic spiritual placement: "I pull the chair up to the corner of the foot of the bed so I can sit between the kitty and the [icon of the] Virgin Mary. The kitty, *la gatta* in Spanish, the little Tathagata [Buddha] of the night. . . . On my right [where the icon is located] the devotional candles flame before the clay wall" (15). Situated in this fashion, an agent of compassionate understanding, truly betwixt and between, Kerouac can draw from either Buddhism or Christianity (or, as he often does, from both at the same time) in order to enrich Tristessa's life in the very midst of her blighted surroundings and hopeless condition. For example, in superimposing basic aspects of the two belief systems—the cycle of continuity and the notion of a personal God, Kerouac writes from inside the hovel: "holy Tristessa will not be a cause of further rebirth and will go straight to her God and He will recompense her multibillionfold in aeons and aeons of dead Karma time. She understands Karma, she says: 'What I do, I *reap*'" (22–23). Similarly, he describes her devotion to the icon of the Blessed Virgin Mary in a manner that further hints at his syncretic sensibility: "Tristessa loves death, she goes to the ikon and adjusts flowers and prays. She bends over a sandwich and prays, looking sideways at the ikon, sitting Burmese fashion in the bed" (23). Whether pivoting separately or in combination, Kerouac employs the forms of Eastern and Western belief to heighten the search for compassionate release from vulnerability and suffering. Once, tracing a singular arc around the genesis of Western meaning (transcendence and loss), Kerouac evokes the very basis for belief in the West: the enigmatic division between visible and invisible realms. "There is only the unsayable divine word. Which is not a Word, but a Mystery. At the root of the Mystery the separation of one world from another by a sword of light" (43).

The complement to this "unsayable divine word" is a concrete human response, an expression of sympathetic understanding of another person's distress. Although such compassion is centered on Tristessa, it also reaches out to her sister Cruz and friend El Indio, as well as to the animals and birds that occupy the same cramped space as this motley crew. In proper Buddhist fashion, and in keeping with the First Precept, reverence for all life, Kerouac expands this fundamental ideal and practice to all sentient beings. In the contemporary words of Thich Nhat Hanh, a Vietnamese Buddhist monk, the First Precept reads as follows: "Aware of the suffering caused by the destruction of life, I vow to cultivate compassion and learn ways to protect the lives of people, animals, plants, and minerals. I am determined not to kill, not to let others kill, and not to condone any act of killing in the world, in my thinking and in my way of life."[5]

In his playful encounters with and meditations on a cat, a hen, a rooster, and a pigeon (perceived as a dove), Kerouac appreciates and honors the beauty of all living beings, dwelling peacefully with them in the present barnyard moment of Tristessa's tenement cell. Throughout the novella, his heightened awareness of suffering and cultivation of compassion demonstrates an ever-widening concern. Even Tristessa's cat has "golden thoughts" and will die a natural death, as opposed to Jack's Pinky, recently flattened on the killing lanes of New York, "run over on Atlantic Avenue by the swerve dim madtraffics of Brooklyn and Queens, the automatons sitting at wheels automatically killing cats every day about five or six a day on the same road" (31).

Typically, Kerouac's consciousness of suffering and expansion of compassionate feeling mingle with his reflections on mortality—the knowledge concerning the ultimate destruction of life that will come to all, sooner or later:

> At dawn in impenetrable bleak Oceanities of Undersunk gloom, [the rooster] blows his rosy morn Collario and still the farmer knows it wont tend that rosy way. Then he chuckles, rooster chuckles, comments on something crazy we might have said, and chuckles—poor sentient noticing being, the beast he knows his time is up in the Chickenshacks

of Lenox Avenue—chuckles like we do—yells louder if a man, with special rooster jowls and jinglets—Hen, his wife, she wears her adjustable hat falling from one side of her pretty beak to the other. "Good *morn* ing Mrs. Gazookas," I tell her, having fun by myself watching the chickens as I'd done as a boy in New Hampshire in farmhouses at night waiting for the talk to be done and the wood to be taken in. (20–21)

What of all those other poor sentient noticing beings in the room with him? Guided by the principle of nonviolence and the wish to protect all life from the tremulous awareness of destruction, Kerouac wants to convey his Buddhist insights to Tristessa, Cruz, and El Indio amid their morphine fixes and faints. "I wish I could communicate to all their combined fears of death the Teaching that I have heard from Ages of Old, that recompenses all that pain with soft reward of perfect silent love abiding up and down and in and out everywhere past, present, and future in the Void unknown where nothing happens and all simply is what it is" (33). However noble this communal intention to share the bliss of knowledge and hope, Kerouac needs initially to address and convince himself of such beneficence by taking the Buddha's advice: "'First level your own mind, and then the earth will be level, even unto Mount Sumeru' (the ancient name for Everest in Old Magadha) (India)" (21). Throughout, it seems as though Jack cannot get beyond the thought of death—*"born to die"*; such a thought (in fact, more of a refrain) always brings him back to the ubiquitous reality of destruction. Like the heifer and bites of veal Cruz prepares on the kerosene stove, we are all viewed as "little pieces of quivering meat" looking nervously over our shoulders. Kerouac extends the metaphor even as he transports it to the other syncretic shore of Christian and Buddhist belief: "soul eats soul in the general emptiness" (34).

In order to level his own mind, Kerouac tries mightily to practice nonattachment. Although distracted by the evil designs of Mara the Tempter (a Buddhist-like Satan), Jack does not break his vow of celibacy—as long as impure thoughts don't count. The conflict between attachment and detachment intensifies at the end of part one, thus clinching the title—"Trembling and Chaste." Reacting to the Buddhist notion that the phenomenal world is dreamlike, its treasures an alluring mirage, Kerouac gripes:

It's the old question of "Yes life's not real" but you see a beautiful woman or something you can't get away from wanting because it is there in front of you—This beautiful woman of 28 [Tristessa] standing in front of me with her fragile body . . . and that face so expressive of the pain and loveliness that went no doubt into the making of this fatal world,—a beautiful sunrise, that makes you stop on the sands and gaze out to sea hearing Wagner's Magic Fire Music in your thoughts—the fragile and holy countenance of poor Tristessa, the tremulous bravery of her little junk-racked body that a man could throw up in the air ten feet—the bundle of death and beauty. (51–52)

Kerouac seems to carry that bundle across his shoulders, weighed down by the dualistic burden of "pain and loveliness." If attachment to this human world promises both joy and sorrow as the inevitable outcome of intimate relationship, then enlightened detachment effects an eerie magic by pulling out of the Buddhist hat the "absolute perfect purity of nobody" (55). Although the latter is Jack's chaste goal, he is certainly drawn naturally to the former position of love and trembling: "I think of the inexpressible tenderness of receiving this holy friendship from the sacrificial sick body of Tristessa and I almost feel crying or grabbing her and kissing her—A wave of loneliness passes over me, remembering past loves and bodies in bed and the unbeatable surge when you go into your beloved deep and the whole world goes with you" (53–54).

Kerouac regards Tristessa as innocent but sees his own desires as tantamount to "murderous lust"—"It's all my sin if I make a play for her" (54). In the end, it is more than mind alone that's leveled here. "I look at Tristessa's leg and decide to avoid the issue of fate and rest beyond heaven" (58). For the moment, exercising his Buddhist resolve of nonattachment, Jack has set that bundle-burden of death and beauty down by the wayside, thereby defeating ignorant craving and its consequences. The result is not simply a platonic conception of their relationship but an incredible lightness of being, as if both he and Tristessa were "two empty phantoms of light." Such a leveling image, which helps Kerouac keep the terrible anxiety of death at bay, results from the positive valence that attends the Buddhist conception of the void. The following exchange between Jack and Tristessa as they descend the hazardous steps leading down from his rooftop hut brings to light the ultimate reality that envelops these two phantoms of the Mexican night.

"We are nothing."
"Tomorrow we may be die."
"We are nothing."
"You and me." (59)

Part two of *Tristessa*, "A Year Later . . . ," reveals the change of heart and mind that time deals out. Kerouac completed the novella in October 1956, after spending the summer "surling in the Wilderness" as a fire lookout on Desolation Peak in Washington's High Cascades (idealized in *The Dharma Bums*). After climbing down the mountain that summer to Seattle, then on down to San Francisco, Kerouac kept descending until he landed back with Garver in Mexico City. By this time, nearly three years since the onset of his Buddhist studies, Kerouac had pivoted in his feelings and convictions once again. For example, in order to reflect the struggle and commitment to nonattachment that he felt one year earlier, Kerouac ended part one of *Tristessa* with the very apt line: "Diminished is the drizzle that broke my calm" (59). Now, the following year, he opens part two with both a discount and a reversal: "DIMINISHED NEVER IS the drizzle that broke no calm" (63). Such a sentence, which turns abruptly on the virtue of chastity, "the perfect purity of nobody," and "empty phantoms" swarming in the bright pure land of nothingness, boldly declares the redefining experience that occurred in the meantime.

What a difference a year makes, as well as a whole summer alone on a mountaintop, for now Jack kicks himself for being "too pious": "I had some silly ascetic or celibacious notion that I must not touch a woman—My touch might have saved her" (65). Now he feels that it is "too late," especially given the fact that, over the course of a year, Tristessa has become junk-sick, hardened, crazily erratic, and unlovable. Having missed the chance to touch and rescue her, Jack hangs around the Mexico Thieves Market, a "befuddled American."

Although his attitude towards Tristessa makes an about-face, and though the regret he feels is genuine, the scene of suffering remains constant. This setting and human condition comprise the real link between part one and part two of the novella. Kerouac wends his way through scene and condition, under "the garbage of the [night] sky," until he hits rock bottom. As for Tristessa, it seems as if the nadir is unfathomable—there's always something else to lose, a deeper level in which to sink. In living up to one of his essentials of spontaneous prose, Jack accepts loss forever in a "blind dazzle of ecstasy" when a "gay gang of thieves" robs him of money, sunglasses, and poems. Of course, he is a witting accomplice to his own demise, for how else could he find the glory of the abyss? He reaches the lowest point (for him) when he leaves the gang to follow his love—his "sad mutilated blue Madonna"—down into the streets where they find their lair for the night: "I've made up my mind to stay with her and sleep where she sleeps, even if she sleeps in a garbage can, in a stone cell with rats. . . . It's the end" (75–76). Typically, it is here, in such squalid zones of human alienation and discard, where Kerouac can earnestly adjust his focus to get a clear image of God and his creation:

> O there's been pulque and vomiting in the streets and groans under heaven, spattered angel wings covered with the pale blue dirt of heaven—Angels in hell, our wings huge in the dark, . . . and from the Golden Eternal Heaven bends God blessing us with his face which I can only describe as being infinitely sorry (compassionate), that is, infinite with understanding of suffering, the sight of that Face would make you cry—I've seen it, in a vision, it will cancel all in the end— No tears, just the lips, O I can show you! (74)

The "Face" of God, which is more important than the pronoun that refers to the transcendent stature of his theistic being (i.e., Him—that Being beyond all beings, that Power beyond all power, that Cause beyond all causes), shows that Kerouac is more interested in featuring the universal quality of compassion itself than in upholding the determinate notion of divinity. He relies on this rather anthropomorphic image of a personal God to underscore the empathetic response needed to coordinate heaven with the valleys of hell on earth below. In doing so, that is, by showing us, Kerouac pictures a desolate state of existence yet wondrously confers a sense of dignity on all those lost, broken ones, who are still angelic despite the fact that they are commonly viewed as unmeritorious. To stretch the compassionate face of God into the world at large, Kerouac imagines a "Garden of Arden," where "everybody . . . devoted himself to helping others all day long, because of a dream or a vision of the freedom of eternity." In such a garden, "Miss Goofball [Tristessa on secanol] would ope her rosy lips and kiss in the World all day, and men would sleep—And there wouldnt be men or women, but just one sex, the original sex of the mind" (89). With that final thought, a gesture towards Essential Mind, Kerouac adeptly complements the previous Christian image of a personal God, and his personalized garden of mutuality on earth, with the all-embracing source of Buddhist indeterminacy.

Although direct references to Buddhism thin out in part two of *Tristessa,* and the notion of a personal God appears to get the nod, in actuality Kerouac's sense of the divine is treated in a more complex manner. On the one hand, when viewed positively, the divine is conceived as love, compassion, belonging, and creative activity—the divine elements in human life. On the other, when viewed critically, the divine is shot back into the heavens to stomp around as mind-stormed creator, the syncretic design of a Christian God tinged with Buddhist oneness. When seen from far below, mired in the quagmire of suffering, this transcendent entity is often the target for a mixture of human awe and complaint:

> Ah Above, what you doin with your children?—You with your sad compassionate and nay-would-I-ever-say-unbeautiful face, what you doin with your stolen children you stole from your mind to think a thought because you were bored or you were Mind—shouldna done it, Lord, Awakenerhood, shouldna played the suffering-and-dying game with the children in your own mind, shouldna slept, shoulda whistled for the music and danced, alone, on a cloud, yelling to the stars you made, God, but never shoulda thought up and topped up tippy top Toonerville tweaky little sorrowers like us, the children—Poor crying Bull [Gaines]—child, when's sick, and I cry too, and Tristessa who wont even let herself cry . . . (88–89)

Adopting the more humanistic conception of divinity, that is, wearing the face of sorrow and compassion, Jack fulfills the design inherent in his "Garden of Arden," particularly when Tristessa collapses convulsively in his arms after getting her shot of morphine in the junk den the morning after. Nursing Tristessa after she collapses, Jack ponders: "I realize I'm there to refuse to let her die. . . . 'She must know that I refused and now she'll be expecting me to show her something better than that—than death's eternal ecstasy'—O Golden Eternity, and as I know death is best but 'Non, I love you, don't die, don't leave me . . . I love you too much'" (81). Certainly, by this time Kerouac's Mount Sumeru has been leveled into a garden, raked with the unpredictable soil necessary for rooting himself back into the world, and properly fertilized for cultivating the "tormented state" of attachment to the other.

Such attachment, however, is qualified by Jack's "majestic coward-ice," for he admits: "All I can do is stumble behind her, sometimes I briefly lead the way but I'm not much the figure of the man, The Man Who Leads The Way" (82). Moreover, Tristessa's increasing decline has made her even more unobtainable. As if giving voice to the pain and loss that accompanies desire, Jack laments: "I never dreamed it could be this bad" (84). After collapsing, and once again on her own, Tristessa falls three times, reflecting the impression that this bleeding icon (donning a purple shawl) is indeed fashioned in the image of Jesus and his passion. Despite this image of undiminished suffering, and though he knows that it is most improbable, Jack still wants Tristessa to be his third wife, even if this means descending with her into the void of human affect: "Give me a shot of morphine so I can think the way you do." But he loses her, had already lost her (in fact, has never had her) to morphine. Madame Poppy wins out. As Gaines reiterates: "'She don't want love—You put Grace Kelly in this chair, Mucky-muck's morphine on that chair, Jack, I take the morphine, I no take the Grace Kelly.'" Tristessa chimes in, "'Yes, . . . and me, I no awanta love'" (90–91).

When he realizes that morphine will remain their lifelong substi-tute for love, Jack abruptly takes leave of Gaines and Tristessa, this "pair of love-thieves," "moaning over their razor-blades and white junk and pieces of broken mirror to act as the pan. . . . Quiet evenings at home" (91–92). However, before quitting the scene of his discontent, Kerouac distinguishes between two forms of attachment: "Some people are all guts and no heart—I take heart" (95). Love, then, is the preferred basis for one's connection to the world, and Kerouac dem-onstrates this amid the drug-induced fragments that conclude the no-vella. First of all, as his attitude towards the pair of love-thieves soft-ens, his tone alters from sardonic to endearing, and he finds a graceful yet credible way to honor these sentient knowing beings by finding an aspect of human love, some residual passion, coursing from their guts to both their hearts and groins:

> But O the grace of some bones, that milt a little flesh hang-on, like Tristessa, and makes a woman—And Old Bull, spite of his thin hawky

body nobody, his gray hair is well slicked and his cheek is youthful and sometimes he looks positively pretty, and in fact Tristessa had finally one night decided to make it and he was there and they made it, good—I wanted some of that too, seein's how Bull didnt rise to the issue except once every twenty years or so— (96)

Secondly, Kerouac ends the novella with a final pivot and affirmation that gives new meaning to the notion of bearing witness. All along, the author has been showing us, making good on his earlier claim, as if the book were reels of a movie being projected onto a screen. But in this case producer, director, and viewer are all one and the same: "O movie—A movie by God, showing us him—him,—and us showing him,—him which is us—for how can there be two, not-one?" Kerouac's conflation of the sacred and profane into a holy "us" relates both the truth of the present personal horrors he has witnessed as well as his attribution of grace and worth to that human experience. In humanizing a personal God in this manner, Kerouac emphasizes the direct subjective experience of the divine as a living reality—an immanent divinity within us conceived as love, compassion, belonging, and creative endeavor. If "God is love," as John wrote in his first letter,[6] and his face "infinitely sorry," as Kerouac pictures it, then we may pivot freely between the living Christ and the living Buddha, for each, whether risen or enlightened, manifests an immanent holiness in humankind. Kerouac's closing sentences make good on his phrase—"him which is us"—by taking this last chance to show that his version of events is by nature incomplete. "I'll write long sad tales about people in the legend of my life—This part is my part of the movie, let's hear yours[.]" There is no final period, since the ending is intended as the point of departure for embarking on new beginnings. In making this democratic gesture to the reader, Kerouac suggests that we are necessary to complete the puzzle of spirituality—that is, "showing us him—him,—and us showing him,—him which is us." Such expressions of the subjective lives and inner spirits of a multitude of authors are necessary to heighten the awareness and practice of sympathetic understanding. The generous prod to the reader is bound to be returned, if such intersubjectivity works to turn the arc of Kerouac's own individual triangle into a more immense collective circle. As Tristessa, this icon showing faintly in the void, put it, "My Lord, he pay me back *more*."

7

Ethereal Flower

In one of his confessional letters to Neal Cassady, Kerouac likened himself to Judas Iscariot and his brother, Gerard, who died of rheumatic heart disease at nine years of age, to Jesus Christ. The vehicle he used to symbolize this opposition between sinner and savior was Titian's painting, *Tribute Money.* (Jack mistakenly views the painting as Jesus and Judas immediately after the Last Supper; in fact, it is not Judas but a pharisee featured with Jesus in the painting.)[1] Nonetheless, in describing his perception of the painting, Kerouac projected a strong sense of survivor guilt that gnawed at him over the course of his life. In identifying with who he thinks is Judas, Jack claims irrationally that he betrayed Gerard by the sheer fact that the former lived and the latter died.

> Judas loves him; he wishes he could be forgiven even as he betrays;— the well known cake-and-eat-it-rule. Jesus seems to be wondering how

a man could be so dense, or so greedy, or so paradoxical, and so mad, sad, gone, and wild. . . . Judas is me, Jesus is Gerard. What have I gone and done; and what hath God wrought? . . .

He was an angel, I was a mortal; what he could have brought to the world, I destroyed by my mere presence; because if I had not lived, Gerard would have lived.

Isn't it mad, that I sense this now, and sensed it as a child, and all of it completely devoid of rational meaning; all of it merely a "sense" and a hidden conviction, and a fear, and perhaps a hope, and a thousand-and-one-mysteries. (*SL*, 281–82)

Five years later, during ten days in January 1956, Kerouac expanded upon what he "sensed" as a man-child and wrote his eighth novel, *Visions of Gerard*, an idealization of his brother and the earliest account of the Duluoz Legend. In fact when he finished the novel, Kerouac had wanted to title it "ST. GERARD THE CHILD."[2] Fortunately, he changed his mind. If *Tristessa* proclaimed the mortal fact that we are all "BORN TO DIE," then *Visions of Gerard* can be seen as its fulfillment; for the latter deals with the actuality of death and dying, a death in the family French-Canadian style. But this is not simply any death defined by a distinct ethnicity. In Kerouac's mind, it means the passing away and salvation of a spiritual hero, a child and youth who embodied humility, kindness, and patient suffering—a pure soul destined to be an angel of heaven. Yet, from another vantage point, death also signifies the unreality of being-in-the-world: ethereal flower. Kerouac frames this Buddhist perspective with essential Catholic concepts; in doing so, he both states a conviction and manifests the method behind his madness:

Bless my soul, death is the only decent subject, since it marks the end of illusion and delusion——Death is the other side of the same coin, we call now, Life——The appearance of sweet Gerard's flower face, followed by its disappearance, alas, only a contour-maker and shadow-selector could prove it, that in all the perfect snow any such person or thing ever did arrive say Yea and go away——The whole world has no reality, it's only imaginary, and what are we to do?—— Nothing—— *nothing*——*nothing*. Pray to be kind, wait to be patient, try to be fine. No use screamin. The Devil was a charming fool. (123)

As evinced by this passage, *Gerard* is Kerouac's most sentimental novel, somewhat cloying both in terms of its nostalgic depiction of

Lowell (and the Duluoz family) during the 1920s and in the spiritual idealism that the novel portrays. However, the sentiments expressed are not false. The novel is simple without being simplistic. In his ingenuous glorification of Gerard, Kerouac writes a very unusual yet genuine "book of sorrows," as he put it in a letter to Gary Snyder, one that, despite an account of intense pain and extreme suffering, sows goodness and showers tenderness. Moreover, *Visions of Gerard* reflects the ramifications of Kerouac's spiritual journey on his worldviews— the intersection of the belief system he inherited and the one he discovered along the way. The task he set out for himself in this novel is not without difficulty, for Kerouac must present the immigrant Catholic sensibility of a saintlike individual, his family, and community while reinterpreting events and their significance from a Buddhist perspective, and placing little Ti Jean (two to four years old) into the scene of Gerard's angelic suffering—all told from the present "sick-aim" state of adulthood. A tall order, indeed.

"Lord bless it, an Ethereal Flower, I saw it all blossom," Kerouac writes with respect to Gerard (132). He also sees the blooms wither and collapse and so, throughout the novel, must confront the endless comings and goings, the inevitability of "living-but-to-die." And, again, as with part one of *Tristessa,* Kerouac steps to the beat of "Samsara's sorrow parade" while hitting those flats that awaken him to the sounds of detachment—another flower in need of cultivation. The melody of sorrow (as melancholic as Sinatra in his pure tone-indigo prime) and the loud background hum of detachment that characterize *Gerard* are prefigured in the 114th chorus of *Mexico City Blues*:

> You don't have to worry bout death
> Everything you do, is like your hero
> The Sweetest angelic tenor of man
> Wailing sweet bop
> On a front afternoon
> When not leading the band
> And every note plaintive,
> Every note Call for Loss
>   of our Love and Mastery—
>   just so, eternalized—
>
>   (*MCB,* 114)

Strike up the band. Gerard, a peculiar flower sprouting from a swollen heart, blossoming amid the gross heap of the world. That is the plain gist of it. Kerouac's stereoscopic vision of his brother, however, enriches the view by combining the religious images of Buddhism and Catholicism: "I see there in the eyes of Gerard the very diamond kindness and patient humility of the Brotherhood Ideal propounded from afar down the eternal corridors of Buddhahood and Compassionate Sanctity. . . . My own brother, a spot of sainthood in the endless globular Universes and Chillicosm——His heart under the little shirt as big as the sacred heart of thorns and blood depicted in all the humble homes of French-Canadian Lowell" (15). The optics Kerouac trains on his brother add a certain solidity and depth to the virtues associated with Buddhism (karuna: wisdom and compassion) and Christianity (agape: love and justice). Through Kerouac's remembrance and construction, Gerard's "sainthood" integrates the worldviews of East and West, bringing home to both Ti Jean and Jack the lessons of idealism, love of God, compassionate kindness towards all sentient beings, and the holiness of all life.

Such beneficent lessons are set against the grim and bleak setting of Lowell to prove that goodness grows out of the mean streets of life and those who reside there, "repenting over losses, gloating over gains——pot-boys, bone carriers, funeral directors, glove wearers, fog breathers, shit-betiders, pissers, befoulers, stenchers, fat calf converts, utter blots & scabs on the face of it the earth" (16–17). The mouse is a case in point:

> Behold: — One day [Gerard] found a mouse caught in Scoop's mousetrap outside the fish market on West Sixth Street. . . . The hung-jawed dull faces of grown adults who had no words to praise or please little trying-angels like Gerard working to save the mouse from the trap. . . . The little mouse, thrashing in the concrete, was released by Gerard——It went wobbling to the gutter with the fishjuice and spit, to die——He picked it tenderly and in his pocket sowed the goodness—— (15–16)

While the men of Lowell make their daily rounds, "rounding up paper beyond their beans," thus making that materialistic leap from use value to exchange value, Gerard takes the creature home and nurses it back to its old mousekin self. Empathetic toward all sentient beings, Gerard "could feel the iron snap grinding his little imagined birdy bones and squeezing and cracking and pressing harder unto worse-than-death the bleak-in-life" (16). Who among the raving citizens of the republic would take the time to nurture a rodent? Kerouac presents the reigning viewpoint: "'Mouse? Who cares about a gad dam mouse——God musta made em to fit our traps'" (17). But, in actuality, the traps set for mice and men are those triggered by our own insatiable hunger and inhumanity, animals lower on the food chain excused, for that is instinct, not ignorance.

Lo and behold, Gerard returns from school one afternoon soon after the rescue and rehabilitation to see only a mouse tail curled in the little hospital basket. Hi ho, it's the old Tom and Jerry affair whereby the cat ate the mouse—no cheese. In excusing the innocent cat, and the whole unconscionable food chain to boot, Mother Duluoz explains to her anguished son that no one's to blame—"such was life." From Father Duluoz, Gerard gets more harsh detail regarding the menu of predator and prey inscribed in that food chain, which engulfs humankind as well: "'I'll tell you, Ti Gerard, little one, in life it's a jungle, man eats man either you eat or get eaten——The cat eats the mouse, the mouse eats the worm, the worm eats the cheese, the cheese turns and eats the man——So to speak——It's like that, life.'. . . Life, another word for mud" (21–22). (No wonder that, in *Tristessa*, Kerouac takes this principle to its logical conclusion, remarking syncretically that "soul eats soul in the general emptiness.") This all strikes Gerard as one pathetic situation that he would like to rectify. With the cat in his lap, and holding her jowls, the exhortation he delivers to her is also meant allegorically for that knowing creature: humankind. As Gerard shouts angrily the moral lesson to this cruel fable called life, the reader sees Kerouac melding the Sixth Commandment with the First Precept. Throughout, Ti Jean cowers in the corner, astonished and frightened, "as one might have felt seeing Christ in the temple bashing the moneychanger tables everywhichway and scourging them with his seldom whip":

> "*Mechante!* Bad girl! Don't you understand what you've done? When will you understand? We don't disturb little animals and little things! We leave them alone! We'll never go to heaven if we go on eating each other and destroying each other like that all the time!——without thinking, without knowing!——wake up, foolish girl!——realize what

you've done!——Be ashamed! shame! crazy face! stop wiggling your ears! Understand what I'm tellin you! It's got to stop some fine day! There won't always be time!——Bad girl! Go on! Go in your corner! Think it over well!" (18–19)

What comes of all this? Gerard and Ti Jean talk it over the following morning while nestled in bed. Ti Jean wonders, "Where is she the little mouse now?" Gerard, now calm and natural, no dummy when it comes to the nitrogen cycle, explains: "'The cat has shat her in the woods *(Le chat l'a shiez dans l'champ)*'" (23). Such is life—the lesson now complete.

For Kerouac, life in general is a compost heap, a prison house of decay. His fatalism and pessimism about the menacing world at large reflects his particular ethnicity and the historical oppression and diaspora of the Quebecois. There is no ethnic glamorization in Kerouac's account of the French-Canadians residing in the "raw, gricky hopelessness, cold and chapped sorrow of Lowell" (13). The sense of desolation and inferiority, fundamental attributes of the scene of discontent (Quebec/Lowell) and the culture, reinforces his despairing moans and groans. He'd rather not be associated with them—"that crew of bulls——the particular bleak gray jowled pale eyed sneaky fearful French Canadian quality of a man. . . . Lay me down in sweet India or old Tahiti, I don't want to be buried in *their* cemetery——In fact, cremate me and deliver me to *les Indes,* I'm through" (17).

Thus the need for a spiritual hero to scoop people out of the bottomless muck of life. In projecting the French-Canadian sensibility, Kerouac views the world as if it were a sinkhole, dragging one into the depths of one's own weakness (through temptation and sin). "But you bumbling fool you're a mass of sin, a veritable barrel of it, you swish and swash in it like molasses——You ooze mistakes thru your frail crevasses. . . . Sin is sin and there's no erasing it——We are spiders. We sting one another" (41–42). Such an ethno-religious perspective is modulated by Kerouac in order to first present *la condition humaine* at the Catholic "altar of repentance," then shift the point of view to subsume this belief system into a Buddhist worldview.

Even Gerard is a sinner and must subject himself to the traditional Catholic cycle (sin—repentance—redemption). His sins are so minor they are hardly worth mentioning. But he does whisper them, mainly because, as Kerouac writes, "sin's so deeply ingrained in us we invent them where they aint and ignore them where they are" (45). In bringing Gerard into the confessional to unburden himself of what amounts to "pale lenten farts," Kerouac heightens the lad's innocence, faith, and devotion. The dim, secretive atmosphere he creates in describing the scene in the confessional is amusing and endearing. Throughout, Kerouac presents the sacrament with respect and tenderness; however, in the process, he allows certain questions to be raised rather naturally, as when he extends the priest's words in the confessional into a thoughtful conjecture, "'When all is said and done, why do we sit here and have to admit the sinningness of man'" (47). A fine sense of wonder and a good reason for pause. But the moment passes, and Gerard, absolved by the priest, completes the ritual by doing his penance at the altar rail. Kerouac uses this opportunity not only to wax poetic on the mercy of God and the "blisskindness" of purity restored, but to reveal the emptiness (shunyata) that absorbs the definite Catholic architecture of the scene into an undifferentiated whole, or the All, dissolving form and ego in the process. Both Gerard and Ti Jean are swept away into this endless and beginningless stream of Buddhist ecstasy:

> All alone at the rail [Gerard] suddenly becomes conscious of the intense roaring of the silence, it fills his every ear and seems to permeate throughout the marble and the flowers and the darkening flickering air with the same pure hush transparency——The heaven heard sound for sure, hard as a diamond, empty as a diamond, bright as a diamond——Like unceasing compassion its continual near-at-hand seawash and solace, some subtle solace intended to teach some subtler reward than the one we've printed and that for which the architects raised.
>
> Enveloped in peaceful joy, my little brother hurries out the empty church and goes running and skampering home to supper thru raw marched streets. . . .
>
> I'm sitting stupidly at a bed-end in a dark room realizing my Gerard is home, my mouth's been open in awe an hour you might think the way it's sorta slobbered and run down my cheeks, I look down to discover my hands upturned and loose on my knees, the utter disjointed existence of my bliss.
>
> Me too I'd been hearing the silence, and seeing swarms of little lights thru objects and rooms and walls of rooms.
>
> None of the elements of this dream can be separated from any other part, it is all one pure suchness. (50)

Through the eyes of a child, Kerouac daydreams about the way things sometimes are—worldly forms, like the castles of the Gandharvas, vanishing amid the sea wash of *shunyata*. A bit further on in the novel, the Buddhist sensibility of the adult writer comes into the foreground for a brief moment, as if to cash in on the proposition that form and emptiness are coemergent (and all things a manifestation of mind itself): "I curse and rant nowaday because I don't want to have to work to make a living and do childish work for other men . . . but'd rather sleep all day and stay it up all night scrubbling these visions of the world which is only an ethereal flower of a world, the coal, the chute, the fire and the ashes all, imaginary blossoms" (62). Such a view reminds us that a blossom by any other name would seem as impermanent. Given the painful transiency of life and the inevitability of death, the sense of the world as an ethereal flower helps Kerouac cultivate detachment from distress and equanimity of mind.

The alternation between Christian conception and Buddhist reinterpretation (albeit poeticized) allows Kerouac to ensure the integrity of Gerard's vision ("his way") while at the same time enriching the novel's scope of religious belief and spirituality. By creating this pattern, Kerouac not only weaves an alternative worldview into the pages of the novel, but also works to strengthen the security one gains from the experience of the holy. For Kerouac, living without faith in the transcendent, whatever form that might take, leaves one exposed and at risk, like a homeless person cast away among the utilitarian designs of civil engineers: "the protection you'd get tonight huddling against an underpass" (58).

Gerard's vision of heaven, and Kerouac's take on it, rescues the subject from such helplessness. The dream of heaven comes to Gerard after he nods off in catechism class: he is received by the Virgin Mary, "beauteous beyond bounds and belief, like snow," and ascends in a white wagon drawn by two lambs, and with two white pigeons perched on each of his shoulders (65). Gerard is abruptly awakened by Sister Marie and reprimanded for sleeping. Ironically, after he reveals his vision of heaven to the startled Sister he is forced to take his turn in reading the catechism—as mundane and inert as the window-opening pole that leans in the corner of the room, or the stillness of erasers on the ledge of the blackboard, or the dust motes stranded in rays of sunlight. Kerouac interprets the strange scene from another angle:

"The whole pitiful world is still there! and nobody knows it! the different appearances of the same emptiness everywhere!" (68).

Once the Sister finally awakens to Gerard's dream, she asks him to describe it. At this point, Kerouac begins to make the transition from the theistic Christian immortality of the soul to Buddhist immediacy and indeterminacy, equating heaven with nirvana in this life-and-death world; and he does so at first by using his brother as his mouthpiece. Gerard responds to the nun: "'Yes my good sister——don't be afraid my good sister, we're all in Heaven——but we don't know it'!—— 'Oh,' he laughs, *we don't know it!*'" (68). Then, several pages later, Kerouac leaves the inspired boy behind and gets on his own high horse to humorously evoke and decenter the hierarchy of value that underlies traditional Western thought (i.e., that Great Chain of Being) as compared with the Buddhist sleight of hand:

> Hearken, amigos, to the olden message: it's neither what you think it is, nor what you think it isn't, but an elder matter, uncompounded and clear——Pigs may rut in field, come running to the Soo-Call, full of sow-y glee; people may count themselves higher than pigs, and walk proudly down country roads; geniuses may look out of windows and count themselves higher than louts; tics in the pine needles may be inferior to the swan; but whether any of these and the stone know it, it's still the same truth: none of it is even there, it's a mind movie, *believe* this if you will and you'll be saved in the solvent solution of salvation and Gerard knew it well in his dying bed in his way, in his way—— And who handed us down the knowledge here of the Diamond Light? Messengers unnumberable from the Ethereal Awakened Diamond Light. And why?——because is, is——and was, was——and will be, will be—t'will! (71)

It is typical of Kerouac that his Buddhist perspective is intuitively evoked rather than rationally stated. In this manner, he avoids forcing his views onto the reader; he does not take sides but, rather, grants Gerard "his way" even as he hints at another path. By not being absolutist or exclusive, Kerouac errs on the side of confusion rather than dogmatism. But that, in itself, is part of his purpose—to blur elements of two belief systems, so that, in the final lines of the previous passage, Kerouac enlightens the reader with respect to an illimitable Buddhism (the Diamond Light) by fusing it with those eternal terms of the Glory Be.

About midway into the novel, Kerouac signals the fundamental motive for religious belief, namely, to protect one from the finality of death, and to justify the anguish and lamentation that surround death and dying. By juxtaposing and, at times, combining references to Catholicism and Buddhism, Kerouac in effect reinforces those protective devices. His role, therefore, is twofold: to enhance the dimensions of spiritual sustenance and consolation; and to play the part of an uninvited messenger, announcing a mournful vision of our ultimate fate: "All the living and dying creatures of the endless future wont even wanta be forewarned——wherefore, I should shut up and close up shop and bang shutters and broom my own dark and nasty nest" (60).

Obviously, Kerouac keeps the office open, though the image of this writer brooming his own tangled mess of fears and gloom-webs is self-knowing and accurate. His obsession with forewarning the reader about death is understandable in light of the family's trauma over the plight of Gerard. "For my part," Kerouac writes, "the news about the truth [resident in the bones of the dead] came from the silence of my predecessor diers' graves. Sicken if you will, this gloomy book's foretold" (89). His task, then, is simply to particularize what is already a well-known fact of existence. He concentrates his attention on the surrounding context in which this fact is embedded—pain and pity:

> Lancing pain in the legs and vague pain in the chest wakes Gerard in the mid of night. . . . "Aw it hurts, it hurts!!" he groans, and grabs his pain, which wont stop——It comes on and off like a light.
> "Lance, lance, lance, why is this happening to me, what'd I do?" Hands to face, about to cry. Like a load of rocks dumped from a truck onto a little kitty, the pitiful inescapability of death and the pain of death, and it will happen to the best and all and most beloved of us, O——Why should such hearts be made to wince and cringe and groan out life's breath?——*why does God kill us?* (83–84)

With a childish pout, Kerouac raises a vexing question. His skepticism about the stain of sin, especially original sin, leaves him perplexed and, at times, indignant. "If his mortality be the witness of Gerard's sin," Kerouac writes earlier in the novel, "as Augustine Page One immediately announced, then his sin must have been a great deal greater than the sin of mortals who enjoy" (57–58). Several months before writing *Visions of Gerard,* Kerouac concluded in one of his blues choruses:

Unless my guess is wrong,
We are all in for it
And our time
Is Life,
The Penalty,
    Death.

                           (MCB, chorus 129)

In another chorus, he admonishes the reader:

Think of pain, you're being hurt,
Hurry, hurry, think of pain
Before they make a fool of you
And discover that you dont feel
It's the best possible privilege
To be alive just to die
And die in denizen of misery.

                           (MCB, chorus 212)

These religious and existential sentiments from *Mexico City Blues* are implicit in *Gerard*. Mostly out of exasperation over Gerard's fatal sickness, but also due to the deaths of predecessors, Kerouac speaks through his father, Emil Duluoz, who challenges the very nature of the game as given in the original scenario of our mortality. Disgusted by such an injustice—that sentence of life and punishment of death, Emil complains about the dubious tactics employed from on high: "'Go on, God, don't call yourself God in my face——Doin business under conditions like that, we'll never win——'" (96).

Is God a shyster, Jack? Kerouac makes one wonder, which recalls that old saying: you can lead a horse to wet, but you can't make it water. Kerouac's genuine response to Gerard's excruciating pain is to dig a hole in the backyard of Catholic Lowell and come up in ole Buddhist India. The result is an excerpt from the closing lines of "The Great Dharani," a long prayer that appears at the end of the *Surangama Sutra*. Thought to have magical powers, the incantation of this dharani is meant to transmit spiritual strength to someone who is falling through the cracks of extremity. In light of his brother's condition, and when one considers the architectonic weakness Kerouac finds in Catholic structure, it is understandable that he adopts a small part of this Buddhist prayer to offer encouragement. (In Buddhism, words that signify extinction are regarded positively, since they are meant to curtail the cycle of continuity: karma and rebirth; or, in Kerouac's apt poetic phrase, "The wheel of the quivering meat / conception.") The closing lines of "The Great Dharani" Kerouac uses are set in italics; these lines are preceded and followed by Kerouac's own that blend in with the prayer:

> "O Lord, Ethereal Flower,
> Messenger from Perfectness,
> Hearer and Answerer of Prayer
> *Raise thy diamond hand,*
> *Bring to naught,*
> *Destroy,*
> *Exterminate—*
> *O thou Sustainer,*
> *Sustain all who are in extremity—*
> Bless all living and dying things in
> the endless past of the ethereal flower,
> Bless all living and dying things in
> the endless present of the ethereal flower,
> Bless all living and dying things in
> the endless future of the ethereal flower,
> amen."
>
> (86)[3]

With this prayer, Kerouac offers yet another Buddhist reinterpretation of events. Interestingly, he frames the dharani by introductory and concluding narrative lines. With respect to his brother's pain that Kerouac has been writing about in the novel, he admits the difficulty of forging an empathetic link between reader and subject: "Words cant do it, readers will get sick of it——Because it's not happening to themselves——." He then clinches the matter with an example of spiritual strength and resolve coming from someone whom you would not think capable: "Unceasing compassion flows from Gerard to the world even while he groans in the very middle of his extremity" (86). Taken as a whole, the dharani as well as the framework Kerouac devises put us all to shame for our reflexive cynicism and, at best, furious indifference toward the tormented state of the other.

Gerard is dying; "his breath smells like crushed flowers," a sure sign that the end is near (127). When he does pass away, Ti Jean is initially joyful, misunderstanding the irreversibility of death. He is bank-ing on the second coming of his older brother: "He would reappear, following his 'death,' so huge and all powerful and renewed." Greet-ing his father on the sidewalk as Emil rounds the corner of Beaulieu Street, Ti Jean yells gleefully, *"Gerard est mort!"*[4] In response, the child gets a weary acknowledgment, which leads Kerouac to comment: "I had that same feeling that I have today when I would rush and tell people the good news that Nirvana, Heaven, Our Salvation is *Here* and *Now,* that gloomy reaction of theirs, which I can only attribute to pitiful and so-to-be-loved Ignorance of mortal brains" (129–30).

The blank face of death / puff'd, powdered, and breathless / "why does God kill us?" This is the portrait and lament that come to mind. And the Duluozes, especially Gerard's mother, Ange, and old pitiful Uncle Mike from *Sax,* lament and give vent to their hearts' discon-tent. The wails, cries, screams, and sobs all flow into "One Woe." Uncle Mike swiftly sizes up the situation: "finished, bought, sold, washed, brought to the great heaven!" The mother's lament, on the other hand, is much more chilling and gut-wrenching, as if the only sound she hears is that of the undertaker blowing a futile horn. No shelter in this storm. The sense of defeat and utter hopelessness is complete. The injustice of it all comes crashing down, the feeling that Gerard was simply "a little lame boy dying without hope——'It's *that* that's tear-ing my heart out and breaking my head in two!'" yells Ange. "'He died *without* a chance!'" (134–35). In the midst of all this, Kerouac has Ti Jean relieve the "gloom shrine" of the wake and funeral by unveiling the luminous Buddhist "scene behind the scene," which detaches the viewer from appearances and dissolves the illusory nature of both existence and nonexistence into the encompassing void:

> I see the whole house and woe open up from within its every molecule . . . as if a curtain had opened, and innumerably revealed the scene behind the scene . . . shows itself compounded be, of emptiness, of pure light, of imagination, of mind, mind-only, madness, mental woe, the striving of mind pain, the working-at-thinking which is all this imagined death & false life, phantasmal beings, phantoms finagling in the gloom, goopy poor figures haranguing and failing with lack-hands in a fallen-angel world of shadows and glore, the central entire essence of which is dazzling radiant blissful ecstasy unending, the un-

believable Truth that cracks open in my head like an oyster and I see it, the house disappears in her Swarm of Snow, Gerard is dead and the soul is dead and the world is dead and dead is dead. (130–31)

A glimpse of this scene, however, is all that Kerouac offers the audience. The curtain closes abruptly, as if samsara's long hook had somehow yanked the "blissful ecstasy" off stage. As the narrative shuffles back to the common beat, we return to the grime and perplexity of existence, to the "stain of earth, where we all, human brothers and sisters, pop like flower after flower from the fecund same joke of unstymied pregnant earth and raise standardbearers of fertility and ego-personality" (140). In short, we return to the incessant comings and goings of life and the belief in a persisting self. Kerouac's image of this condition is that of "a self-believing butcher with a handlebar mustache standing in the door, full of human hope and realistic sentimentality among the charnels and hacked thighs of his own making, . . . his hands raw from blood-juice, red in fact———." Standing these victuals on their stumps, Kerouac wants to know where to find a "[p]rovision made for a 'cessation and a truce' to all this sprouting of being just so it can wilt and be sacked, canned———." For the moment, Kerouac's only answer is to catapult the multiplicity of being/nonbeing into "angel spirits" that return to earth in awe at the sight of unreal "living beings": "we see man there ghostly crystal apparition juggling as he goes in selfmade streets inside Mind a liquid phantom glur-ing on the brain ectoplasm———A vision in water" (140–41). Once again, Kerouac, magician-like, parts the curtain ever so slightly. In doing so, he unmasks our illusion of embodiment, relying on both a Christian image of angels and a linguistic trick of the Buddhist trade in order to pull it off—to liquefy the solid rock of independent ego-identity. In Buddhist thought, only by surmounting ignorance and attachment to world and self, the very sources of delusion, can there ever be an escape from suffering.

Much easier said than done. Emil's critique—"Doin business under conditions like that, we'll never win," aimed, of course, for the ears of the Judeo-Christian God, can be justifiably applied to the Buddhist quest for supreme enlightenment. For how on earth does one pursue the quest for ultimate perfection when submerged in this quagmire of loss and grief we call life—"another name for mud." The condition of suffering, endemic to earthly existence, creates hindrances that seem impossible to surmount. Mr. Groscorp, the classic image of our imperfect material being, is a case in point. Eating his "necessitous Samsara dinner" in an apartment across from Gerard's funeral service, and looking down on the scene, Groscorp is Kerouac's choice symbol of just how hemmed in we are by the constraints of our surroundings, our very bodies, the bulk of our ignorance, and our insatiable attachment to being-in-itself. All in all, not a very positive evaluation of living in the world, for Kerouac likens the facticity of life to feeding one hole and being laid to rest in another. Here is Kerouac's final glimpse of doing business with the beast in us, Groscorp:

> His face is huge, muckchop rich as kincobs, sleek as surah, gray pale and fetid to make-you-sick, a great beast, with small mouth makes an oo of simpery delight, and great hanging jowls——A bathrobe, slippers, a fat cat——Winebottle and chops laid out——His huge paunch keeps him well away from his fork, and makes it necessary for the eating-chair to be scraped a good deal of the way back, so that he stoops, or rather hunches forward with huge mountainous determination, like a tunnel, to his about-to-be-eaten lunch——"Ah," he interrupted, "another corpse! . . . In all this rain they're gonna bury another one,——aw dammit, it's a pity, it spoils all my meal——It all goes down the same hole, why make such a great ceremonial fuss? . . . That, there's plenty more where it came from, the comin and the goin—— Outa my way, I'm eating——We'll think about it later——" (142)

To his credit, Kerouac has confronted death, not denied it; he has allowed his uncanny memory of Gerard to broaden into visions of near saintliness, brotherly love, familial unity, the pain of loss, personal and communal grief, and ultimate reality—that which lies beyond the flatulent footsteps of Mr. Groscorp as well as the grave digger's shovel, which "closes the book." The final memory turned vision presented in the novel is actually the very first of Kerouac's life (at age one). The memory entails entering a shoe repair store in a baby carriage with Ma on a rainy day and seeing the shelves cluttered with "innumerable battered shoes." Out of this emerges a formative vision "of the great Gloom of the earth and the great Clutter of human life and the great Drizzly Dream of the dreary eternities" (145): in short, the conditions that wear us down. "The tearful beatness of the scene" is accented and relieved by the sight of "an ordinary man, in a strangely slanted gray hat, in coat, presumably, walking off up the dreary and endless boulevard of the drizzle dump. . . . And it seems to me that the little man is going towards some inexpressibly beautiful opening in the rain where it will be all open-sky and radiant, but I will never go there, as I'm being wheeled another way in my present vehicle———He, on foot, heads for the pure land" (145–46). So, with this vision in the mind's eye, it seemed to Ti Jean "that Gerard, now motionless in the central presented bier at the foot of the main aisle and by the altar rail, with his long face composed, honorably mounted and all beflowered and anointed, was delivered to that Pure Land where I could never go or at least not for a long time" (146).

Such deliverance does not imply that Kerouac concludes the novel with a facile resolution of Catholic and Buddhist worldviews; but he does point to a provision, a "cessation and a truce," for doing business under conditions that would be far more favorable for working out one's salvation. In other words, a chance to win. Kerouac locates this provision in the Pure Land School, the devotional spirit of Mahayana Buddhism, which emphasized salvation from karma and rebirth through an exclusive reliance on faith alone. A much later development in the history of Buddhism, somewhat contemporaneous with Ch'an (in China) and Zen (in Japan), this school offered the masses hope for pursuing supreme enlightenment under far more propitious circumstances.[5] What are the requisites? Simply sincere faith and trust in the compassionate bodhisattva, Amitabha (Amida in Japan), who grants eternal happiness in his Western Paradise to whoever invokes his name with devotion, especially at death. (In Japan, the invocation of Amida is called the *nembutsu*.) Those who call on Amitabha in this manner and praise him, especially at death, will be reborn in the Pure Land, where escape from suffering is not only possible but imminently attainable.

It is not surprising that Kerouac banks on the Buddhist conception of the Pure Land for deliverance, since it is well suited to both his pietistic upbringing and mature antinomian sensibility. Also, by the time he wrote *Visions of Gerard*, Kerouac had spent two intensive years on his Buddhist journey; although he had not given up disciplined effort (meditation) or rejected the value of merit-producing acts, he may have seen salvation by faith alone as the only way out. Furthermore, the description of the Pure Land, a rather lush Buddha-field located in the western realm of the universe, brings to mind the opulent account of the heavenly Jerusalem as given in John's Revelation and recalls Dante's Earthly Paradise as well. Thus it presents a vision of an afterlife more familiar than foreign to Kerouac. Replete with fruits, banana and palm trees, lotus flowers ten miles in circumference, and fragrant jewel trees that line the banks of great rivers, the Pure Land is a pleasantly sensuous paradise; even the sound of the rivers rise like music and "always agrees with one and one likes to hear it, like the words 'Impermanent, peaceful, calm, and not-self.'" Moreover, and most relevant to that grotesque scene of sloughing through the material necessities of life on earth, beings in the Pure Land "do not eat gross food, . . . but whatever food they may wish for, that they perceive as eaten, and they become gratified in body and mind, without there being any further need to throw the food into the body." Finally, and this is the capper to putting beings on a much better footing in order to secure spiritual perfection, those carried away to the Pure Land become naturally receptive to Buddhist teachings and practices. In time, questing without any encumbrances,

> one gains the exalted zest and joyfulness which is associated with detachment, dispassion, calm, cessation, Dharma, and brings about the state of mind which leads to enlightenment. And nowhere in this world [of the Pure Land] . . . does one hear of anything unwholesome, nowhere of the hindrances, nowhere of the states of punishment, the states of woe and the bad destinies, nowhere of suffering. Even of feelings which are neither pleasant nor unpleasant one does not hear here, how much less of suffering! . . . And the beings who have been born, who are born, who will be born in this Buddha-field, they all are fixed on the right method of salvation, until they have won Nirvana.[6]

In light of these vastly improved conditions, Kerouac's conflation of a Buddhist Pure Land and a Christian Heaven makes eminent sense. Amid the sound of Latin and the smell of incense, Gerard is delivered to that Pure Land; and, all in all, to little Ti Jean the funeral mass seemed like a show: "It's a vast ethereal movie, I'm an extra and Gerard is the hero and God is directing it from Heaven———." Although Kerouac gives the omnipotent eternal God of Christianity his proper due—a respectful nod to Gerard, the Duluoz family, and Western belief in the immortality of the soul, he ends this novel of last things by reaffirming his own journey East as the ultimate destination for his quest.

> I see nothing but the swarm of angels in the church in the form of sudden myriad illuminated snowflakes of ecstasy——I scoff to think that anybody should cry. . . .
>
> I want to express somehow, "*Here* and *Now* I see the ecstasy," the divine and perfect ecstasy, reward without end, it has come, has been always with us, the formalities of the tomb are ignorant irrelevancies most befittingly gravely conducted by proper qualified doers and actors and Latin-singers—— (147–48)

In this final reinterpretation, Kerouac bends Catholic ceremony to Buddhist bliss. The reader is left with a glimpse of eternity in the very midst of time, and the feeling that both Ti Jean and Kerouac want us to understand that such rewards are available to everyone; or, as the priest intones before Gerard's casket, with his own version of eternal life in mind, *et pro omnibus* (and for all).

8

Kindred Spirits

A complement to *On the Road, The Dharma Bums*—Kerouac's ninth novel—was written from November 26 to December 7, 1957, four years after Kerouac embarked on his Buddhist studies. *The Dharma Bums,* which deals with the year September 1955–August 1956, was one those literary efforts that got typed. (Half of Kerouac's novels were actually handwritten in pencil in spiral notebooks.) Upon completion of the work, Kerouac posted a letter to his editor Malcolm Cowley:

> I'm mighty proud to let you know that I have just finished a new novel, written like *On the Road* on a 100 foot roll of paper, single space, cup after cup of coffee, the last chapter infinitely more sublime than anything in *Road* and the whole think quite different. . . . I realized I wanted to tell the story of Gary Snyder that great young Rucksack Wanderer and translator of Chinese poems and mountain climber and logger and hitch hiker and poet of the West Coast. I've done a credit-

able job delineating this great new personality in our literature, not a
sensational job . . . like Dean Moriarty.

Justifiably pleased with the result, Kerouac went on to explain to
Cowley the meaning of dharma bums, which he fashioned as "religious bums," or "bums of the true meaning." (In Buddhism, dharma
means the truth; the saving doctrine or the way; also, in Mahayana,
it refers to the essential quality of any reality.) The climax of the novel,
of course, features Kerouac's stint as a fire lookout on Desolation Peak
in the High Cascades of northern Washington, "the final exhilirated
[*sic*] moments of the book dealing with descriptions of that top-of-
the-world the best I've ever done. The whole thing wrapped up in a
nice ribbon. . . . In it are . . . accurate descriptions of a new thing in
American culture ultimately a hell of a lot more important than 'beatness' altho it is beatness but no 'hipness' at all, just good oldfashioned
early-Christian John the Baptist wilderness though sensitivity, Zen
lunacy, in short, The Dharma Bums of America."[1]

References to Christianity notwithstanding, *The Dharma Bums* is
Kerouac's Buddhist shrine; in Ginsberg's estimate, a "brilliant Buddhist exposition."[2] Shortly after the novel was published, Snyder sent
Kerouac an appreciative letter, most likely written in between the meditation bells at one of the major Zen temples in Kyoto: "Dharma Bums
is a beautiful book and I am amazed and touched that you should say
so many nice things about me because that period was for me really a
great process of learning from you, not just your vision of America
and of people but your immediate all-embracing faith."[3] Snyder reminds us that the Buddha shrine Kerouac constructs in *The Dharma
Bums* is built from the clay of Emersonian self-reliance and set on a
high rocky ledge along one of Muir's western trails. In "keep[ing] that
earlier, wilder image bright," Kerouac tells a story of self-willed religious heroes—kindred spirits—with a penchant for Zen rigor and
lunacy who cast themselves away to rucksack up and down, and to
and fro as they make their pilgrimage through the wilderness of nature and culture. Still in the throes of excitement from writing the
novel, Kerouac closed his letter to Cowley with the following claim:
"It's a real American book and has an optimistic American ring of the
woods in it."

Though loose and rambling, *The Dharma Bums* is not without a
fine sense of craft and development to show Ray Smith's spiritual

progress with the dharma. As with *Road,* the aesthetic distance between Kerouac and the narrator of the story brings out the innocent, enthusiastic naivete of the main character, conveying the nature of Smith's exhilarated quest, along with its defining qualities, hindrances, and results. With a sense of hindsight, the narrator reflects this distance in order to gain perspective on the fervent search:

> I was very devout in those days and was practicing my religious devotions almost to perfection. Since then I've become a little hypocritical about my lip-service and a little tired and cynical. Because now I am grown old and neutral. . . . But then I really believed in the reality of charity and kindness and humility and zeal and neutral tranquility and wisdom [the Six Paramitas] and ecstasy, and I believed that I was an oldtime bhikku in modern clothes wandering the world (usually the immense triangular arc of New York to Mexico City to San Francisco) in order to turn the wheel of True Meaning, or Dharma, and gain merit for myself as a future Buddha (Awakener) and as a future Hero in Paradise. (5)

As the passage indicates, the narrator's identity in the novel is simply and humbly that of a religious wanderer. In contrast to the other novels that comprise the Duluoz Legend, the narrator of *The Dharma Bums* is neither writer nor artist. At best, Smith is viewed as a sort of religious poet, whose lines naturally emanate from his ongoing travels and devotions. In fact, the reader's first glimpse of Smith is that of a homeless man, a bum or hobo, hopping a freight train out of L.A., yet another classic American image to enrich the novel. It is September 1955, one and a half years after Kerouac's immersion in Buddhism, and he is heading north to San Francisco and Berkeley from Mexico City. The religious feeling of the story immediately takes off as "the little bum of Saint Teresa" climbs into the gondola and finds Smith at the other end of the gon. Smith shares his wine, cheese, bread, and conversation with this fellow traveler, who pulls out a prayer by St. Therese of Lisieux, the little flower of Jesus, which he reads daily while squatting in boxcars. The little bum confirms Smith's faith in the wanderlust of the holy, and the underlying essence of spirituality that finds form in various beliefs and individuals, especially those figures who are so hollowed out they don't even cast a shadow on Skid Row.

In the opening chapter, whether with this fellow traveler or alone, Smith evokes the mystery of life and eternity, the condition of solitude, and the joy that comes from living deeply within the guts of one's experience. Right off the bat, Kerouac offers several proofs of Emerson's famous line from "Nature": "The foundations of man are not in matter, but in spirit."[4] Whether meditating on the "actual warmth of God" to withstand the cold of the moving train, or swigging wine— hootin' and hollerin' and spittin' on the Santa Barbara beach at night— or contemplating his life and times, or filling up all that matter with hot dogs and beans, Kerouac expresses an all-embracing feeling of spiritual beauty; like Saint Theresa's roses, his words seem to shower the reader with the grace of compassionate kindness. Mimicking the rhetorical style of *The Diamond Sutra,* Smith wonders about the incalculables: grains of sand, human beings, living creatures "'since before the *less* part of beginingless time?'" How many were there anyway? "'I don't rightly know but it must be a couple umpteen trillion sextillion infideled and busted up unnumberable number of roses that sweet Saint Teresa and that fine little old man are now this minute showering on your head'" (8). And if that image is too Christian for you, then cut to the close of the first chapter when, sleeping and dreaming in his blankets on the beach, Smith wakes up suddenly to see "the horizon shift as if a sceneshifter had hurried to put it back in place and make me believe in its reality. . . . 'It's all the same thing,' I heard my voice say in the void that's highly embraceable during sleep" (9). Once again, the mix of worldviews given in the opening chapter reiterates Kerouac's conviction that "all things are different forms that the same holy essence takes."

However, as in a shifting figure/ground scene, Buddhism, and Zen Buddhism in particular, swiftly occupy the foreground of this novel's spiritual perspective as soon as the sleeper rolls into action. Then the "little Saint Teresa bum" becomes "the first genuine Dharma Bum I'd met." The second dharma bum Smith encounters is the one in Berkeley who coined the phrase—Japhy Ryder (Gary Snyder). Even in the opening chapter, one can see how Smith, already in a Buddhist state of readiness, exhibits aspects of the Four Jnanas, or rapturous holy states: compassion, joy, peace, and equanimity. As mentor, friend, and dharma bum *par excellence,* Japhy will help Ray stay focused on these states, guiding Smith along in his ragged quest for enlightenment. Throughout the novel, Smith strives to tame and train his mind and aspires to the Four Nobilities. Although he is partial to the First Noble

Truth (all life is suffering) and to some extent the Third (the cessation of suffering), the Second and Fourth Truths are naturally interwoven (the origin of suffering and the way to its cessation).

What then does Smith do in the Bay Area and its environs? Well, he reads *The Diamond Sutra* daily, studies, meditates, rucksacks around in the hills and mountains, and partakes of occasional poetry readings, parties, and sloppy yabyums. There is some uneasiness about the sexually promiscuous yabyums, since they violate Smith's vow of celibacy ("'pretty girls make graves'" [*DB*, 29]) and interrupt the detached feeling of a "new peaceful life."[5] But he goes along with the sexual rite in his own detached and "hincty" (i.e., suspicious) way. Afterward, sitting under a tree beneath the night sky, Smith tries to recover his Buddhist equilibrium. Soon Alvah Goldbook (Ginsberg) joins him, making his purpose all the more difficult. Smith explains to Goldbook: "All Japhy's doing [in yabyum] is amusing himself in the void" (33). When Alvah continues to criticize "all this Buddhist bullshit" Smith has been doling out, Ray tries to make him understand the unaccountably illusory nature of reality by recounting the five aggregates (the integration of senses, feelings, and perceptions), which make life only appear solid and the self persisting. "'There is no me, no airplane [flying overhead], no mind, no Princess [the Berkeley bodhisattva of yabyum], no nothing, you for krissakes do you want to go on being fooled every damn minute of your life?'" Alvah relents somewhat but follows with a discount: "'Well sometimes I see a flash of illumination in what you're trying to say but believe me I get more of a satori out of Princess than out of words.'" Ray, in turn, delivers a frank and fiery sermon on the boomerang of desire, the basic cause of suffering: "'It's a satori of your foolish flesh, you lecher. . . . Balls, when I thought like you, Alvah, I was just as miserable and graspy as you are now. All you want to do is run out there and get laid and get beat up and get screwed up and get old and sick and banged around by samsara, you fucking eternal meat of comeback you you'll deserve it too, I'll say'" (34).

There are more words exchanged, then Alvah ends the altercation by returning to the cottage; Smith remains outside in the yard. Soon Ray douses those three-fold fires that blazed and rippled through his mind (passion, hatred, infatuation). As he recovers his equilibrium, he takes comfort in a form of wisdom that subdues sensuality and argumentation: "there did come over me a wave of gladness to know that all this perturbation was just a dream already ended. . . ." Casting his character in the role of disciple, Kerouac is concerned with getting through to others—not just passing through, but passing on some kind of vital knowledge that will equip others for the tough job of living. This is why Smith prays to be given "enough time and enough sense and strength to be able to tell people what [he knows] . . . so they'd know what I know and not despair so much." Under his own self-fashioned bodhi tree on the West Coast, Smith thinks on a bit more before all this thinking stops and segues into dream: "The old tree brooded over me silently, a living thing. I heard a mouse snoring in the garden weeds. The rooftops of Berkeley looked like pitiful living meat sheltering grieving phantoms from the eternality of the heavens which they feared to face. By the time I went to bed I wasn't taken in by no Princess or no desire for no Princess and nobody's disapproval and I felt glad and slept well" (35).[6]

The struggle over yabyum highlights the fundamental problem that drives Smith's Buddhist devotions—that old difficulty of finding the concrete mean between self-indulgence and self-mortification, the same struggle that led to Shakyamuni's enlightenment under the bodhi tree after thirty years in the palace among pleasure-seekers and seven years in the forest among strung-out skeletal ascetics. (The string on the instrument was either too lax or too taut.) In Smith's words, the problem he faces is "how to cast off the evils of the world and the city and find my true pure soul" (156). The question is reminiscent of the one raised by Kamo no Chomei in his beautiful Buddhist sketch, "An Account of My Hut," written in 1212 during the early part of Japan's Kamakura period: "Wherever one may live, whatever one may do, is it possible even for a moment to find a haven for the body or peace for the mind?"[7] After documenting the disasters and hardships that befell the end of the classic Heian era (fires, typhoons, earthquakes, famine, and the like), Chomei answers his own query by eventually renouncing the world and removing himself to a ten-foot-square hut— "like the cocoon spun by an aged silkworm"—on Mt. Hino in Toyama. After highlighting the calamities and sense of impermanency that underscore the First Noble Truth, Chomei works successively through the remaining three in a graceful style, practicing nonattachment with ease and enjoying tranquility.

Despite the absence of comparable hardship, the road to Ray Smith's mountain hut on Desolation Peak is much steeper and rougher than Chomei's. Perhaps this is why, though coming into the West fully armed with his Buddhist sensibility, Smith draws sustenance and guidance from Japhy Ryder, who is the true cultural hero of the novel. Ryder, the number one dharma bum of them all on the West Coast, teaches Smith the knack of casting himself away amid the breeding booming confusion of the world.

The sharp contrast between the heroic aspects of Moriarty and Ryder speaks for the huge chasm Kerouac had leaped across in his inward journey. Japhy Ryder embodies a whole new set of qualities and values that are particularly appealing to Smith's current stage of development; they are also useful in charting the course for where he has yet to go. First of all, Ryder is a constructive model: intelligent, disciplined, rugged, and, like Han Shan (the Chinese Zen recluse of the T'ang dynasty to whom the novel is dedicated), a poet and Buddhist mountain man easy with solitude. Secondly, it is only appropriate that Ryder inhabits two huts in the novel—the twelve-by-twelve-foot hut in Berkeley and the one in Corte Madera (in actuality, the Mill Valley cabin behind Loche McCorckle's house). Such dwellings represent the values of the simple contemplative life, expressing the clarity, efficiency, and order that are rooted in the aesthetic and spiritual ideals of traditional Asian belief. The overall sense of peace, stability, good sense, and charity rubs off on Smith as he takes these examples to heart. Finally, Smith finds Ryder an attractive American character who combines willy-nilly the influences of the Great Northwest logging camps, Wobblie anarchism, the frontier spirit (including indigenous cultures), and East Asian scholarship. In many respects, the novel is very much like its hero: earnest, strong, and humanly hopeful.

One result of this fertile synthesis is Japhy's social critique and religious vision of the "rucksack revolution"—the original blueprint for the 1960s counterculture. The nature of the revolution Japhy espouses is one that advances spiritual values over materialism and its discontents. We must remember that the postwar period of the 1950s was the renewed takeoff of American consumer society, after the prolonged interruptions of the Great Depression and World War II. According to Japhy, we need only to turn our backs on the materialistic cycle and thereby drive a wedge into it. Such resistance is the very basis for a new direction in American culture:

> See the whole thing is a world full of rucksack wanderers, Dharma
> Bums refusing to subscribe to the general demand that they consume
> production and therefore have to work for the privilege of consum-
> ing, . . . work, produce, consume, work, produce, consume, I see a great
> rucksack revolution thousands or even millions of young Americans
> wandering around with rucksacks, going up to the mountains to pray,
> making children laugh and old men glad, making young girls happy
> and old girls happier, all of 'em Zen Lunatics who go about writing
> poems that happen to appear in their heads for no reason and also by
> being kind and also by strange unexpected acts keep giving visions of
> eternal freedom to everybody and to all living creatures. (97–98)

If humankind lost the use of its feet when civilization built the
coach, as Emerson claimed in "Self-Reliance," then what price did we
pay for stimulating consumer culture? A very high one, indeed: we
have sacrificed not only our pocketbooks and our simple definition
of *necessity,* not only our neighborhoods and downtowns, not only our
natural environment, but our pursuit of happiness as well. Perhaps this
is why every Fourth of July celebration since the modern takeoff has
been a mixed toast: to life, liberty, and the pursuit of quiet desperation, to quote from one of Emerson's good friends who was never too
far from his dinner bell, even when living in the woods.

An unusual, itinerant citizen of the republic, Smith speaks for the
mid–twentieth century and the truth he sees through the complacent
shadows of Japhy's vision, and among the "Zen Lunatics" in general.

> But there was a wisdom in it all, as you'll see if you take a walk some
> night on a suburban street and pass house after house on both sides of
> the street each with the lamplight of the living room, shining golden,
> and inside the little blue square of the television, each living family
> riveting its attention on probably one show; nobody talking; silence
> in the yards; dogs barking at you because you pass on human feet in-
> stead of on wheels. You'll see what I mean, when it begins to appear
> like everybody in the world is soon going to be thinking the same way
> and the Zen Lunatics have long joined dust, laughter on their dust
> lips. (104)

We see, we see what you mean, only now, Jack, they have cable television, and families surf sometimes hundreds of channels, riveted to
distraction and bad programming, and it all gets crammed down the
optics of your mind and cancels any vision save one: buy now, pay

later. For TV is the insidious extension of consumer capitalism into the living room and bedroom. The real meaning of remote control. You'll see.

Ready, willing, and able, Smith is outfitted for the rucksack way by Ryder, who helps to supply pack, sleeping bag, poncho, cooking gear, and, most importantly, the trail to "cold mountain"—both an evocation of the high country's rugged terrain and a Zen symbol of one's self and state of mind derived from Han Shan. On the climb up Mt. Matterhorn in the Sierra Nevadas with Ryder, Smith leaves the sensuality of the road and alienation of the railway for the mountain trail and surrounding forest—a new haven for revising ecstasy, which now has a soothing and dreamy quality to it. Nature complements Smith's quest to cast himself away, providing the conditions of peaceful solitude and contemplative awareness, especially as IT combines with the self-sufficient Muir-like vigor of wandering through raw American wilderness:

> The woods, . . . they always look familiar, long lost, like the face of a long-dead relative, like an old dream, like a piece of forgotten song drifting across the water, most of all like the golden eternities of past childhood or past manhood and all the living and the dying and the heartbreak that went on a million years ago and the clouds as they pass overhead seem to testify . . . to this feeling. Ecstasy, even, I felt, with flashes of sudden remembrance, and feeling sweaty and drowsy I felt like sleeping and dreaming in the grass. As we got higher we got more tired and now like two true mountainclimbers we weren't talking any more and didn't have to talk and were glad. (61–62)

The rigorous climb, with Japhy leading the way, is lightened by a sense of idle joy, as the two climbers spin haikus, and is given a sacred quality during campsite meditations and prayers, such as Ray's offering: "'Japhy Ryder, equally empty, equally to be loved, equally a coming Buddha'" (68). Smith also learns about the practice of charity as Ryder gives him his juju beads and performs other acts of kindness. The whole experience grants Ray a deep sense of solace: "just to be sitting there meditating and praying for the world with another earnest young man—'twere good enough to have been born just to die, as we all are. Something will come of it in the Milky Ways of eternity stretching in front of all our phantom unjaundiced eyes, friends" (71). Japhy's oneness with nature and his heartiness also help to restore Ray's idealism, and he vows to begin a new rucksack way of life, which he refers to as "the pure way." Perhaps the most valuable lesson for Smith, who does not make it all the way to the top of Matterhorn, huddled in a ledge of fear, is this: "'You can't fall off a mountain'" (86), provided that mountain is contained within the center of one's Essential Mind. Moreover, the experience is good preparation for Smith's later stint as a fire lookout in Washington's Mt. Baker–Snoqualmie National Forest, and it also gives him the taste for leading the lone rucksack life of the Buddhist bo in the deserts of the southwest. For Smith, the rucksack way is, in essence, the path of self-sufficiency and spiritual urgency; therefore, even without subscribing to Japhy's social vision and Alvah's clinging to the world, the way is well-suited to the eremitic life of a religious wanderer.

> I wanted to get me a full pack complete with everything necessary to sleep, shelter, eat, cook, in fact a regular kitchen and bedroom right on my back, and go off somewhere and find perfect solitude and look into the perfect emptiness of my mind and be completely neutral from any and all ideas. I intended to pray, too, as my only activity, pray for all living creatures; I saw it was the only decent activity left in the world. To be in some riverbottom somewhere, or in a desert, or in mountains, or in some hut in Mexico or shack in Adirondack, and rest and be kind, and do nothing else, practice what the Chinese call "do-nothing." (105–6)

After coming off the mountain, Smith rejoins the freewheeling intellectual-poetic-artistic yabyum world of Berkeley and San Francisco before heading back to the relative peace and quiet of his mother's home in North Carolina—a long freight-hopping/hitchhiking adventure through the Southwest and Mexican border towns. Once home, Smith is able to pursue his Buddhist insights and rucksack way to the limit of his ability during his regular midnight meditations in the piney woods. It is a restful, comfortable time filled with devotions, family life, idle play, and the hardy atmosphere of the outdoors. At times, especially at Christmas, Smith's confluence of Buddhism and Catholicism comes into play as he reads St. Paul, coming across a passage "more beautiful than all the poetry readings of all the San Francisco Renaissances of Time: 'Meats for the belly, and the belly for meats; but God shall bring to naught both it and them'" (135). It is more beautiful than the mad, ranting howl over rooftops of Harlem cold-water flats because we are back to the mortal fundamentals of life; everything else pales in comparison. But there is more than beauty at work here. In light of Rosie's recent suicide in San Francisco and his mother's visit to New York for a funeral, the real suffering that stems from the inevitability of death soon overwhelms Smith. He collapses to the ground in a fit of depression, crying "'I'm gonna die!' because there was nothing else to do in the cold loneliness of this harsh inhospitable earth." However, no sooner does Smith hit the earth then he is suddenly rescued from his despair by the truth implicit in two protective devices—"the Tree of Buddha as well as the Cross of Jesus. *Believe* that the world is an ethereal flower, and ye live. I knew this! . . . The diamond light was in my eyes" (137).

The root system of suffering is what connects Buddhism with Catholicism in Smith's mind. Despite the philosophical and doctrinal contradictions between the two world religions, confronting or justifying or surmounting everyday human suffering is at the heart of both the New Testament and the Four Noble Truths. The fact that Ray Smith could bounce right back off the ground indicates that his earnest faith—his willingness to believe—was indeed intact, effectively shielding him from utter helplessness. "O Buddha thy moonlight O Christ thy starling on the sea" (117). Whereas Japhy makes sharp distinctions between Christianity and Buddhism, distinguishing fastidiously between Buddhism and Zen as well, Smith takes a more open-souled, come one, come all approach. Although traditional Buddhism is his way, and, in deference to Japhy, Zen and rucksacking the special dharma bum path for now, Ray still accepts spiritual lessons and insights from anyone who can reveal truth and beauty, whatever stripe, such as the Ma Rainy–like street preacher in San Francisco, spitting to the side— *"sploosh"*—every now and then while delivering a resounding Christian blues-sermon.

With mortal hopelessness once again at bay, Smith's meditations become more and more fruitful in his efforts to tame the mind and pursue its insights. Initially, the bliss of samadhis that accompany a cessation of the mind's activities settles over Smith. This most basic form of meditation—sitting still with vacant mind—does not necessarily divest one of an ego-entity. A persisting attachment to the self may exist as one seeks to attain emancipation by the mere ceasing of thought. "A blessed night," Smith recounts of one midnight meditation session. "I immediately fell into a blank thoughtless trance where-in it was again revealed to me 'This thinking has stopped' and I sighed because I didn't have to think any more and felt my whole body sink into a blessedness surely to be believed, completely relaxed and at peace with all the ephemeral world of dream and dreamer and the dream-ing" (134). After a period of concentrated meditation (dhyana), Ray raises his level of awareness and experiences a sudden awakening, one which parallels the famous lines from *The Heart Sutra*—"Form is emptiness and the very emptiness is form."[8] For Smith, it is put thus: "'Everything is empty but awake!'" It is a fine, spare phrase for point-ing to a factor in the nature of things: the blissful drift into nothing-ness (All-At-One-Ment) while remaining mindful of entering into the undifferentiated state. Although the conscious mind is still aware, it is not snared by attachment or desire. Curiously, Ray's attainment is similar to the Sixth Bodhisattva Stage (there are ten in all): "While still being in touch with the passions and discriminations of the Saha world, he turns his mind inward by his faculty of intuitive insight to the realization of the intrinsic emptiness and silence of the mind's pure essence."[9]

What ruins the awakening of this higher state of meditation, how-ever, is Smith's insistence on wearing his Buddhism on his sleeve. Ironi-cally, he is too self-conscious about his attainments, his own purported egolessness: "I figured it all out and the next day feeling very exhila-rated I felt the time had come to explain everything to my family" (144). Not only is Smith's explanation somewhat lame, he is much too full of self, too attached to his own enlightenment and views and beliefs to mine the potential of the insight. By clinging to the sheer enjoyment of samadhis and samapattis (intuitive realization and tran-scendental powers or graces, respectively), Smith proves that he has only caught the cow (mind), the fourth stage of spiritual progress rep-resented by Kakuan's *Ten Cow-Herding Pictures* (one picture for each phase of Zen Buddhist development). But he has not yet begun to herd the cow and ride it back home (the fifth and sixth stages).[10] Nevertheless, Smith's insight translates into the following: "'It means I've become a Buddha.' I really felt that and believed it and exulted to think what I had to tell Japhy now when I got back to California" (145). Not only does Ray's family turn a deaf ear, but the reader has the distinct feeling that Kerouac exaggerates the scene to reveal the writer's own knowledge of his main character's self-consciousness. (This also applies to the "pure egolessness" of Smith's "Transcendental Vistas.") The intention appears somewhat parodic—in the sense of drawing a caricature of enlightenment—and one is immediately reminded of those delightful lines from the *Tao Teh Ching*: "He who knows does not speak / He who speaks does not know."[11]

If form is emptiness and emptiness form, is Smith's cup half-empty or half-full? At this stage in the novel, Kerouac highlights the hindrances to Smith's further progress. Smith's certainty about his own spiritual attainment is, to say the least, premature and fraught with self-centeredness and prideful assertion. The reader is reminded of Ray's arrogance and insensitivity with respect to Rosie's suicide (i.e., "If she had only listened to me"). Rather than transcend personality and ego, Smith still seems to harbor some cherished sense of the self as a persisting, determinate element within the phenomenal world. As Kerouac confessed in a letter to Carolyn Cassady (17 May 1954) about being under the influence of Buddhism: "Biggest trouble is hangup on self, on ego-personality" (*SL*, 428). This all amounts to a case of big-fuss Buddhism, what Alan Watts referred to as the lack of *wu-shih* (no fuss) in his critique of beat Zen.[12] The need for self-justification is too strong, a dead giveaway that all is not well in obtaining deliverance from the ontological divide between ego and environment. When this is combined with lust and restlessness, which Smith still struggles with, the reader sees that the hindrances to maintaining his sense of peaceful equilibrium are formidable. A further hindrance, which echoes the conflict between flesh and spirit, presents itself once Smith leaves North Carolina to hitch cross-country and hook up with Japhy Ryder again. Rucksacking in the desert and making forays into Mexico, ping-ponging from self-indulgence to self-denial, his comparison of the "evil city" to the "virtuous desert" appears too rigidly dualistic. Such discriminations suggest that Smith is still stuck in the web of arbitrary conceptions and that he has a way to go before herding and riding the cow, let alone forgetting it, attaining to nothing, returning to the origin, and, finally, entering the city with bliss-bestowing hands. Whether or not his cup is half-full or half-empty, he is clearly halfway there.

Despite the fact that Kerouac was drawn more forcefully to Mahayana in general rather than to Zen Buddhism in particular, he was highly conscious of Kakuan's *Ten Cow-Herding Pictures* and incorporated them into the thematic development and imagery of the novel in order to help chart the progress of Ray Smith's spiritual journey. In the novel, Ryder shows and explains the "famous Bulls" to Smith while they share the Corte Madera cabin before Japhy heads off for the Zen temples of Kyoto and Ray for Desolation Peak. During this time there are more chances to meditate, work, share insights, drink green tea, party, hike, and gather in the lessons from a mature friendship between kindred spirits. Ray also uses this hiatus in the action of the story to confront the hindrances that lay in his path. For instance, after one of the long parties, when everyone is asleep, Ray considers the figures huddled on the floor and begins to question the very solidity of other selves as well as the identity of his own self: "Who were all these strange ghosts rooted to the silly little adventure of earth with me? And who was I?" (199).

Appropriate to the design of the novel's symbolic terrain, the remainder of those "famous Bulls" (pictures 5–10) don't start to appear until Smith is on his way up to the majestic solitude of Desolation Peak, where he will spend the summer as a fire lookout in the third and final hut of the novel—"a funny little peaked almost Chinese cabin." The fifth and sixth stages, herding the cow and coming home on the cow's back, signify mastery over one's self-deceiving mind and the growing lack of concern with gain and loss. Near the end of the novel they are merged as Smith rides his mare up the mountain trail: "I got off the horse and simply led her up the trail, she grunted a kind of groan of relief to be rid of the weight and followed me obediently" (231). The seventh stage—the cow forgotten, leaving the man alone— is reached when the party of forest rangers who accompanied Smith up the mountain return down, leaving him to his desolation on a pinnacle 6800 feet above sea level. "The windows howled as they rode out of sight in the mist among the gnarled rock-top trees and pretty soon I couldn't see them and I was alone on Desolation Peak for all I knew for eternity. . . . And it was all mine, not another human pair of eyes in the world were looking at this immense cycloramic universe of matter" (233–35). Taking in the whole panoramic vista from the roof of the earth day after day gave Smith a dreamlike feeling about the soft, illusory nature of the world he once inhabited and the encompassing rock-hard emptiness that he now faced. The effect was particularly pronounced when he stood on his head, a remedy for thrombophlebitis that a bum had taught him in an L.A. freight yard, which he practiced regularly: "Then the mountains looked like little bubbles hanging in the void upsidedown. In fact I realized they were upsidedown and I was upsidedown! There was nothing here to hide the fact of gravity holding us all intact upsidedown against a surface globe of earth in infinite empty space. And suddenly I realized I was truly alone and had nothing to do but feed myself and rest and amuse myself, and nobody could criticize" (235).

Defamiliarizing his sense of perspective, Smith soon feels a Thoreauvian sense of being "deliberate and glad and solitary" (236). Even Mt. Hozomeen, the menacing peak staring in Smith's window from the north, the very embodiment of the void, grows on him, and he comes to appreciate its beauty. Finally, that boundary between ego and world begins to dissolve and a lightness of being results, whereby Ray acknowledges the impotency of the ego: "In bed at night, warm and happy in my bag on the good hemp bunk, I'd see my table and my clothes in the moonlight and feel, 'Poor Raymond boy, his day is so sorrowful and worried, his reasons are so ephemeral, it's such a haunted and pitiful thing to have to live' and on this I'd go to sleep like a lamb" (239). This is equivalent to the eighth stage, that of egolessness, in which the cow and man are both gone out of sight. Before long, Ray has altogether stopped trying to improve himself—living out a form of effortless effort—and the ninth and tenth stages of spiritual development are quickly realized: returning to the origin, back to the source (pure lucid mind), and entering the city with bliss-bestowing hands (and drinking with the butchers to spread the dharma).

In the concluding chapter, barely five pages, Kerouac attains an *aesthetic* and *idealized* form of enlightenment for his main character; dualism is transcended and serenity prevails. There are no longer any profound answers because there are no longer any searching questions. As Smith remarks, "'Poor gentle flesh,' I realized, 'there is no answer.' I didn't know anything anymore, I didn't care, and it didn't matter, and suddenly I felt really free" (240). An overall sense of nonattainment (or Non-Ado) characterizes these final days on the mountaintop. "'When you get to the top of a mountain, keep climbing,'" Smith had yelled up to Ryder on Matterhorn (83–84). Now it is his turn, and he does keep climbing, for he wills nothing, knows nothing, desires nothing. Recall Kamo no Chomei's perfect lines emanating from his own mountain hut to express the same condition: "My body is like a drifting cloud—I ask for nothing, I want nothing. My greatest joy is a quiet nap."[13] Smith, too, abides in the peacefulness of nonassertion— do nothing—and he pleasantly goes about observing life on the pinnacle while carrying out his fire lookout chores. Here is the sound of the fifty-fifth day on Desolation Peak: "I called Han Shan in the mountains: there was no answer. I called Han Shan in the morning fog: silence, it said" (242).

Smith's transcendence is celebrated by the hues of a rainbow, as if to consecrate the moment: "I went outside and suddenly my shadow was ringed by the rainbow as I walked on the hilltop, a lovely-haloed mystery making me want to pray. 'O Ray, the career of your life is like a raindrop in the illimitable ocean which is eternal awakenerhood'" (241). A vision of Japhy Ryder, merging with the figure of Han Shan, comes to Smith as a tribute to his guides for leading him "up the Cold Mountain path":

> The moss is slippery, though there's been no rain
> The pine sings, but there's no wind.
> Who can leap the world's ties
> And sit with me among the white clouds?[14]

On Desolation Peak, Smith reaches the summit of transcendental ecstasy. In the process, he seems to refine those rapturous states of Buddhist enlightenment (i.e., the Four Jnanas: compassion, joy, peace, and equanimity). The hindrances disappear; there is no need for self-justification on a mountaintop, no temptations from the leering world, and no way to satisfy them even if there were. Desolation Peak is the only location in the novel where Ray Smith can tether both his body and mind and cast off the world. Yet it is to that world that he must return—to drink with the butchers and complete his spiritual journey: "'Now comes the sadness of coming back to cities and I've grown two months older and there's all that humanity of bars and burlesque shows and gritty love, all upsidedown in the void'" (244). As if driven by an instinct to right himself, Kerouac makes three references to God on the last page of the novel. It is simply a reminder to the reader of a desired complement to this "Buddhaland splendor," that is, a wish for a "Personal God in all this impersonal matter" (237). Perhaps

Kerouac is right when he remarks, "To the children and innocent it's all the same" (244).

In the *Ten Cow-Herding Pictures,* the cow gradually turns from black to white until the cow and the man are both gone from sight. Purification is a natural result of taming the mind—originally pure but blackened by extraneous impurities that lead one astray. Thus there is a need to seek the mind, trace and catch it, and bring it back home to be cleansed. Since the world is the litmus test for Ray Smith's spiritual stick-to-it-iveness, one wonders about his downgoing. When Ray returns down that trail to the world, when he passes through, will IT—the ecstasy and enlightenment—pass through with him? And, in passing through, will he extend love and peace and goodwill to all living beings in fulfillment of his Buddhist teachings? How will it feel to be upside down in the void of the mind-shredding, heart-banging world where the force is centrifugal and everyone and his sister a shattered critic? Will the mind remain in rapture, the form dissolved? Put another way, will the world and corrupt city whiten as a result of Ray Smith being in it, or will the cow/mind begin to blacken all over again in the sooty shelves of dense human habitat? Or will Ray gradually turn half and half, like a plump Jersey chewing its cud by the fencepost? Will those butchers he drinks with be converted within the very slaughterhouses where they work and sweat and stink in, now drunk on the dharma? At the end of *The Dharma Bums* we can only speculate because it's all unknown. The only certain thing is this: we upside down, brother—the void is calling us from eternity and the stripper from the burlesque club in Seattle.

PART THREE

The Lifelong Vulture and the Little Man

Ah Neal, I must tell you of my Lifelong Vulture, precursor to the Adult Snake. . . . My vulture I made myself, by placing third finger over forefinger and thumb below, wiggling thus to make a jaw. First it circled around my head, then dived to my arm, where it took a hearty horrible nip and I yelled the Saxon roar. Then the Little Man began to run up my arm; he was formed, of course, by walking fingers. . . . [As a child] I began creating this endless chase of the vulture and the man. Years, years after I was still doing it, and only recently I remembered it and did it again (willy-nilly hi), only now, being an adult and symbolic fool, I let my little man collapse and the vulture get him. No child in his right mind would let the vulture catch the man!

—Jack Kerouac to Neal Cassady, 10 January 1951

9

Downsizing

Several months before his stint as a fire lookout in the summer of 1956, Kerouac wrote to Gary Snyder about a vague premonition: "Something will happen to me on Desolation Peak . . . as happened to Hui Neng on Vulture Peak, I can sense it" (*SL,* 567). Indeed, something truly did happen to Kerouac while in utter solitude on top of the mountain, but it was not the Buddhist "turning about" that he had idealized and that Hui Neng, the Sixth Chinese Patriarch of Zen, actually experienced. In this phase, commensurate with the Seventh Bodhisattva Stage, one turns away from the self and discards all memory of the thinking mind—all discriminations, attachments, desires, dualisms, and habit-energy, "wholly abiding in the Mind's Pure Essence."[1] This passage into a higher state of awareness (call it noble wisdom) surmounts the selfless pleasures of blissful vacuity attained in the meditative state in order to express a universal sense of compassionate love for all. What Kerouac sensed before climbing the mountain might very well have been the underside of such transcendental intelligence, that is, the tormented state. For when Kerouac, who acts as our cicerone, comes face-to-face with this latter state of existence, he not only reflects the throbbing perturbations of his attachment to the world, but inflicts a Sophoclean torture upon himself as well. On Desolation Peak, Kerouac bottoms out, thereby discovering the meaning of the mountain's namesake.

Kerouac documents the disparity between romantic ideal and actual experience in book one of *Desolation Angels* ("Desolation in Solitude" and "Desolation in the World"), which was written prior to *The Dharma Bums* in Mexico City during the fall of 1956—right after coming down off the mountain. However, the remainder of the work, including all the passing through of book two, was not finished until 1961 (the same year *Big Sur* was written), and the entire book, which covers the period 1956–1957, was not published until 1965. Book one of *Desolation Angels,* which is based on the journal Kerouac kept while atop Desolation Peak, tells the untold story of the whole experience in solitude and then in the worlds of Seattle and San Francisco. Whether on the mountaintop or down at sea level, one thing is for sure: the desolation is constant.

The aesthetic form of enlightenment glamorized in *The Dharma Bums* ("the whole thing wrapped up in a nice ribbon"), especially given the protagonist's sense of progression through well-defined spiritual stages, is very different from the true-to-life experience recounted in *Desolation Angels.* In fact, it is quite remarkable that, just a little more than a year after the agonizing events that transpired while straddling the roof of the world, Kerouac was capable of creating the considerable distance between his misadventure and the novelistic vision realized in *Dharma Bums.* Surely this confirms the difference between image and reality; but, of equal importance, it also affirms the fact that Kerouac's authorial sense of literary mastery and stylization was very much intact immediately after the successful publication of *On the Road* (when *The Dharma Bums* was written). Such confidence and creative reappraisal took Kerouac over the top imaginatively—right before the deluge of fame or, more accurately, infamous notoriety, made it increasingly difficult for him to surface and recapture that critical distance.

In *Desolation Angels,* which contains the most belabored prose that Kerouac has ever published (particularly "Desolation in Solitude"), Kerouac presents Duluoz's ongoing struggles with roaring solitude as well as his exposure to the nagging hindrances—both existential and philosophical—that accompany his Buddhist yearnings. Despite the desultory prose that characterizes the first part of book one, and the undistilled prosaic style employed throughout, *Desolation Angels* is a candid, confessional, and open-book view of a life subjected to such an ordeal and aspiration—and whose progress report, rather than stellar, is just flip-floppingly human. No doubt most men and women attempting to spend two full months in complete isolation would report back in a similar manner; in fact, most would come undone.

If desolation abides in both uninhabited and inhabited places, both on the pinnacle and within the human honeycomb, then the term must refer to the pathos that results from solitude and loneliness—whether amid the deserted airy rock-void or within disconsolate congested fleshpots. Astride Desolation Peak, Duluoz suffers from too much mind; rather than diminishing to the ultimate meltdown point of no self, all the momentum seems to go right into the gray matter and the mind keeps accumulating. Perhaps it is the result of too much standing upside down in the void:

> —Everything goes to the head
> Of the hanging bubble, with men
> The juice is in the head—
> So mountain peaks are points
> Of rocky liquid yearning.

("Desolation Blues," BB, 117)

The juices are ever-flowing on this divide, a virtual watershed of reverberating cerebral circuitry that could power all the valleys below.

But the mind is not at peace. In fact, it shreds into incoherency, an every-which-way Buddhism, as if locked in the third stage of the dialectic of the negative: no persisting personal self; no material world; only the transient associations of the senses and introspections left to project against the craggy screen of Mt. Hozomeen. Since the daily round of chores takes little time, and with no fires threatening all summer, where does the lookout look? He looks up and down and all around, becoming a virtual medium for the flickering of past and future shows: entertaining memories, daydreams, reflections, anticipations, sexual fantasies, and a card game of baseball solitaire, to name a few pastimes. In fact, the chapters in "Desolation in Solitude" alternate between present chores or meditations on the mountain and one of the above mental activities that pull Duluoz off the mountain and back into the world. The alternating pattern of this structure suggests that Kerouac wishes to express, in a manner true to the experience of utter solitude, something basic about noumenal and phenomenal realms of existence, and the conflict he perceives therein. But as Thich Nhat Hanh reminds us, "*Samsara* and nirvana are two dimensions of the same reality. There is a relationship, but it is a phenomena-noumena relationship, not a phenomena-phenomena one. . . . That is why [Buddhists] speak of 'the separate investigation of noumena *(svabhava)* and phenomena *(laksana)*.' And yet, at the same time, they are aware that the two realms are one."[2]

In searching for the purity inherent in the Buddhist diamond of truth, one cultivates detachment from the illusory world—including the notion that one has a persisting self—and seeks a sense of ultimate reality in the noumenal. In *The Diamond Sutra,* Buddha encouraged his followers to reject all phenomenal distinctions: "All Bodhisattvas . . . should develop a pure, lucid mind, not depending upon sound, flavour, touch, odour or any quality. . . . A mind which alights upon no thing whatsoever."[3] Although all alone on Desolation Peak, Duluoz is not truly cast away. He cannot turn his back on the world and consistently breaks the peace by ushering in the phenomenal. This too-much mind—hurling words that head nowhere but the compost heap, momentarily reconstructing that which is absent, remains the biggest hindrance of all. Saigyo, a twelfth-century Buddhist poet-priest who led the eremitic life in his own Japanese mountain hut, would have called such linguistic compulsiveness the "sin of words."[4] But since there is no sin in Buddhism other than ignorance, perhaps instead we should call such tendencies thieves of the mind. It seems an irreconcilable contradiction for a writer who claimed to want to write "all the talk of the world . . . with roars of me / all brain—all world / roaring—vibrating" to settle "upon no thing whatsoever" ("Daydreams for Ginsberg," *Scattered Poems,* 11–12).[5]

Kerouac—and Duluoz—still clings not only to sensual flights of passionate fancy but to ideas, conceptions, words and images, views, and to volition itself, that is, the will to be—to continue, to become, which is the real force of karma. Therefore, as long as Duluoz's craving for the phenomenal remains—and there is no doubt it remains—he will not extinguish desire (the fires of earthly passion) and put an end to the origin of suffering in the strictly Buddhist sense. The deliverance from clinging to existence, which characterizes the conclusion of *The Dharma Bums,* is thus absent from the earlier, pre-aesthetic version of the experience. In "Desolation in Solitude," everything is left to be done, everything remains in the midst of the void, including a thousand imagined details of romps through Seattle and San Francisco. Such heightened self-consciousness and intrusions from the phenomenal realm undermine the serenity of enlightened detachment, fueling instead the linguistic dieselation of restless heady searching. For Kerouac, however, this seems to be necessary to the very act of survival.

The contention between noumena and phenomena is planted very early in the account and grows wildly throughout "Desolation in Solitude." Thinking that he will "come face to face with God or Tathagata and find out once and for all what is the meaning of all this suffering and going to and fro in vain," Duluoz instead confronts himself without the old devices of the past—"no liquor, no drugs, no chance of faking it but face to face with ole Hateful Duluoz Me and many's the time I thought I die, suspire of boredom, or jump off the mountain, but the days, nay the hours dragged and I had no guts for such a leap, I had to *wait* and get to see the face of reality." This face is none other than that of Mt. Hozomeen, and the naturalistic thought that accompanies the visage is this: "'The void is not disturbed by any kind of ups or downs, my God look at Hozomeen, is he worried or tearful? Does he bend before storms or snarl when the sun shines or sigh in the late day drowse? . . . Why should I choose to be bitter or sweet, he does neither?—Why cant I be like Hozomeen and O Platitude O hoary old platitude of the bourgeois mind 'take life as it comes'" (4–5)? Thus admonishing himself to be more neutral, like that majestic mountain-void Hozomeen, itself "beyond serenity, beyond even gladness," flatly indifferent to its own passing through, Duluoz gives himself a good Buddhist pep talk:

> Hold together, Jack, pass through everything, and everything is one dream, one appearance, one flash, one sad eye, one crystal lucid mystery, one word—Hold still, man, regain your love of life and go down

from this mountain and simply *be—be*—be the infinite fertilities of
the one mind of infinity, make no comments, complaints, criticisms,
appraisals, avowals, sayings, shooting stars of thought, just *flow, flow,*
be you all, be you what it is, it is only what it always is—Hope is a
word like a snow drift—This is the Great Knowing, this is the Awakening, this is Voidness—So shut up, live, travel, adventure, bless and
don't be sorry— (5)

In spite of his wise counsel, Duluoz cannot get it together or simply be voidlike or hold back the "shooting stars of thought." In short,
he cannot "shut up." Such self-denial, a contemplative route to the
noumenal, is quickly replaced by the frenetic onrush of the phenomenal, as if to express a fundamental conflict in human nature. For Duluoz in particular, the onrush also serves to fend off the anxiety and
dread of confronting nothingness (i.e., in an existential sense—the
horror and negation within the very core of one's being). Swept away
by images of the phenomenal, Duluoz has great difficulty in keeping
his mind tranquil, the prerequisite for the Buddhist meditative state.
Instead, he admits that the distractions assailing him willy-nilly are
so real they seem to be physiological: "A thousand memories come
like tics all day perturbing my vital mind with almost muscular spasms
of clarity and recall. . . . My life is a vast inconsequential epic with a
thousand and a million characters—here they all come, as swiftly we
roll east, as swiftly the earth rolls east" (11–12).

Before long, the tranquility of the noumenal somehow manages to
return, bringing with it the realization that "the world is a babe's dream
and the ecstasy of the golden eternity is all we're going back to, to the
essence of the Power—and the Primordial Rapture, *we all know it*"
(28). One gets the feeling, however, that the words are getting away
from the experience, spawning a life of their own: the sentiments associated with each realm being played out in the mind without the
spiritual will to back them up. As if to give expression to this very
notion, Duluoz makes the following observation while in his cabin:
"Noumena is what you see with your eyes closed, that immaterial
golden ash, Ta the Golden Angel—Phenomena is what you see with
your eyes open, in my case the debris of one thousand hours of the
living-conception in a mountain shack." From this point, he goes on
to describe the entire contents of his cabin, all the way down to the
jar of pickles left in 1952 that "froze in the winter so that the pickles

are just spicy water husks looking like Mexican greenpeppers" (33–34). And although he wants to resolve matters in a facile way, resorting to *The Diamond Sutra* once again to register the unreality of self, others, worldly appearances, and imaginary judgments, the effort remains unstable, ever shifting (telltale signs of change and its rumblings underfoot), and soon Duluoz is off on another very real subject—the "bottomless horror" of various scenes in this here-and-now, then-and-there world which cannot be vanquished. The litany of horrors leads to a form of pathos rooted in despondency—"Sad understanding is what compassion means—I resign from the attempt to be happy"—before dumping into the void, perhaps from whence it came, and the section finally ends in a prayer: "O golden eternity, these simperers in your show of things, take them and slave them to your truth that is forever true forever—forgive me my human floppings—I think therefore I die—I think therefore I am born—Let me be void still" (45–46). And so we teeter on through the whole unrelieved chilling solitude of Desolation Peak.

Given such flip-flops, what, then, is learned other than the desolation of monotonous solitude, of desolation itself?

> I learned that I hate myself because by myself I am only myself and not even that and how monotonous it is to be monostonos—ponos—purt-pi tariant-hor por por—I learned to disappreciate things themselves and hanshan man mad me mop I dont want it—I learned learn learned no learning nothing—AIK—I go mad one afternoon thinking like this, . . . I want to come down RIGHT AWAY because the smell of onions on my hand as I bring blueberries to my lips on the mountainside suddenly reminds me of the smell of hamburgers and raw onions and coffee and dishwater in lunchcarts of the World to which I want to return at once, . . . let there be rain on redbrick walls and I got a place to go and poems to write about hearts not just rocks— (61)

On the one hand, with one week to go on the mountain, Duluoz realizes that "desolation adventure finds me finding at the bottom of myself abysmal nothingness worst than that no illusion even—my mind's in rags." On the other hand, there is a natural longing for those "lunchcarts of the World" and other more sensual pleasures: "I'd rather undo the back straps of redheads dear God and roam the redbrick walls of perfidious samsara than this rash rugged ridge full of bugs that sing in harmony and mysterious earth rumbles." Above all, Duluoz (and the reader) awakens to a form of *enlightened attachment*. We learn that it is impossible to keep the mind neutral and devoid of the phenomenal world for sixty-three days on a Western mountaintop, especially when one's genius as a writer and artist depends upon the attachment (i.e., concrete expressionism). In fact, Kerouac begins the last chapter of his fire lookout experience with the following observation: "In 63 days I left a column of feces about the height and size of a baby" (61–64). So, rather than the fruition of detached enlightenment, which tops off in the conclusion to *The Dharma Bums,* Kerouac offers here a rather natural inversion of transcendence—shit out the bottom.

This does not mean that the Buddhist spiritual quest was futile (after all, the Buddha died of dysentery), but only that it was not taken by Kerouac to its ultimate conclusion: renouncing the world so as to develop "pure, lucid mind" in the strict sense of the diamond cutter's words. As we have seen, such profound detachment has been preempted by all those wild accompaniments of the mind in mountain solitude, interrupted by all that mixed-up confusion of carrying the real world in one's head and heart—those thousands of characters and events that bring us back to our senses, and, of course, by the unstable, ever-shifting point of view echoing throughout "Desolation in Solitude." Knowing his own temperament, Kerouac had registered doubts about the ideal of Buddhist detachment almost a year before taking the job as fire lookout. In the 225th chorus of *Mexico City Blues,* he wrote:

> In the dark I wryly remonstrate
> With my sillier self
> For feigning to believe
> In the reality of anything
> Especially the so-called reality
> Of giving the Discipline
> The full desert-hut workout
> And superman solitude
> And continual enlightened trance
>
> (*MCB,* 227)

But he tried, damn it, at least he tried! To fail the test of "superman solitude" does not mean that he fell all the way down at once—6800 feet to splatsville. No, he takes it gradually, and, once he starts his descent from Desolation Peak, he never stops climbing down off the mountain. Even at sea level, in Seattle and San Francisco, Kerouac keeps downsizing the ideal, and throughout his travels to Mexico City, New York, Tangier, Paris, London, and America again he seems to pass through like water, seeking its lowest level.

Nonetheless, both on the mountaintop and throughout the process of downsizing the ideal, Kerouac illuminates what—for lack of a better phrase—I call *enlightened attachment,* which is the realization of the selfishness and worldly passions against which one struggles and suffers. First and foremost, enlightened attachment is an acknowledgment of spiritual struggle between noumena and phenomena and the difficulties of cultivating complete, enduring, and gnostic detachment in solitude. As such, it admits rather than annihilates our humanity, that is, our immersion in the experience and language and consciousness of the phenomenal world. Although we may not snuff out desire and liberate ourselves *from* being by failing to renounce the world, what remains is indeed something—a sense of honest compassion— "sad understanding"—of all this coming and going, to and fro, up and down in the world. In this sense, enlightened attachment refers simply to this: an appreciation of one's own limits in finding *the* remedy for this life and knowing it. Freed from self-deception and self-justification, one can then go about seeking the divine amid this world, while occasionally taking a glimpse into the next, what Duluoz calls "the vision of the freedom of eternity" (66). Only in the buzzing world does such a vision get further refined. Furthermore, enlightened attachment also implies a condition of relative solitude, in which human contact and association are imperative. As Duluoz remarks after his first encounter with people in two months, "Talking to a human being is like flying with angels" (80). Finally, using Northrop's philosophical distinction, enlightened attachment can be likened to the determinate or differentiated aesthetic continuum (the sensed qualities and felt experience of the Tao in both nature and culture), rather than to the indeterminate or undifferentiated aesthetic continuum (an encompassing sense of unity that abstracts away from sensation, introspection, and feeling). According to Northrop, the latter concentrates attention (via enlightened detachment) upon this continuum for its own sake, for it alone "'escapes the ravages of death.'" Obviously, given Kerouac's perfervid personality (self-admittedly, "a wondrous mess of contradictions"), and his eternal struggle between restlessness and peace of mind, he was much more attuned to the differentiated aesthetic continuum, in which, as Northrop comments, "emotional, aesthetically immediate, hedonistic, sensuous differences are real and good for their own sake."[6]

Unlike the blithe Ray Smith, Jack Duluoz falls short of the Buddhist ideal. Kerouac makes no bones about it, letting us know this in a thousand and one maddening ways. "Where was the joy?—the joy I prophesied," Duluoz wonders as he heads down the trail back to the world. Instead of happiness, he feels anxiety; and when he tries to muster pleasant thoughts of *la dolce vita*, the only response he gets is a muscular one of chronic pain (the physical correlate of psychic distress). The descent provides no respite; it is yet another chore requiring concentration and effort. Echoing Samuel Beckett's sense of tragic-comic complaint belied by the very act of endurance, Kerouac writes: "'I cant make it' is my only thought as I keep going" (72, 77). For all his ineptitude and determination, it is interesting that the writing acquires clarity, direction, and purpose once the lookout actually notices (as if for the first time) human temporality and events as he begins climbing down the mountain to rejoin the world. As Duluoz later puts it while bouncing around the lower places of the planet, "After all, the only reason for life *or* a story is 'What Happened Next'?" (238). The descent immediately puts Duluoz back into his element—the phenomenal world, or the sensorium of everyday experience, where he rediscovers the necessity of human contact and storytelling.

In part two, "Desolation in the World," Kerouac supplies the narrative play-by-play of character and action as witnessed by a reawakened mind navigating through the rational grid once again. What peeks through the clutter of events and people and haunts in Seattle and San Francisco is Duluoz's inability to transfer his "vision of the freedom of eternity" to his friends. This brings on a sense of abiding desolation that is leavened only by the fury of activity in the beat scene in San Francisco. But even before he hits the littoral moth swarm of those cities, Duluoz anticipates the problem of translation with agitated Elizabethan wonderment: "What a world is this not only that friendship cancels enmity, but enmity doth cancel friendship and the grave and the urn cancel all—Time enough to die in ignorance, but now that we live what shall we celebrate, what shall we say? What to do?" These perennials are well posed in the vase of Kerouac's rhetorical display. After drifting off into "cherubim tendencies" whereby we are all angels—even "itchy Wallace Beery in a dirty undershirt"—Jack comes back to the questions at hand. We get both a semblance of an answer (one that grounds the sweet levity of angelic attribution) as well as a glimpse into the harrower of desolation: "Why else should we live but to discuss (at least) the horror and the terror of all this life. God how old we get and some of us go mad and everything changes viciously—it's that vicious *change* that hurts, as soon as something is cool and complete it falls apart and burns" (66–67). The answer really begs the question; however, the rondure is legitimacy enough for Kerouac's concern, for Q and A both meet in the grave, eventually. But in the meantime he has called for discussion and recognition of the vicissitudes that drive one to the very brink and beyond.

Kerouac apologizes for even bringing this up and driving a wedge into the celebration, let alone the vision he claims was his on the mountain: "Above all, I'm sorry—but my sorriness wont help you, or me." As if to focus the horror and terror more concretely, he confesses in gruesome detail to murder most foul. Two mice were pitifully done away with on Desolation Peak, and a third, though released and probably gone a-courtin', was gobbled up by the rat. What now? Only the angst associated with the fact that he can't become St. Gerard who, we might recall, delivered a mouse from death only to have it eaten by the cat some days later. What's left to assume in the classic dichotomy but the role of sinner, that of common criminal: "Now I had joined the ranks of the murderers and so I had no more reason to be pious and superior. . . . Now I'm just a dirty murdering human being like everybody else and . . . I cant take refuge in heaven anymore and here I am, with angel's wings dripping with blood of my victims. . . . There is nothing but murder in the hearts of men" (67, 69). After bringing himself up short, and dusting off the criminal and the saint as two distinct exhibits claimed by the same dirt, Kerouac still persists in asking, "But what we gonna do?" If Duluoz didn't figure it out after sixty-three days on high, then why beat a dead horse on his way down below? Now the response (so credible in the context of *The Dharma Bums*) seems forced and futile: "'I dont know, I dont care, and it doesnt matter' will be the final human prayer." We are left in the lurch as ever. What to do? The question that goads the quest still remains, desolating all the way down with Duluoz to the very end of the road.

Pragmatically, *what to do?* is quickly altered to *what next?* as Duluoz makes it down to Seattle and checks into a skid row hotel for the night before bussing to San Francisco. Walking the streets with keen eyes, and stopping in a bar or two, Duluoz senses the warmth in humanity and notes its possibilities for love. But then, registering the perversion of such potential, he ducks into a burlesque show to catch the vaudevillian banter and writhing sensual slapstick on stage. One might think that if anything could break that fitful spell of mountain solitude in one fell swoop, this would be it—a trick of the old trade. But the view of the burlesque dancer from the dark and crowded theater is just as unsettling as standing upside down in the void of Desolation Peak, especially when she's "in the coitus position . . . throwing a fit at heaven." Duluoz, dizzily drunk for the first time in two months, takes it in, swirling sinuosity and all, thinking that it's "insane" and recalling "vaguely from the mountains [that] it's upsidedown and wow, sneer, slake, snake, slake of sex, what are people doing in audience seats in this crashing magician's void handclapping and howling to music and a girl?" Squirming in the vulgar seat of samsara, Duluoz conjures fragmentary images of the sacred and profane—a combination of beatness, religious association, and love-lust:

> Ugh, ow, I dont know what to do, Sarina the Naughty One is now on her back on the stage slowly moving her sweet loins at some imaginary God-man in the sky giving her the eternal works—and pretty soon we'll have pregnant balloons and castoff rubbers in the alley and sperm in the stars and broken bottles. . . . The whole world is roaring right there in that theater and just beyond I see files of sorrowing humanity wailing by candlelight and Jesus on the Cross and Buddha sitting neath the Bo Tree and Mohammed in a cave and the serpent and the sun held high and all Akkadian-Sumerian antiquities and early sea-boats carrying courtesan Helens away to the bash final war and broken glass of tiny infinity till nothing's there but white snowy light permeating everywhere throughout the darkness and sun—pling, and electromagnetic gravitational ecstasy passing through without a word or sign and not even passing through and not even being—

But O Sarina come with me to my bed of woes, let me love you gently in the night, long time, we got all night, till dawn, till Juliet's rising sun and Romeo's vial sink, till I have slaked my thirst of Samsara at your portal rosy petal lips and left saviour juice in your rosy flesh garden to melt and dry and ululate another baby for the void, come sweet Sarina in my naughty arms, be dirty in my clean milk. (108–10)

In the end, once the tight grip of Sarina's tease has released him, Duluoz realizes that both vaudevillians and strippers are all *"troupers."* "Just . . . working and making a living in the dark sad earth. . ." No reason to get excited. Located in the cheap and make-do economy of Seattle lowlife, this is the first real lesson Duluoz learns from his journey back to this world. The second lesson is that, at thirty-four, he already feels over the hill. Though at times he longs to refine the purity from love, he knows that love may very well be behind him (111–12). The contrast between high and low speaks for the great divide separating the spiritual ideal from the toothless reality of things as they are.

Till they re-establish paradise on earth, the Days of Perfect Nature, and we'll wander around naked and kissing in gardens, and attend dedicatory ceremonies to the Love God at the Great Love Meeting Park, at the World Shrine of Love—Until then, bums—
Bums—
Nothing but bums— (112)

Even before boarding the bus and moving on down the coast, and gathered from simple observation over a single night and morning, Duluoz gleans this much from his reentry: "That's the way it goes, there's your world—Stab! Kill!—Dont care!" (115). What can the living conception reasonably expect from being stuck in such a place? Perhaps only this for starters: "Eat your eggs and Shut up" (113). Then digest, catch your bus, and get the hell out—to the next stop.

Although Duluoz is only with his subterranean friends in San Francisco for one whirlwind of a week before resuming a life of semisolitude in Mexico City, other lessons become readily apparent to him. In San Fran, he keeps climbing farther down from his ideal, mainly because his expectations always seem to run away with him. Therefore, he needs to continually revise and scale down the nature and scope of his spiritual quest. For instance, in a syncretic enactment of religious influences and subcultural scene, Duluoz puts on a friend's silver crucifix at a beat party and then reads aloud a paraphrased passage from *The Diamond Sutra*, one about not being swayed by passions in order to attain a greater bliss and merit: *"Living ones who know, in teaching meaning to others, should first be free themselves from all the frustrating desires aroused by beautiful sights, pleasant sounds, sweet tastes, fragrance, soft tangibles, and tempting thoughts. In their practice of generosity, they should not be blindly influenced by any of these intriguing shows"* (151, italics in the original).[7] But the words fall on deaf ears. More importantly, though the passage is clearly meant for others, and to tone down sexual jealousies, Kerouac ironically reveals that it is Duluoz (among others) who, "blindly influenced," surrenders that very night to carnal pleasures and the cat's cradle they weave in the loop of a lesser bliss.

So in drinking with the butchers, he is tarnished, his spiritual willfulness weakened; and the Buddhist vision that he articulates either floats by unnoticed by others or backfires in his own flesh. In narrative time, we come to see that this notion of enlightened attachment also works to heighten all of the conflicts that disturb Duluoz's equanimity: flesh vs. spirit; hedonism vs. asceticism; phenomenal vs. noumenal. And there seems to be no end to the desolation that such collisions cause. But that is not the entire story, for Kerouac seems to pivot here regarding the implication of enlightened attachment for his own view on suffering. Rather than trying mightily to escape the clutches of crazy sorrow, he appears to accept it as inevitable, perhaps even preferable (more Christ-like, if you will) to abstracting away from it. As Henrik Vroom reminds us, "Christian faith is not concerned with removing suffering from the world in which we live. . . . Following Christ entails suffering—even if only through insight into how things are: the brokenness of the world, the groaning of the creation, the yearning of all things for the children of God to be revealed, and the cry of the humiliated and wronged."[8] In expressing the naked reality of his own shattered yet still sacred heart, Duluoz wakes up the morning after thinking about the cross around his neck and his own intriguing burlesque show.

> I realize what thicks and thins I'll have to wear this through, and ask myself "What would Catholics and Christians say about me wearing the cross to ball and to drink like this?—but what would Jesus say if I

went up to him and said 'May I wear Your cross in this world as it is'?"
No matter what happens, may I wear your cross? (152)

As a fool for Christ and a jester for Buddha, Duluoz tests out the strength of both the cross and the bo tree. Is it possible, given the wild beatness of the scene, to combine the spiritual values associated with agape and karuna? In his own inimitable way, Duluoz gives it a go. And, throughout the week in San Francisco, the world does actually whiten by virtue of his presence—particularly brightened by the goodwill that he shares with others and also by his assumed role as peacemaker for the old gang. Since there seems to be no end to the friction and growing divisions among members of his tight circle, Duluoz manages—whenever the moment is right—to extend compassionate understanding to his friends, mending and patching up the rifts between Cody (Neal Cassady) and Raphael (Gregory Corso), Raphael and McLear (Michael McClure), Garden (Ginsberg) and McLear, and so on. In fact during one escapade, the bohemian rabble gets a little out of hand; while Cody calls for order, Duluoz insists on mercy: "'Let us have forgiveness everywhere—try as hard as you can—forgive—forget'" (205).

However, Duluoz's presence, though beneficent, is ever fleeting. The bus must move on, and so he bids farewell to his blessed beats. After hopping a freight train from San Francisco to L.A., he catches a bus for Arizona; the final destination is Mexico. Along the way, another bus pulls up alongside the one Duluoz is riding. It turns out to be a prison bus with several armed guards and twenty men, "and two of them turn and see me and all I do is slowly lift my hand and slowly wave hello and look away as they slowly smile." At the very end of *The Dharma Bums,* Ray Smith turns away from his shack to take the trail back to the world of possibility—and to drink with the butchers. Now, at the end of *Desolation Angels* (book one), we realize that the experience of reentry into this world (wandering amid its hacked slaughterhouses) is framed by two notorious institutions: the burlesque house and the penitentiary. In other words, by seduction and entrapment. No wonder the resulting state of mind is one of desolation. On the bus, Kerouac rounds out book one by returning for a moment to the summit. With ample evidence in hand, he poses the question: "Desolation Peak, what more do you want?" (216).

Nearly five years later, in 1961, Kerouac wrote book two of *Desolation Angels* "in a filthy room in Mexico [City]." Feeling that his privacy had been "invaded" over the past four years since the publication of *On the Road,* Kerouac was deeply disturbed by the consequences of his notoriety. In one of his notebooks for 1961, he brooded: "Nobody should invade the writer's study. . . . Balzac wrote in solitude, lived in solitude with a man servant who went to bed at midnight when Balzac got ready to write till noon!—That's the only way—The rest is nothing but conscious sabotage by 'visitors' and 'admirers' and even uninvited 'friends' & relatives—Uninvited brother artists also—How can Vulcan forge his sword when someone holds his arm?"[9] Kerouac did not mention the extent to which self-sabotage was also at work in the crashing wake of his commercial and popular success. The disillusionment that eventually sunk him was a complex process that was instigated by the ignominious fact that he was never taken seriously as a literary artist during his own lifetime. As Holmes aptly put it: "He realized he wasn't famous, he was only notorious and that's quite different."[10] Kerouac was sent spinning by the overload of public attention that resulted from the popularity of *Road,* and he quickly tumbled into the trappings of success—the pressures of money, recognition, adulation by the youth culture, and monstrous media attention. The deluge of admirers at his door and the constant misunderstanding of his mission as a writer promulgated by critics and the media at large ruptured Kerouac's resolve as a writer. From 1958 to 1961, except for the eight prose sketches that made up *Lonesome Traveler* (a collection of published and unpublished pieces, the longest of which—"The Railroad Earth"—was composed in 1952), he had written nothing but letters, some poems, journal or notebook entries, and his dreams. "You think it's glamorous," Kerouac wrote in 1962 to Stella Sampas, his future third wife, "but I think this 'fame' is all a big interruption of my original simple soul."[11]

In 1961, the acute sense of disillusionment that resulted from this nagging interruption colored Kerouac's writing of book two. During the intervening years in which books one and two were completed, Kerouac grew older (climbing from thirty-four to thirty-nine), put on weight (gaining forty pounds in four years), lost the anonymity that, according to Michael McClure, made each novel "an act of desperation and an act of vision," felt that "fruitful illusion" so necessary to a writer slipping away, and appeared to have altered Milarepa's Buddhist principle—"The notion of Emptiness engenders Compassion"—into the following existential mantra: The notion of nothingness engenders despair.[12] All of these had a profound impact on the truncated reach of Kerouac's spiritual quest. In the opening chapters of book two, Kerouac sums up the state of affairs: "Nowadays [1961], after all the horror of my literary notoriety, the bathtubs of booze that have passed through my gullet, the years of hiding at home from hundreds of petitioners for my time (pebbles in my window at midnight, 'Come on out get drunk Jack, all big wild parties everywhere!')—oi—As the circle closed in on this old independent renegade, I got to look like a Bourgeois, pot belly and all, that expression on my face of mistrust and affluence" (221).

The crisis of identity and thwarted sense of purpose that gnawed at Kerouac in 1961 are traced back to their origin in the year 1956–57. The first order of business in book two is to reconsider the ideal, or the pinnacle, and begin the painful process of change. As we have seen, though the process had been underway during book one, Kerouac's first major attempt to clearly articulate the downsizing of the ideal into a manageable endeavor does not occur until the opening of book two. After leaving San Francisco, and just prior to passing through Mexico City, Duluoz redefines the nature of his quest. Despite the lapse of memory regarding his attainment of "absolute peace" on Desolation Peak, a.k.a. that "airy dungeon," such stock-taking reflects a mature sense of compromise and a more flexible (hence realistic) conception of the relationship between self and world:

> Now, after the experience on top of the mountain where I was alone for two months without being questioned or looked at by any single human being I began a complete turnabout in my feelings about life— I now wanted a reproduction of that absolute peace [of the mountaintop] in the world of society but secretly greedy too for some of the pleasures of society (such as shows, sex, comforts, fine foods & drink), no such things on a mountain—I knew now that my life was a search for peace as an artist, but not only as an artist—As a man of contemplations rather than too many actions, in the old Tao Chinese sense of "Do Nothing" (Wu Wei) which is a way of life in itself more beautiful than any, a kind of cloistral fervor in the midst of mad ranting action-seekers of this or any other "modern" world. (217)

Letting go of his role as bhikku, and accepting the inherent vagaries of the artist, Duluoz now seems to want both the road and the hut embedded within the same accessible landscape. His new self-ideal, which alternates between attachment and detachment, is reflected in that phrase—"a search for peace as an artist," and as a man more given to contemplation than one "imbroglio'd in [the world's] actions, which have by now become famous for their horror & abomination" (220).

The revision expresses both a worthy sentiment and a reasonable set of expectations but, once again, the will is unable to pull it off. Reminiscent of Sal Paradise's picture of Dean Moriarty "bearing down" on him, Duluoz is pursued in Mexico by several of his artist-writer friends from San Francisco. Chief among them is Irwin Garden (Ginsberg), who tells Duluoz about his own "'Blakean message for the Iron Hound of America,'" and insists that this is the time for Jack to *"make it!"* Duluoz responds, "'Make *what?*'" Viewed retrospectively, Garden paints an ironically prophetic picture of success for him: "'Get published, meet everybody, make money, become a big international traveling author, sign autographs for old ladies from Ozone Park. . . . "Road" is a big mad book that will change America! They can even make money with it. You'll be dancing naked on your fan mail'" (252–53).

The reader comes across this exchange just pages after Duluoz lays claim to being an American romantic at the time he began writing book one of *Desolation Angels* in 1956. Clearly, Kerouac wants us to view the great divide between the fruitful illusion then still intact (which he no doubt embellishes) and the impending, bare-ass realism of making it in America. With respect to the former, there is no false modesty in the recollection: "I was an Ambitious Paranoid— Nothing could stop me from writing big books of prose and poetry for nothing, that is, with no hope of ever having them published—I was simply writing them because I was an 'Idealist' and I believed in 'Life' and was going about justifying it with my earnest scribblings— Strangely enough, these scribblings were the first of their kind in the world" (229). The self-absorption that immediately follows concerning the invention of spontaneous prose, confessional influences, and method of composition ("cheap nickel notebooks by candlelight in poverty and fame—*Fame* of self") is relieved only by reference to Gerard and his lesson of "reverence of the *idea* of life." By the end of the passage, Kerouac finally works his way out of the narcissistic flourish by equating such reverence with the Holy Spirit: "That we all wander thru flesh, while the dove cries for us, back to the Dove of Heaven." This speaks for another very important change linking identity and belief, for by 1961 Buddha, though still a major hero-figure for Kerouac, has taken a back seat to Christ; and, after 1960, Kerouac is introduced to his readers not as "beat," but as a "strange solitary crazy Catholic mystic."[13]

In the midst of these continual revisions of identity and belief, the bohemian party that swoops down on Mexico disturbs the peace of the artist writing in his Orizaba rooftop hut and travels with him to New York City, where they continue "passing through" (in the Buddhist sense of impermanence). Hopelessly mixing Buddhist and Catholic sensibilities, Kerouac places both in the same travel car: the word made flesh appears to be doing the driving here, but not without taking heed of the navigator in the backseat, who insists on simply passing through the sites of this world without as much as leaving a breath. Traveling like this, the party makes New York and, before long, Duluoz is caught up in the revelry of those "mad ranting action-seekers" once again.

Passing through Tangier does not offer any escape; his cronies are hot on his heels—intense, vigilant, curious, strident in their aim for publicity. However, *en route* (it's now January 1957) Duluoz travels solo on a freighter, which gives him ample time to reassess the situation. He discovers an immense change has occurred inside himself, what he calls a "complete turningabout." This really amounts to a strong sense of "nausea concerning the experience of the world at large, a *revulsion* in all the six senses." Once again, rewriting personal history, Duluoz claims that the initial turn of this about-face took place on Desolation Peak. "And the same feeling came to me: Avoid the World, it's just a lot of dust and drag and means nothing in the end" (300). Yet, even if he could pull it off, it isn't enough to simply renounce the world, because the persistent question remains: "What to do instead?" Moreover, there is an unstated irony to this notion of "complete turningabout," since—in the Buddhist sense—"turning about" refers to that Seventh Bodhisattva Stage where Kerouac could not go. At best, he entered the Buddhist stream, but because of his abiding self-centeredness and clinging to his own ego he could not attain the turning about so necessary to the Buddhist ideal. Also, those who do turn away from self and toward universal compassion have surmounted black and white conceptions (i.e., the dualistic trap of either/or) and remain undisturbed by suffering. Duluoz (and Kerouac) was clearly affected by his anxiety and desolation; in fact, he becomes increasingly attached to his own suffering throughout the course of book two. As Augustine wisely stated the matter: "The difference is not in what people suffer but in the way they suffer." And the Buddha admonished those who deceive themselves by viewing nirvana as simply "an escape and a recompense" from suffering.[14] Since Duluoz (and Kerouac) does not pass muster with respect to these transcendental qualities, the "complete turningabout" he has in mind refers to something quite different.

While in Tangier, helping Hubbard (Burroughs) arrange and type out *Nude Supper* (*Naked Lunch*), Duluoz has awful nightmares brought on by that novel's grotesquely surreal scenes—"like of pulling out endless bolognas from my mouth, from my very entrails, feet of it, pulling and pulling out all the horror of what Bull saw, and wrote" (311). When the rest of the old gang catches up with Duluoz in Tangier, the situation gets even more desperate. Duluoz becomes disenchanted with any and every form of experience in the world. Quite frankly, he is simply beat and overwhelmed by a state of *nada*: "Nothing, nothing, nothing O but *nothing* could interest me any more for one god damned minute in anything in the *world*" (303). Bored and fed up with all the talk of the Beat Generation, coolness, and the faddishness that would soon sweep over the masses of American middle-class youth upon publication of his novel, Duluoz reflects: "To think that I had so much to do with it, too, in fact at that very moment the manuscript of *Road* was being linotyped for imminent publication and I was already sick of the whole subject" (321). Given this pervasive sense of ennui, compounded by an overdose of opium that clinches his resolve to turn things around, one wonders—wither goes that wigwam?

The answer is immediate—*home,* which is a place to be sought somewhere in America: "All I had to do was stay home, give it all up, get a little home for me and Ma, meditate, live quiet, read in the sun, drink wine in the moon in old clothes, pet my kitties, sleep good dreams" (302). This further downsizing of the quest is accompanied by something other than the simple joys of sweet domesticity, namely, a cry of regression: "The best thing to do," Duluoz concludes, "is be like a baby. . . . All I wanted somehow now was Wheaties by a pine breeze kitchen window in America, that is, I guess a vision of my childhood" (316–17).

Yearning for the consolation of a Personal God and for the recovery of lost bliss, Duluoz realizes that the only earthly substitute for such elusive comforts would be his mother—Memère, who is the one constant in his life, the one concerned with "the mending of torture and folly and all loss, mending the very days of your life with almost glad purposeful gravity" (334). Duluoz's intense attachment to Memère is in one sense a return to the safety of the womb, and he frankly acknowledges and defends the fixation, pointing out the "peace and good sense" that Memère provides him. Not only does she offer a needed sense of order and design to life, a gracious periodicity, but she embodies continuity with the very idea of familial togetherness and ethnic heritage, which have all but vanished for Kerouac since the days recalled in *The Town and the City*, especially given the deracination that had set in by the mid-1950s. In fact, Duluoz notes that it would make "some neurotics go mad to see such sanity" exhibited by his mother's resourcefulness and nurturing manner, not to mention the self-indulgence of lazing around like a bum all day while someone serves you. This is a very traditional vision, mostly obsolete now in the West, except perhaps for the recent increase of *mammones* in Italy (i.e., adult men living with their mothers or, idiomatically, "mama's boys"). However, in Japan, where dependency—known as *amae*—is still highly valued and positively viewed, particularly in the mother/son relationship, Duluoz's devotion to Memère would not seem odd at all. It is surprising that, given the trend of ethnographic analysis, no one has cut Kerouac any slack on this issue. In part, the attachment is a direct result of *de facto* French-Canadian matriarchal structure, one in which the childhood father/son relation is replaced by the strong mother/son bond. Granted, the prefeminist role that Memère fulfills seems to the contemporary viewer an unlikely combination of Beatrice and a dutiful French maidservant. But for Duluoz, she offers both escape from the furies of romantic entanglement and protection against the encroaching shadow of the lifelong vulture.

For Duluoz and Memère, seeking home is much easier said than done. After desolating on the mountain and along the West Coast, and while passing through to the point of turnabout, what else could possibly alleviate the grief of this lonesome traveler's weary soul? The particulars of home and the vision of himself as householder come to Duluoz only after an arduous yet endearing cross-country bus trip with Memère. But as one might predict by now, the trip and plan to settle together in the Bay Area turn into yet another misadventure, for Memère—as restless as her son—does not feel *at home* in Berkeley. Even before they get there, along the journey west, Duluoz confronts an ever-closing frontier, one that restricts the very territory in which the quest can roam, thus paving the way for the final downsizing of the ideal:

> God how right Hemingway was when he said there was no remedy for life. . . . No remedy but in my mind I raise a fist to High Heaven promising that I shall bull whip the first bastard who makes fun of human hopelessness anyway. . . . I'm talking about human helplessness and unbelievable loneliness in the darkness of birth and death and asking, "What is there to laugh about in that?" "How can you be *clever* in a meatgrinder?" "Who makes fun of misery?" There's my mother a hunk of flesh that didnt ask to be born, sleeping restlessly, dreaming hopefully, beside her son who also didnt ask to be born, thinking desperately, praying hopelessly, in a bouncing earthly vehicle going from nowhere to nowhere. . . . Where is the rock that will sustain us? (339)

Attempting to provide an answer to that last question, and with his Catholic sensibility now restored, Duluoz suggests that we find our cleft by emulating Memère, including her simple peasantlike virtues and devout faith in God. This renewed belief in a supreme being (of finding a dwelling place in Thee) and in the notion of an immortal soul that seeks an eternal and supreme peace are reflected in Duluoz's conviction: "If the soul cant escape the body give the world to Mao Tse-tung" (285).

In the meantime, and during a moment of rare good sense in the novel, Memère—now on the West Coast—asks to go back home. When Jack asks where such a place exists, she outlines a simple and elegant vision of home for him back there, back in those old-fashioned values that underlie the *town*: "'Home is with your family—You've only got one sister—I've only got one grandson—And one son, *you*— Let's all get together and live *quiet.* People like your Ben Fagan, your Alex Poorbrother, your Irwin Gazootsky, they dont *know* how to live!—You gotta have *fun,* good food, good beds, nothing more—*La tranquillite qui compte!*—Never mind all the fuss about you worry this and that, make yourself a *haven* in this world and Heaven comes after'" (359–60). That last line is a wonderful update of Chomei's classic and enduring question: "Is it possible . . . to find a haven for the body or peace for the mind?" Although Duluoz remarks that "there can be no haven for the living lamb but plenty haven for the dead lamb," he follows Memère's advice because, as he considers her words, he realizes that "she is really delivering to me . . . a message about quietude" (360).

By the end of the novel, Duluoz and Memère have returned to their version of the origin, back to their source of consolation, making a home in the busy world but "miles from [New York] city." At last, he has stopped climbing down from the mountaintop. However, this final scaling-down of the quest is not a happy resolution; it is the final note of qualified desolation that Kerouac sounds in the novel. Although this form of the simple life is accompanied by success and fame for Duluoz and several of his friends, he seems to them "so sunk now" and "unexcited." In the end, when Desolation Peak flattens into Long Island, the potential of enlightened attachment finally empties out into a domestic form of the soulful life as one last hope. In keeping with the quietude of this arrangement, Duluoz tones down the once-shrill quest to a bare murmur: "A peaceful sorrow at home is the best I'll ever be able to offer the world, in the end, and so I told my Desolation Angels goodbye. A new life for me" (366).

This "new life" became Kerouac's *way* as well—"home life, as in the beginning, with a little toot once in a while in local bars," as he put it in an interview.[15] Call it the Modified Lush Life (a complement to the "Modified Ascetic Life"). Evidently, by the end of 1957, and as viewed from the writer completing *Desolation Angels* in 1961, Kerouac was no longer under the influence of Buddhist teachings. Perhaps he finally took seriously some advice from his good friend William S. Burroughs, who thought in 1954 that Kerouac was going too far with the *practice* of Buddhism, writing the following in a letter to him:

> Buddha is only for the West to *study* as *history,* that it is a subject for *under standing,* and Yoga can profitably be practiced to that end. But it is not for the West, An Answer, not A Solution. WE must learn by

acting, experiencing, and living, that is, above all by Love and by Suffering. A man who uses Buddhism or any other instrument to remove love from his being in order to avoid suffering, has committed, in my mind, a sacrilege comparable to castration. (SL, 439)

Such an admonishment must have triggered Kerouac's family motto, which was always close to his heart: *Aimer, Travailler, et Souffrir* (Love, Work, and Suffer). In any case, from 1958 on, and particularly after 1961, Buddhism would lose its hold on Kerouac as *the way* to cracking that "transcendental mystery of existence" that so bemused him. Instead, it would become history, "a subject for *under standing.*" Nonetheless, the questions—what to do? what next?—would still remain.

10

The Old Rugged Cross

As we know, Kerouac's whittled down yet shapely ideal of "a peaceful sorrow at home" was viciously stomped on by the unsettling spectacle of American fortune. The engagement with the bitch goddess Success left Kerouac in a state of "drunken hopelessness" that characterized the years 1958–1961, and—to varying degrees—the years remaining to him thereafter. This form of disillusionment was as total as his idealistic yearning for mystical union with a transcendent reality that fueled the energetic thrusts of the quest during the 1940s and for most of the 1950s. (Although the forms changed, the underlying motive had remained the same.) What to do? What next? Nothing, it seems, but exist in the depths of drunken hopelessness, which is simply the distillation and sum total of "physical and spiritual and metaphysical hopelessness."

> The feeling when you wake up with the delirium tremens with the *fear* of eerie death dripping from your ears like those special heavy cobwebs spiders weave in the hot countries, the feeling of being a bentback mudman monster groaning underground in hot steaming mud pulling a long hot burden nowhere, the feeling of standing ankledeep in hot boiled pork blood, ugh, of being up to your waist in a giant pan of greasy brown dishwater not a trace of suds left in it——The face of yourself you see in the mirror with its expression of unbearable anguish so hagged and awful with sorrow you cant even cry for a thing so ugly, so lost, no connection whatever with early perfection and therefore nothing to connect with tears or anything: it's like William Seward Burroughs' "Stranger" suddenly appearing in your place in the mirror—— (7–8)

In this introductory passage from *Big Sur,* Kerouac's eleventh novel, which was written in the summer of 1961 at the height of Kerouac's maturity as a writer, Duluoz is seething in the stew of the tormented state—this is the everyday world you find. On one hand, the deep sense of hopelessness and self-estrangement results from the facile codification of Kerouac by the popular media and critics as "King of the Beats." In a notebook entry made one year before writing the novel, Kerouac complained about being pigeonholed into such a counterculture role: "The Monster they've built up in the papers is beginning to take shape inside my body like Burroughs' 'stranger'—by simple process of endless repetition & insinuation—They're going to INSIST that I fit their preconceived notion of the 'Beatnik Captain' as tho I was some degenerate Bearded Insurrectionist—."[1] No doubt Kerouac felt bastardized by the misunderstanding of his work and by the commercialization of the beats, which distorted something beatific, genuine, and original into a marketable commodity for the dominant culture's pleasure or ridicule. Consider, for instance, the popular image of the beatnik (bearded, blue-jeaned, sweatshirted, and bongoed out) probably best exemplified by Maynard G. Krebs on television's "The Dobie Gillis Show."

On the other hand, the helplessness and alienation that consumed Kerouac in his later years were direct results of the quest itself when making that final turn before the road flattens out into a line of endless arid nothingness: the sometimes slow yet sure process of sobering up from the ecstasy of being. As Tolstoy relates from the nadir of his own spiritual search in *A Confession,* "It is only possible to go on living while you are intoxicated with life; once sober it is impossible not to see that it is all a mere trick, and a stupid trick! That is exactly what it is: there is nothing either witty or amusing, it is only cruel and stupid."[2] The Kerouac of *Desolation Angels* (especially book two) and *Big Sur* would certainly agree with Tolstoy's sobering definition of "it." As Kerouac became increasingly disillusioned, giving in to despair and losing faith in life, his fruitful illusion of himself as a modernistic mystic altered, along with the personalist messages in his writing that aspired to spiritual meaning, the mysteries, and the awe and wonder and beauty they engendered.

As a modernistic mystic, Kerouac believed that direct knowledge of God, spiritual truth, or ultimate reality could be attained through subjective experience (conceived as intuition or insight). This was both his wager and means for being intoxicated—drunk with life—(helped along, as always, by alcohol and/or drugs). His aim, however, was not to get smashed; rather, it was to get a higher purchase on the ecstasy of being in order to forge a mystical bond with the divine or ultimate. In fact, Kerouac's sobering-up phase of the late 1950s and 1960s was accompanied by far more excessive consumption of alcohol than the various stages of the quest when fully engaged, thus testifying to the misplaced thirst of despair in comparison to ecstasy. Kerouac's modernism—his interest in authenticity and baring one's soul—enhanced his mystical yearnings, especially in an age of vulgar materialism, complacency, and standardization. He was passionate about turning away from the conventional notion of the good life and towards that essential role of a writer revealing the spiritual urgency of a transparent self—someone immersed in the everyday world yet seeking personal meaning in the mysterious relationship between the finite and the infinite.

As for the mystical yearnings themselves, they reached back to the Hebraic myth of creation, to Eden and to the implications of original sin (as set forth by Augustine), or what Kerouac referred to in *Vanity of Duluoz,* his last novel, as "Original Sacrifice" (274).[3] The cost of such primordial sin, as given in the Baltimore catechism Kerouac had read growing up, was this: having forfeited happiness in this life and everlasting glory in the next (both preternatural and supernatural gifts granted by God), humankind was thus "doomed" to sickness and death. This fall from grace, and the necessary corruption of all through sexual intercourse, explains much of Kerouac's abiding interest in restoring lost innocence—the purity of such holy origins; it also accounts for the repining echoes of Kerouac's groans. How else to register the distance between now and then? Recall that telling line from *Big Sur* quoted previously that evokes such estrangement from the ideal: "no connection whatever with early perfection."

The mystic in Kerouac also adapted the spiritual works of mercy and beatitudes to the secularized cash nexus of late Western civilization (i.e., the neglected Christian values of humility, mercy, justice, forgiveness, consolation, patience, compassion, and universal love; in short, he expressed a "*beatific* indifference to things that are Caesar's" ["Aftermath: The Philosophy of the Beat Generation," *GB*, 50]). Of course, for Kerouac the primary beatitude that drove his work onward was the following: "Blessed are they that mourn, for they shall be comforted." This explains both his calling and pilgrimage, initially voiced by the prophet in *On the Road* and elaborated upon in *Visions of Cody*: "*Go moan for man. . . .*" All of this explains why the most frequently occurring word in Kerouac's oeuvre is "sad." Finally, in order to escape the tormented state of original suffering, and the misery that attends one's attachment to the transient desires of the world, Kerouac turned to Buddhism as an alternative way to reclaim the transcendent, hoping to secure a measure of spiritual peace and contentment. And true to the mystical impulse, Kerouac (up until his embittered late period) was far more interested in the inner experience of such spiritual truths gathered from East and West than in the organized assembly of external phenomena displayed in religious form and ritual.

Even as late as 1959, in the midst of his public disaster, Kerouac felt it necessary to clarify the breadth and direction of his mystical embrace. Recalling a TV interview with Ben Hecht, Kerouac complained: "All he wanted me to do was speak out my mind *against* people . . . *against* the world he wanted, this is his ideal of freedom, he calls it freedom":

> Who knows, my God, but that the universe is not one vast sea of compassion actually, the veritable holy honey, beneath all this show of personality and cruelty. . . . No, I want to speak *for* things, for the crucifix I speak out, for the Star of Israel I speak out, for the divinest

man who ever lived who was a German (Bach) I speak out, for sweet Mohammed I speak out, for Buddha I speak out, for Lao-tse and Chuang-tse I speak out, for D. T. Suzuki I speak out . . . why should I attack what I love out of life. This is Beat. Live your lives out? Naw, *love* your lives out. ("On the Origins of a Generation," GB, 56)

By 1961, however, the effusiveness of Kerouac's affirmative spirit had nearly vanished. From 1958 to 1961, Kerouac drank more heavily than in any other period of his life. Evidently, the forces of self-indulgence and self-destruction, which were always there but held in check, were cut loose by fame and notoriety. Distraught by the fact that he was hung rather than crowned by the laurel wreath of culture, Kerouac apparently forgot what he once said to his first publisher Bob Giroux back in the summer of 1949 when they were working on the final revisions of *The Town and the City*: "I told him there were 'no laurel wreaths,' i.e., the poet did not find ecstasies in worldly fame, nor in fortune, nor even in anything like acclaim or regard. He quite sensibly told me that the laurel wreath is worn only in the moment of writing."[4] Although wildly popular as a beat figure among the youth of America coming of age in the late fifties and the sixties, Kerouac did not enjoy critical acclaim or regard until well after his death. With few exceptions, the literary establishment dismissed him as a rebellious juvenile delinquent—a sensation-seeking "high school athlete who went from Lowell, Massachusetts to Skid Row, losing his eraser en route," in the words of John Ciardi.[5] And, of course, the crude, devolutionary view of Kerouac (inspired by Truman Capote)—that "neanderthal with a typewriter"—dogged Kerouac his entire life.

Seen in this light, *Big Sur* marks Kerouac's rite of passage from modernistic mystic to hopeless drunkard. At the time when Kerouac composed the novel, he made the following journal entry: "All day I've been sick—Who can ever heal me? I'm a drunkard—Even rum won't do to ease the pain I feel—And I cant tell anyone how bad I feel, they would never believe me—Why is consolation a joke in this dry world? It's consolation I seek from rum."[6] The condition of "drunken hopelessness" manifested in the novel was thus unwittingly refined into a mode of being—one fortified by the identities of literary monk and *"farceur"* ("honest goof-off"),[7] which carried Kerouac through the anguish of those embittered years (from 1962 to his untimely death from alcoholism in 1969). In *Big Sur*, which recalls Duluoz's total breakdown (physical, spiritual, and metaphysical) during the summer of 1960, it is clear that the quest has finally turned into crisis, culminating in an explicit renunciation of Buddhism as *the way* and a return to Catholicism. However, in the meantime, between the peaceful sorrow that ends *Desolation Angels* and the vision of the Cross that Duluoz embraces at the very end of *Big Sur*, the reader is deprived of that spiritual solace Kerouac customarily offers in his role as "madman bum and angel"—a guarantor of hope that somehow the defiled gutter will rise and transform itself into the holy eaves of heaven. Throughout *Big Sur*, Duluoz (and the reader) is left bereft of any "protective devices" that could both cushion his fall and steer the better part of himself to higher ground.

Big Sur is Kerouac's most carefully crafted novel. As one perceptive reviewer of the time commented, the novel has "a sense of structure and pacing which the early books lack. The scenes absolutely click for a change. They 'signify.' An orgy is no mere orgy; it has motive and consequence."[8] From the very opening of *Big Sur*, Kerouac reveals his interest in subverting his role as "King of the Beats" and thereby invalidating the game of achievement. Duluoz wakes up in a San Francisco skid row flophouse hung over, listening to the maudlin tones of "I'll Take You Home Again Kathleen" ring out from a nearby church belfry: "I've hit the end of the trail and cant even drag my body any more even to a refuge in the woods let alone stay upright in the city a minute" (4). It's the first big cross-country trip since the publication of *Road*, the last attempt to span the continent and recover a sense of community with the old gang as well as some peace of mind. The going itself is revealing; rather than reinforce the beat image of hitchhiker, Duluoz takes the cushy—though well-deserved, for a man nearing forty—passage on a train, staying in his bourgeois berth for three straight days to watch the countryside flash past his window. The purpose of the trip is to retreat to the haven of a solitary cabin owned by Monsanto (Lawrence Ferlinghetti) amid the extraordinary natural beauty of Big Sur. Duluoz's notion is simply to reclaim his sanity after the maddening assault of fame that sent him staggering into the public arena over the past few years. Instead of enjoying a sense of contentment and triumph after so many desperate years of laboring in anonymity, Duluoz now feels besieged and defeated by the grotesque distortions of success. With Kerouac as modernistic mystic in mind, Holmes, always the astute observer, accurately assessed the nature of this public misrecognition: "And the man who [once] wrote me . . . , 'Life is drenched in spirit; it rains spirit; we would *suffer* were it not so'. . . , lived to see the books which embodied this credo on page after page used as bibles of hipness by the Beatniks, derided as incoherent mouthings by the critics, and treated as some kind of literary equivalent of rock 'n' roll by the mass media."[9] Perhaps this is why *Big Sur* is also Kerouac's most dire novel, for Duluoz seems to be hankering for some kind of deliverance from the rock bottom of the tormented world, for some way out—a bum's rush to the eternal and untroubled peace of heaven.

However, from the beginning it is clear that there will be no easy way out of this worldly mess. For starters, Duluoz blows his cover. Instead of sneaking off to the cabin undetected as planned upon arrival, he bursts drunkenly into Monsanto's bookstore (City Lights) and is immediately swept away on the shoulders of the subterranean crowds of Saturday night. In this false start, Duluoz returns cravenly to the very madness that he sought escape from, thereby sabotaging the subversion of his beat image and fate as well as his own good intentions to seek sanctuary. Back in skid row, he does offer payment for his folly the morning after; obviously, he has fallen overnight from the high and mighty counterculture figure to the lowly, down-and-out bum trying desperately to rise to the occasion once again, just like all the other bums in the flophouse, awakening to the pungent odor of decay, to the aching rebellion of stomachs, and to voices half-hidden in smoke, in bottles, in the consuming moisture of desolation. Naturally, Duluoz joins this purgatory and becomes an Everyman figure for the polluted dancing above the abyss:

> I wake up drunk, sick, disgusted, frightened, in fact terrified by that sad song across the roofs ["Kathleen"] mingling with the lachrymose cries of a Salvation Army meeting on the corner below "*Satan* is the cause of your alcoholism, *Satan* is the cause of your immorality, Satan is *everywhere* workin to destroy you unless you repent *now*" and worse than that the sound of old drunks throwing up in rooms next to mine, the creak of hall steps, the moans everywhere——Including the moan

that had awakened me, my own moan in the lumpy bed, a moan caused by a big roaring Whoo Whoo in my head that had shot me out of my pillow like a ghost. (5–6)

"Go moan for man." Moan for self who is man. And, in doing so, wake up to one's own groaning existence amid the multitudes tossing and turning in the "lumpy bed" of earth. The whole sorry and miserable scene of skid row and, in particular, the Salvation Army's rhetorical emphasis on cause and conversion, foreshadows the crisis and resolution that mark the novel's progression towards expiation and purgation. This scene also suggests that the problem (or sin) of drunken hopelessness is placed squarely within a Christian context. The attribution of causality voiced by the Sally meeting implies the traditional Western notion of free will and the knowledge of good and evil as a basis for cause and effect and the need for redemption. As Dante put it in *Purgatorio,* "Thus, if the present world has gone astray, in you is the cause, in you it's to be sought."[10] Therefore, from the opening chapter of *Big Sur,* Kerouac reestablishes a Christian outlook, one that presupposes the existence of a persisting self (and immortal soul) that is not beyond the construct of good and evil but, rather, caught in its very teeth. This worldview also accepts human fallibility, sin, punitive consequences, and joining with one's neighbor in this very real and valuable world to learn through love and suffering (recall Burroughs's injunction to Kerouac). Finally, to complete this Christian context, one turns to God in humility and pain with the enormous wager that His mercy is greater than His judgment.

"'One fast move or I'm gone,'" Duluoz realizes and so—to get on with his own personal mission for coming out west—shoots himself out of San Francisco skid row and into the wild open spaces and surf of Big Sur. Initially, once settled into Monsanto's cabin and its surroundings, he seems to find some needed respite from the turmoil of his life. "In the flush of the first few days of joy I confidently tell myself . . . 'no more dissipation, it's time for me to quietly watch the world and even enjoy it, . . . no booze, no drugs, no binges, no bouts with beatniks and drunks and junkies and everybody, no more I ask myself the question *O why is God torturing me,* . . . no more self-imposed agony'" (24). Both the spectacular natural setting and the sage self-counsel help Duluoz to recover the lost innocence, purity, joys, and

anonymity of his life. Whether baking muffins, rolling his own cigarettes, scouring pans, recalling the "endless use" he gets out of an
old T-shirt rescued years ago from a railroad dump, or improving a
waterhole in the creek, Duluoz expresses the importance of the simple
virtues of life so necessary to self-reliance and well-being. The spirituality associated with simplifying one's life (as if taking a vow of
poverty) returns to him at this time and strikes Duluoz as perhaps "the
best way to get to Heaven"; and, as a result, he is able to momentarily
escape from the trap of self-consciousness, making keen observations
and having clear insights into the nature of things. Reminding one of
the naturalistic poetics of Thoreau, Duluoz contemplates the look of
the valley centuries ago, recent and ancient Indians who once lived
there, the changing depth of the creek over the decades, the ancestors
of rocks, the silt that will cover Sur a billion years from now, the fog,
leaves, trees, sand, sea, and the transiency of all life. The meditations
end in a lyrical flourish that enfolds all of creation into an animistic
paradise in the here and now. All the more reason to wonder about a
man who, despite these engaging reflections, cracks up within a few
weeks, losing it completely—a gone bird.

Although Duluoz is slated to stay at the cabin for three uninter-
rupted weeks, boredom begins to set in by the end of the first week,
and before the end of the third, he abandons his solitary post—heading back north to Monterey and San Francisco. It's not just his appetite for people and places and the high-tingled noise and jam of cities
that sends him back to his desire. No, there is something else, something in the air of Sur, something he inhales in the very breath he
takes, which is the first of several "signposts of something wrong," of
something that has gone awry. These signposts proclaim a general
distress which, according to William James, is the common denomi-
nator of all religions. "The uneasiness, reduced to its simplest terms,"
writes James, "is a sense that there is *something wrong about us* as we
naturally stand. The solution is a sense that *we are saved from the wrongness* by making proper connection with the higher powers." According to James, to be aware of the signposts, to read and interpret the
messages clearly, reveals that the individual who suffers from his
wrongness is already a step beyond it. In this case, ignorance is not
bliss. Individuals are thus divided selves:

Along with the wrong part there is thus a better part . . . , even though it may be but a most helpless germ. With which part he should identify his real being is by no means obvious at this stage [of uneasiness]; but when stage 2 (the stage of solution or salvation) arrives, the man identifies his real being with the germinal higher part of himself; and he does so in the following way.

He becomes conscious that this higher part is conterminous and continuous with . . . more of the same quality, which is operative in the universe outside him, and which he can keep in working touch with, and in a fashion get on board of and save himself when all his lower being has gone to pieces in the wreck.[11]

James very accurately describes Duluoz's condition both in terms of the impending crack-up (the wreck and wrongness of his lower being) and his conscious preoccupation with suffering—the fallout from Duluoz's uneasiness concerning his helpless natural standing in the world. Such awareness will eventually put Duluoz "in working touch with" a greater spiritual authority to save him from the shards of his shattered self, just in the nick of time. But for almost all of the novel the reader witnesses the agony and distress of Duluoz's lower self going to pieces, as if Kerouac were implicitly stating that, when it enters one's being (or when one becomes aware of its existence), suffering from wrongness should not be dismissed outright. It is not something to rid oneself of. Rather, one might as well join with it and ride it out to the end of the trail, hoping that—in the meantime, before meeting up with that other pale rider—a taller, more capable rider will have emerged in the saddle to take the high ground.

The idea of a divided self works effectively to set up the tense oppositional rhythm of the agonist: the hope of an inspired sanity vs. the despair resident in the drunken madman; strength vs. sickness; and the simple joys of self-reliance vs. the stressful complications of helplessness. Duluoz spends most of his energy throughout the novel fending off the latter of each pair and attempting to reclaim physical, spiritual, and metaphysical well-being. That first signal alluded to—what Duluoz refers to as "this horrible sinister condition (of mortal hopelessness)"— tips the scale of these oppositions towards Duluoz's feeling that something is fundamentally wrong in the nature of humankind. This breeds an uneasiness that enters Duluoz's being through his very breath, through what we normally associate with life itself:

When I went to the sea in the afternoon and suddenly took a huge deep Yogic breath to get all that good sea air in me but somehow just got an overdose of iodine, or of evil, . . . my heart suddenly beating——Thinking I'm gonna get the local vibrations instead here I am almost fainting only it isnt an ecstatic swoon by St. Francis, it comes over me in the form of horror of an eternal condition of sick mortality in me——In me and in everyone——I felt completely nude of all poor protective devices like thoughts about life or meditations under trees and the "ultimate" and all that shit, in fact the other pitiful devices of making supper or saying "What I do now next? chop wood?——I see myself as just doomed, pitiful——An awful realization that I have been fooling myself all my life thinking there was a next thing to do to keep the show going and actually I'm just a sick clown and so is everybody else——" (41)

Sitting on the sand, staring out to sea, Duluoz seems to hear the steady onrush of Pacific waves yelling at him—what he takes to be "secret knowledge" about the real sound of the sea: "GO TO YOUR DESIRE DON'T HANG AROUND HERE." And so he does, packing up the cabin, leaving food for the creatures of Sur who don't have to bother with such drastic thoughts, and heading back to civilization with his discontents heavy in his rucksack and with a sense of certainty about the great divide between nature and culture: "the sea has its waves, the man has his fireside, period" (42).

The other signals reinforce the foundation of wrongness from the cornerstones of both nature and culture. For instance, the second sign occurs while Duluoz hitches the fourteen miles from the Raton (Bixby) Canyon cabin to Monterey; from there he'll catch a bus to San Francisco. But getting a ride is not so easy, and Duluoz ends up walking half the distance to Monterey as thousands of cars, mainly station wagons filled with vacationing families, speed suspiciously by, thinking he must be the crazed "Hollywood hitch hiker"—a killer on the road. It's been a while since Duluoz has stuck his thumb out and this stretch along the coastal highway gives him a glimpse into an altered America: one less generous and more paranoid as it pursues its leisure; an America thoroughly domesticated, ruled by "wifey" in the passenger seat and driven on to endless consumption by the hordes of children in backseats; and finally, an America that squeezes out the romantic hitchhiker from the soft shoulder of the road. Finally, a folk-singer in an old car going in the opposite direction picks him up and takes him the other way to the Monterey bus station to save his feet from further blistering. By the time he arrives at the station, Duluoz has seen America progress from the natural intimacies of the "Big Two Hearted River" to all the trappings of the interstate. The result: "[It's] the last time I ever hitch hiked—And NO RIDES a sign" (48).

The third sign, which shifts back to nature, is the death of Duluoz's cat, Tyke. This news from New York brings the feeling of "sick mortality" back home to Duluoz, reminding him of the early death of his brother Gerard as well the love of cats they shared together. Tyke's fate also combines with the death of other animals during the course of the novel: an otter, a mouse, goldfish, not to mention the makeshift grave of a car's rusted chassis that fell a thousand feet from the bridge spanning the Raton Canyon—the first fright that visits Duluoz. The other signs return to the cluttered realm of culture, to the population explosion, the growing urban sprawl extending from San Francisco to San Jose, and to the unchecked multiplicity of life that has nowhere to go but up (imagining housing tracts stacked in ever-ascending levels)—the "too-much-ness of the world," which will make the planet look like "'a prickly ball hangin in space'" (63–64). All of these various signs simply document the uneasiness and wrongness that exist in the natural world, in society, and within the heaving breast of man.

These signs also spark a restlessness that drives Duluoz out of his relative peace and quiet, then nearly out of his mind. Yet there is a rough symmetry to the novel, for the six weeks he spends out West are almost equally divided between the mostly contented solitude of Big Sur and the maddening torture that increasingly claims him thereafter. Once Duluoz leaves the cabin, there seems to be no escape from the horrors that tighten their grip upon him. After he returns to San Francisco and hooks up with the beat scene of Zen, jazz, booze, pot, and endless parties, he's off to visit Cody (Cassady) in Los Gatos, then detours to see a friend at the hospital before heading back to San Francisco; another visit to the cabin in Big Sur is made but this time with carfuls of friends and fellow beat poets whose general rowdiness desecrates the quietude of the cabin and its hermetic idyll. Another reunion at the cabin follows the long weekend and an awkward moment of sickness and relief before Duluoz returns to San Francisco, where he hooks up with a lover. They make one final trip to the cabin with another couple before Duluoz bids good-bye to Monsanto and friends in San Francisco and returns to New York. It is as if the questions—what to do? what next?—have become utterly meaningless terms in the syntax of human folly. In a way, we have come full circle to the screeching charge of *On the Road*—Go!—but with these telling exceptions: the landscape for continental adventure is delimited to a chip off the new coast, the route narrowed down to a single lane of self-preoccupation, and the impulsive swings made far more predictable and disturbing. As Duluoz sums it up—"the backs and forths and pains of me in City and Sur."

During one of these strained oscillations, Duluoz finds himself alone at the cabin for a brief time with a young beat zealot, Ron Blake. At this point in the novel, it is no longer necessary for Duluoz to keep reading the signs for, by now, he clearly embodies them; the collapse of signifier and signified is thus fleshed out. Once again, he has traveled three thousand miles only to face the very reason for his departure: "I'm sick and tired of all the endless enthusiasms of new young kids trying to know me and pour out all their lives into me so that I'll jump up and down and say yes yes that's right, which I cant do any more. . . . Like those pathetic five highschool kids who all came to my door in Long Island one night wearing jackets that said 'Dharma Bums' on them, all expecting me to be 25 years old according to a mistake on a book jacket and here I am old enough to be their father" (109–10). Naturally, trying not to disappoint, Duluoz obliges the beat protege. But, after consuming too much sweet port wine on top of previous Manhattans and with very little to eat between drinking bouts over the past few days, Duluoz wakes up with the "final horrors," reminiscent of his rise in the skid row flop before his first trip to Sur. These "horrors," and the "sick mortality" they portend, are instigated by the onset of delirium tremens that strangle his mind. The moaning and groaning begins anew, Blake or no Blake, and the pathetic sight and sound of this little trauma in nature turns the idealistic beat image of the "King" into that of a deranged fool.

Kerouac not only strengthens the subversion of his popular image through this descent but evokes in a startling manner the fragile state of Duluoz's hold on reality. In the process, he certainly answers the question posed by one of his successors: how does it feel?

The mental anguish is so intense that you feel you have betrayed your very birth . . . , you feel a guilt so deep you identify yourself with the devil and God seems so far away abandoning you to your sick silliness—You feel sick in the greatest sense of the word, *breathing without believing in it,* sicksicksick, your soul groans, you look at your helpless hands as tho they were on fire and you cant move to help, you look at the world with dead eyes, there's on your face an expression of incalculable repining like a constipated angel on a cloud—— (111)

This sickening feeling helps to define the condition of "mortal hopelessness" that Duluoz exemplifies: that is, taking one's breath mechanically and for no apparent reason other than it's free (who wouldn't exploit such a bargain?); being emotionally bound up inside; and betraying goodness, mercy, faith, and the efforts of those who have made one's life and future possible. All of this makes Duluoz bury his face in his hands and cry out for help, in turn addressing his mother, father, brother, and friends in French-Canadian *joual,* the first language of his childhood. As for Blake, his young beat companion, Duluoz is doubly distraught that he had to bear witness to this ordeal: "but methinks and mayhap he took away a lesson in temperance, or a lesson in beatness really" (114). Although Duluoz comes out of his turmoiled state when Blake momentarily leaves the premises, recalling childhood reveries, the reader realizes that this agonizing episode is simply a prelude to the breakdown that follows.

The only relief from Duluoz's bleak and deteriorating condition comes in the form of an affair and in several brief interludes with friends. At first, the affair with Billie (Cody's mistress) amounts to a momentary stay against any further skidding down. For a short time, the love interest not only prevents further catastrophe but actually helps Duluoz forget his troubles simply through the "unbelievable surrendering sweetness" of entering into another's body and soul. "Because a new love affair always gives hope, the irrational mortal loneliness is always crowned, that thing I saw (that horror of snake emptiness) when I took the deep iodine deathbreath on the Big Sur beach is now justified and hosannah'd and raised up like a sacred urn to Heaven in the mere fact of the taking off of clothes and clashing wits and bodies in the inexpressibly nervously sad delight of love" (147–48). However, despite such rapturous delights of the honeymoon period, the real import of the love affair is that in no time it turns disastrous, adding to the lethal mix of Duluoz's madness. After only one week with Billie and her little son Elliott in their San Francisco apartment, the chair Duluoz sits on day in and day out (smoking cigarettes, drinking wine and entertaining guests while Billie's at work) suddenly collapses. "I'm sprawled on the floor with surprise, the chair has gone" (167)—as if this were the only way to get his lazy parasitic arse out of the seat of nada. Kerouac pulls a very effective stunt here, a moment of authentic slapstick that suggests, first of all, a tragic-comic view of human folly and, secondly, that romantic love cannot qualify as the vital agency of one's salvation.

Billie, however, doesn't seem to get it. As she closes in on Duluoz, there are echoes of Leo's relationship with Mardou in *The Subterraneans*. For instance, Billie not only attributes Duluoz's wrongness to "withhold[ing]" his love from women, but she accuses him of losing sight of the essence as he busily and blindly constructs possibilities: "'all you've been doing is wasting life really sitting around sad wondering where to go and all the time it's right there for you to take'" (169). She keeps pressing Duluoz, attempting to convince him that the nature of his uneasiness can be remedied by a committed love for a woman: "'O Jack it's time for you to wake up and come with me or at least come with somebody and open your eyes to why God's put you here.'" Although she offers a compelling argument, pulling on one of the main arteries of Duluoz's malaise, he is much too pitiful a figure to take on such a hopeful offer of human love and relationship (even on principle: "at least come with somebody"). Duluoz looks deeply into her eyes only to see his own stinking self: "'I'm a helpless hunk of helpful horse manure looking into your eyes saying Help me.'" And though clearly beyond the verge of rescue by another human being, he does present an apt picture of "mortal hopelessness" pleading for assistance. Despite his own self-absorption, Duluoz at least acknowledges that Billie may be right, and that life itself can be sympathetic to those in need. Wondering if she's right, that is, whether or not marriage is a means for deliverance from suffering, Duluoz feels that now and then life itself offers a tender bone from under its sleeve, and this "fills [him] with love to realize that life so avid and misunderstood nevertheless reaches out skinny skeleton hand to me and to Billie too" (175). Later, at the oceanside, he imagines her distant figure to be "ST. CAROLYN BY THE SEA" and recalls her words, bringing himself up short: "Can it be I'm withholding from her something sacred just like she says, or am I just a fool who'll never learn to have a decent eternally minded deepdown relation with a woman and keep throwing that away for a song at a bottle?" (183).

That is the Duluoz Legend's sixty-four-thousand-dollar question. But before he can even formulate an answer the rubber ducky squats on his head. Once again, it seems that only fertilizer saves Duluoz from being utterly useless. If not playing the fool, he assumes another negative role—phantom of the Opera, the haunting shadow slicing across the aspiring idealism of a brightening JFK America. As previously mentioned, Kerouac seems rather insistent on turning Duluoz into an amalgam of all the "signposts of something wrong." Perhaps the most troubling sign is Duluoz's own relentless self-absorption, which Billie, alluding to the breakout of cultural narcissism across America, likens to a "'curious disease a lot of us have anyway only better hidden'" (186). Duluoz escapes only momentarily from the affliction of such a disease, once when goofing in the spirit of glad freedom with his old friend George Baso (Al Saijo) while paying him a visit at the T.B. hospital; another time at the cabin when engaging in spontaneous repartee with Arthur Ma; and once when passed out in the park with guardian Ben Fagan (Philip Whalen) watching over him—as well as "unexpected events"—all afternoon. Although this last event turns into the most restful day he's spent in California (a little piece of heaven in the clover), it is very telling that, as soon as Duluoz wakes up, the incessant chattering of the monkey mind takes off, swinging from one tangled cerebral branch to another. Fagan offers some sound Zen advice, but to no avail: "'Stop thinking about yourself, will ya, just float with the world'" (162).

> [Jack] "What are we gonna do with our lives?"
> [Ben] "Oh, . . . I dunno, just watch em I guess." (164)

But to simply exist and watch the show, detached from one's own intruding ego monopoly, has become an activity now beyond the helpless reach of Duluoz's mind. There is nothing left for him to do other than return to Go—to the distressing self-absorption of fallen man, "nude of all protective devices," as advertised by that first signpost at Sur. Only this time Duluoz cannot run away to his desire, but must nakedly confront the horrors bouncing off the walls of that "insane

shivering canyon" and see it through once and for all. So he decides
to return to the cabin at Big Sur one final time accompanied by Billie,
Elliott, Dave Wain (Lew Welch), and Romona (Lenore Kandel).

Duluoz's antiromantic view of nature is more than simply colored
by his breakdown; a prime example of the pathetic fallacy at work,
Kerouac projects his character's soul sickness and overwrought self into
his surroundings. The natural setting of Big Sur thus takes on a "Gar-
gantuan leprous face of its own with wide broad nostrils and huge bags
under its eyes and a mouth big enough to swallow five thousand jeep-
ster station wagons and ten thousand Dave Wains and Cody Pomerays
without a sigh of reminiscence or regret" (90). At best, in a moment
of levity, this monstrous visage of wilderness is modified into a paradoxical vista of "gruesome splendor," or what Kerouac would later
refine into the phrase, "brute creation," to evoke the promise of death
emerging out of life (*VOD,* 273).[12]

To make matters worse, once back at the cabin Duluoz cannot even
rely upon the device of art in order to secure an aesthetic distance from
the penetrating willies of unmediated nothingness. Again this is similar
to Tolstoy when, floundering amid his search for meaning (for something to sculpt out of the massive absurdity of existence), he finds "this
mirror [of art] either unnecessary, superfluous and ridiculous, or tor-
menting."[13] For Duluoz, who is "sick and tired," the awareness comes
rather abruptly: "I suddenly remember James Joyce and stare at the
waves realizing 'All summer you were sitting here writing the so called
sound of the waves not realizing how deadly serious our life and doom
is, you fool, you happy kid with a pencil, don't you realize you've been
using words as a happy game—all those marvelous skeptical things
that you wrote about graves and sea death it's ALL TRUE YOU
FOOL! Joyce is dead! The sea took him! it will take YOU!'" (182).
Like Milarepa, the Buddhist monk whom Kerouac quotes earlier in
the novel, Duluoz has been emptied of all pretension and hope. But,
for Duluoz, this void is not placed in the service of Buddhist solitude
and bliss; rather, it is seen anxiously as loss and artifice. Ironically, Duluoz now views his engagement with Buddhist teachings as having
evolved to a state of sheer emptiness: the spiritual substance of the
religious worldview has turned into "'empty words,—I realize I've been
playing like a happy child with words words words in a big serious
tragedy'" (187).

Thus disabused of his last line of defense, the uneasiness and wrongness that have plagued his being finally erupt into full-blown madness, replete with the d.t.'s, sleeplessness, sweats, weakness, and wretchedness. Billie and Elliott only exacerbate the psychic implosion and spiritual desperation: while Billie threatens suicide and repeatedly hits her son, Elliott, the wise and persistent child, attempts more than once to break up the intimacy between mother and lover. Once while the couple is actually making love, Elliott tries to pull his mother off of Duluoz, yelling, "'Billie dont do it dont do it Billie dont do it'" (190). Driven beyond the brink of paranoia, Duluoz feels evil forces closing in on him from everyone and everything. In an attempt to purify himself of this craziness, he keeps returning to drink water from the creek and interpret its babble, which has somehow flowed into his mind: "it's telling me to die because everything is over." Duluoz thinks that the only way to stop this incessant chattering from coursing through the channels of his mind is to perform a lobotomy and snip away "all that agony in my forehead" (201).

As James assayed, the turning point finally comes right before Duluoz has "gone to pieces in the wreck." In moving from the stage of maddening uneasiness to that of salvation from a consuming wrongness, the "higher part" of Duluoz emerges to make a vital connection with the powers that be. This is why *Big Sur* culminates with a vision of the Cross—to keep the spiritual being alive as it springs from the dark night, and despite the departure from previous teachings, influences, and aspirations. At the end of *Big Sur,* after all that gritty "passing through" and "peaceful sorrow" of *Desolation Angels,* Duluoz truly comes home to settle down in mind, body, and spirit after roaming so far and wide. Tapping the spiritual innocence of Ti Jean, Duluoz returns to an old familiar dwelling. An image of the Cross comes to him, simply and clearly defined, alone by itself; there is no bodhi tree along its side, although the devil is close behind and angels laughing from on high. The image appears in Duluoz's waking hours, amid "all the turmoiled universes I see tilting and expanding suddenly exploding suddenly clawing in to my center, faces, yelling mouths, long haired yellers, sudden evil confidences, sudden rat-tat-tats of cerebral committees arguing about 'Jack' and talking about him as if he wasn't there" (204). Rising to a vision of clarity from this immense inner racket, the Cross brings immediate relief and consolation, along with some consternation:

> I see the Cross, it's silent, it stays a long time, my heart goes out to it, my whole body fades away to it, I hold out my arms to be taken away to it. . . . "I'm with you, Jesus, for always, thank you"——I lie there in cold sweat wondering what's come over me for years my Buddhist studies and pipesmoking assured meditations on emptiness and all of a sudden the Cross is manifested to me——My eyes fill with tears——"We'll all be saved——" (205–6)

Of course, it doesn't end there. That would be a peace too easily won for Kerouac. In order to ensure fulfillment of the novel's telos (expiation, atonement, and salvation), the battle rages on through the night with devils, bats, and flying saucers swooping down on Duluoz. Then, at last falling asleep, an oppressive nightmare follows, amounting to the final purgation of his soul. The nightmare, an eerie confluence of the Buddhist mountaintop and beat scene (mingling with the grim reduction of love to sheer mechanics and conflict) appears to deliver an unconscious form of justice to Duluoz for going astray. It begins with a job (similar to fire lookout) in the same ridge where Desolation Peak is located but, instead of promising enlightenment and spiritual liberation, the experience results in trickery and entrapment. Arriving at Mien Mo Mountain, which resembles Sur's Raton Canyon, Duluoz spies "huge brooding vultures" on the rocks of a dried-out river and hundreds more "slowly fornicating vulture couples on the town dump":

> These are now humanly formed vultures with human shaped arms, legs, heads, torsos, but they have rainbow colored feathers, and the men are all quietly sitting *behind* Vulture Women slowly somehow fornicating at them in all the same slow obscene movement. . . . As I pass I even see the expression on the face of a youngish blond vulture man eternally displeased because his Vulture Mistress is an old Yakker who's been arguing with him all the time——His face is completely human but inhumanly pasty like uncooked pale pie dough with dull seamed buggy horror that he's doomed to all this enough to make me shudder in sympathy, I even see her awful expression of middleaged pie dough tormentism——They're so human! (208)

As the nightmare progresses, all the desolations of the mountaintop and beat settings merge in a final torturous image of rot, decay, and punishment. Duluoz and a couple of other young workers are taken to a cavernous and disgusting apartment in town, with "dirty beatnik beds and mattresses everywhere. . . . An endless walk thru long and greasy pantries and vast washrooms a block long with single filthy little sink all dark and slimey." Set to work in the kitchen, amid "uncooked chickens lying around on the floor, among garbage and bottles," the crew realizes that the Vultures are plotting to carry them down to the "Underground Slimes to walk neck deep in steaming mucks pulling huge groaning wheels (among small forked snakes) so the devil with the long ears can mine his Purple Magenta Square Stone that is the secret of all this Kingdom. . . . If you succeed you can become a pasty Vulture Person obscenely fornicating on the dump above" (209–10). The whole grotesque nightmare takes on added significance when we remind ourselves of two essential points: first, that Vulture Peak was a venue where the Buddha discoursed on the sutra to the holy congregation assembled there; and, secondly, that the game Kerouac played throughout his childhood and, occasionally, as an adult was called "the lifelong vulture and the little man" (and remember that, when playing as an adult, he was captured).

Finally, after Duluoz wakes up, the novel moves from climax to resolution, that is, from desolation to consolation. The final gesture of madness is given when Jack seems to enact an image from the nightmare, turning himself into a kind of Vulture Man when he "tromps" the dirt down on a garbage pit dug wittingly or unwittingly by Billie to look like a child's grave. (In supplementing the nightmare, real life hammers in those final nails of the coffin, burying the possibility of salvation through human love and sexuality.) Then, utterly shot through, completely exhausted, Duluoz falls back asleep for just a moment in the hot sun. At last, in the span of a minute's rest, "blessed relief has come" and the madness stops, "and there's the golden swarming peace of Heaven in my eyelids——It comes with a sure hand a soft blessing as big as it is beneficent. . . . Just a golden wash of goodness has spread over all and over all my body and mind——All the dark torture is a memory. . . . Something good will come out of all things yet——And it will be golden and eternal just like that—— There's no need to say another word" (215–16).

No other words except for these: *hope*—that one imperfect device for pulling one through. Not to mention divine grace—that perfect device for landing on one's feet. In the end, Duluoz (an otherwise depraved embodiment of Augustine's fallen man) returns to the protective Christian fold and is reconciled with its higher powers. And just in time, before the tangled parts ("King of the Beats," writing bhikku, and besieged lover) consumed the whole. Although the ending brings a sense of relief and recovery, a testament to human resiliency and the importance of keeping one's spirituality alive in some form (even if barely alive), one wonders about the degree of conviction necessary to back up the words, less they too become empty. If Kerouac's final deliverance seems somewhat facile, then perhaps we should look into the poem that serves as a coda to the novel—"Sea: Sounds of the Pacific Ocean at Big Sur." In the sound-poem, Kerouac does offer some convincing proof that he cannot accept the profound disenchantment of being—not yet. About midway through the poem, there is a cry against nihilism:

> God I've got to believe in you
> or live in death!
> Will you save us——all?
>   Soon or now?
> Send illumination
> to our drowning brains
> ——We're pitiful, Lord,
> we need yr help!

(233)

This raw craving for belief is Kerouac's own interpretation of the sea's resonant rage for order; it's also reinforcement for Tolstoy's own cry: "God is life."[14]

Afterword

In the end, as in the beginning, Kerouac instructed by example—a muscular lump of flesh made somewhat wordy and subjected to the holy terrors of existence. Make of this legend what you will. On the man's gravestone: "He Honored Life." It is a tribute not only to the imprint of Gerard but to the true meaning of life: a tormented ride of ups and downs, joy and sorrow, tenderness and folly, hope and complaint, flight and entrapment. Life and legend, what were they? An enormous comedy, as Kerouac wrote in the preface to *Big Sur*? Something to do in the meantime, before one reaches the Protective City?

Despite its twists and turns and various vehicles, Kerouac's quest emerged out of a preexisting "condition of time." As early as 1953, Kerouac blamed "God for / making life so / boring." Then he quickly took it back: "It isn't anybody's fault that I'm bored—it's the condition of time—the burden of putting up & filling in with tick tack time in dull dull day."[1] Time itself was always the first meaning of *beat*, as Ginsberg's double entendre from the first section of *Howl* makes clear: "the madman bum and angel beat in Time, unknown, yet putting / down here what might be left to say in time come after / death."[2] In this heroic reference to Kerouac (the consummate "madman bum and angel"), beat is both an essential bohemian rhythm and an inescapable condition of human defeat. But transcendence via the word—putting it down—is the only possible way others (including future generations) can come to know time and be illuminated by it.

Of course, Kerouac wanted to leave something behind—his own shelf space in the stacks. However, that in itself was not what drove the quest forward, onward and up. His belief that spirit was both the foundation and flying buttress of human existence blew the dust off the cover of literature. "Man can die," Kerouac wrote in 1951, "& not only live in others but give them life, and not only life but that great consciousness of life that made cathedrals rise from the smoke and rickets of the poor."[3] If Kerouac accomplished this feat, that is, gave life and inspiration to others (a Kesey, a Dylan, a Pynchon, a Cohen, a Thompson, a Morrison—Jim or Van—and so on) let alone an entire counterculture, then there is no question about whether or not he succeeded as "a man of stature." But we must take the spiritual quest on Kerouac's own terms as well, for it was lived (embodied) and provoked into action by taking the following question to heart: how does one beat time?

For Kerouac, the mundane and existential burden of being in time prompted metaphysical preoccupations and incited the spiritual desire to transcend (or sidestep) both the calendar and the clock. The purpose of springing oneself from the prison house of time had always been to restore a state of lost bliss through belief in either a Christian afterlife (where one is saved from sin and hell) or the holy Buddhist void (delivered at last from karma and rebirth). Kerouac knew deep in the marrow of his bones that boredom was the minimal counterpart to that enormous burden of time ticking off our mortality; and his quest sought to evade or surmount the solemn awareness of such final human matters. Either one conquers death via resurrection of the body or by dissolving one's being into the All-at-One. If this either/or proposition of a living Christ/living Buddha could not meet the challenge, then both would reappear under more auspicious circumstances in the Pure Land. And if either/or and a combination of

Catholicism and Buddhism failed to do the trick, then one could always resort to the hedonistic blur of the tormented state (i.e, the necessary intensification of experience that emerges from the preexisting condition of time).

Of course, the turning point can be traced to the ending of *Big Sur*; it is here that the varieties of Kerouac's spiritual quest give way to the singular image of the Cross. Recall that the "peace of Heaven" comes only after he purges himself of the sordid vision—the bestial vulture people fornicating on the dump and the huge greasy beat kitchens below ground. Not only is the "sudden [and actual] vision" a desolate caricature of libertine excesses committed in the past, but also (considering the tortuous episode in the novel) a way of offering atonement for them.[4] Thus cleansed, Kerouac returns home in mind, body, and spirit—to the "blessed relief" of the Cross and all that it stands for. But such relief proved short-lived, for his reembrace of the Cross soon turned into a fixation. Although Kerouac always had a devotion for the Cross, and was throughout his life preoccupied with the crucifixion of Christ, his later years (from 1960 to 1969) signal a far more unmitigated attachment to the sorrows and sacrifices of Jesus. "As Jack grew older," Ginsberg observed, "in despair and lacking the means to calm his mind and let go of the suffering, he tended more and more to grasp at the Cross. And so, in his later years, he made many paintings of the Cross, of cardinals, popes, of Christ crucified, of Mary [and pietas]; seeing himself on the Cross, and finally conceiving of himself as being crucified. He was undergoing crucifixion in the mortification of his body as he drank."[5]

It is only after the experience at Big Sur (and the writing of the novel) that Kerouac fully assumes the role of penitential martyr and finally relinquishes the conceit of being a bhikku, let alone a bodhisattva. (In short, he concludes the process begun in book two of *Desolation Angels,* clinching his peaceful sorrow at home.) From here on in, Kerouac weaves and reweaves a spiritual bouquet out of his clinging to suffering and colors it purple. This is his way of sobering up from the long ecstasy of being. Ironically, this leads to more and more heavy drinking and, naturally, to an ever-deepening sense of disenchantment and despair. Kerouac's condition was obviously reflected in his declining productivity as a prose artist and poet. Although nineteen of his books were published in a sixteen-year span (from 1958 to 1973), all but about five were written before 1958. To aggravate matters, from 1960 on, Kerouac became more and more isolated and withdrawn, rarely traveling for the sake of adventure and only occasionally running into his former beat friends. Memère, with whom Kerouac now lived throughout the entire year, substituted for his old beat community, especially Cassady and Snyder. Whether out of extravagant pride or utter faith in self-reliance, Kerouac's unwillingness to submit himself to a master that would guide his Buddhist quest (as Ginsberg, Snyder, and Whalen had done) reflected Jack's inability to decenter the self, to put it into the hands of another. His withdrawal only enhanced the self-absorption that resulted from virtually going it alone all those years. Under the influence of American and European romantics, Kerouac took the solipsistic vow as early as 1945: "I dedicate myself to myself, to my art, my sleep, my dreams, my labours, my sufferances, my loneliness, my unique madness, my endless absorption and hunger—because I cannot dedicate myself to any fellow being. And if it were in my power to dedicate myself to fellow beings, I would not have myself. . . . This is the idea I take with me to my grave."[6]

Over time, the tyranny of self that finally emerged from such dedicated pursuits proved a major hindrance. Kerouac's *peccatos*—deadly indeed—were the traditional ones: most of all pride, gluttony, and lust. His self-indulgence, which at times joyously led or abetted the quest, eventually spun out of control, chasing and finally catching its own tail and spiraling down. Once the self-destruction had accelerated after 1958, it bored into a hell of Kerouac's own invention—one that he could not extricate himself from. Alcohol (and drugs) played a dual role in this process, for it both fueled the soaring trajectory of the quest and burned it out with a vengeance. Kerouac lived and died by the Dionysian double-edged sword (having lost sight of that very fine line between ecstasy and destruction). Holmes, who felt that Kerouac would not live much beyond forty, wrote the epitaph to his quest back in the mid-sixties: "Such voracious appetites, such psychic vulnerability, such singleness of purpose, must . . . ream a man out at the end, and the Kerouac I knew was as incapable of turning away from his own consuming consciousness, as he was of living for long once he had been burned out by it."[7]

Although the result of questing on the edge, as stated in *Big Sur,* was "adulthood disaster of the soul through excessive drinking," the original intention was just the opposite: that is, alcohol, in particular, was meant to serve the quest and not be an avenging master to it. William James's understanding of the uses of alcohol to further religious ecstasy and spiritual insight applies directly to Kerouac's temperament and to the purity of his aim to transcend the "sober hour":

> The sway of alcohol over mankind is unquestionably due to its power to stimulate the mystical faculties of human nature, usually crushed to earth by the cold facts and dry criticisms of the sober hour. Sobriety diminishes, discriminates, and says no; drunkenness expands, unites, and says yes. It is in fact the great exciter of the *Yes* function in man. It brings its votary from the chill periphery of things to the radiant core. It makes him for the moment one with truth. Not through mere perversity do men run after it. . . . And it is part of the deeper mystery and tragedy of life that whiffs and gleams of something that we immediately recognize as excellent should be vouchsafed to so many of us only in the fleeting earlier phases of what in its totality is so degrading a poisoning. The drunken consciousness is one bit of the mystic consciousness, and our total opinion of it must find its place in our opinion of that larger whole.[8]

Kerouac drank the poison, imbibed the totality. The integration of mystic and drunken consciousness was a classic example of *spiritus et spiritus* (spirit and spirituous). For a while, in that "earlier phase," such an incorporation of part to whole fortified Kerouac's intoxicating affirmation of life and the mystic reach of his spiritual quest. This yea-saying altered state was always set against the dreary, self-abnegating sobriety of dull gray everydayness. However, over time the "deeper mystery and tragedy" James alludes to occurs: the increasingly bloated part becomes equal to the whole, then, eventually, the reversal is complete as drunken consciousness subsumes mystic consciousness into a new (and degrading) totality.

Of course, glimpses of the latter phase can be seen in the excesses that sometimes tipped the balance of the former stage of relative equilibrium. "I drink to destroy myself," Kerouac wrote in his Dharma notebook for 1954. He continued: "Drinking heavily, you abandon people—and they abandon you—and you abandon yourself—It's a form of partial self murder but too sad to go all the way" (*SOD*, 112). For the most part, however, the interplay of mystic and drunken consciousness during this stage led to his relentless swings between the ascetic impulse to renounce the world and the hedonistic desire to mount it. Kerouac was unable to resolve the contradictions inherent in the era's forced choice between the paths of purity and impurity. If he felt defiled by bouts of drunkenness and promiscuity, Kerouac often tried to make amends *in extremus* by setting purifying though unrealistic goals for himself, such as the "Threefold Personal Path" (*SOD,* 167): "one meal a day; no drinking of intoxicants; no maintaining of friendships." Since Kerouac likened his history of drinking, which began in 1940, to being plunged into "insensitive ignorance," the rationale for such self-denial was eminently sensible from a Buddhist point of view:

> Not drinking preserves contemplative strength
> Eating once a day, contemplative sensitivity
> No friends or lusts, contemplative serenity
> Strength, Sensitivity, Serenity = Joy. (SOD, 127)

However, the vows were always broken when the pendulum invariably swung back in the other direction. Keenly feeling unsettled by the hopelessness of this vacillation, Kerouac pleaded and prayed in his notebooks for some kind of help as early as 1954. Though he wrote then that "the time for understanding is short," he was painfully aware of the debilitating effects of drinking: "I want DRY STRONG HAPPINESS instead of all this WET WEAK UNHAPPINESS (hangover)——Drinking like that ruins my physical strength, mars my morning joy, breaks the back of my resolves, blurs my clear reflection, dulls my shiver of bliss" (*SOD, 325*).[9] About a decade later, once the reversal of being had toppled his mystic sensibility, Kerouac tried medication to stop drinking and "escape that dratted liquore." In a letter to Dan De Sole (11 August 1966), Kerouac knew that the hour was getting late: "It may very well be true that I can contribute great stuff to American Lit if I can stay away from getting blind drunk (don't even remember what our closing hours were with Tony last time)."[10]

The likelihood of genetic predisposition to alcoholism notwithstanding, we must keep in mind that Kerouac would never have hit rock bottom had he not aspired to the high heavens. After the publication of *Big Sur,* Kerouac was no longer a "naive overbelieving type," which he had once thought appropriate as an epitaph for his tombstone. Rather, undergoing mortification (i.e, not self-abnegation but the infliction of pain, shame, and humiliation on himself), he became a transcendental pessimist, spending most of the sixties taking in the divine by "digesting grief."[11] Not only were his pride and self-respect wounded but his idealism was shattered as well. Disillusioned with the outcome of his own vigorous pursuit of heroic success and the Faustian-inspired American dream, Kerouac ended by questioning the whole game of achievement and the goad of success. In the final novel he completed, he seems to ask: Why should I strive for aught when it's naught I know? "'Vanity of vanities . . . all is vanity,'" Kerouac writes. "You kill yourself to get to the grave. Especially you kill yourself to get to grave before you even die, and the name of that grave is 'success,' the name of that grave is hullaballoo boomboom horseshit" (*VOD,* 23–24). In a piece published just nine days before his death, Kerouac offers his final take on the meaning of life: "What *is* existence? A lifelong struggle to avoid disaster" ("What Am I Thinking About," *GB,* 198). That impulse to evade catastrophe rather than pursue joy and pleasure speaks for the resignation of his consciousness at the very end of the sobering-up process. In many ways, it resembles James's rendering of an advanced stage of naturalistic Epicurean despair: "'Seek not to be happy, but rather to escape unhappiness; strong happiness is always linked with pain; therefore hug the safe shore, and do not tempt the deeper raptures. Avoid disappointment by expecting little, and by aiming low; and above all do not fret.'"[12] James discerns a sense of dignity in such a restrained and temperate position. Although non-naturalistic in religious orientation, we might also regard Kerouac's grave purchase on the whole as worthy in its own right—a justified slap across the contorted face of ecstatic being.

Although Kerouac's intense identification with Epicurean, Christian, and Buddhist forms of transcendence abruptly leveled off in the sixties as drunken consciousness superseded mystic consciousness, he never abandoned all hope. After *Big Sur,* Kerouac wrote two other novels—the slim *Satori in Paris* was published in 1965 and *Vanity of Duluoz* in 1967. Both novels reflect the dieselation of the quest, the engine still kicking and sputtering even though the motor had been turned off. *Satori* recounts ten drunken days in France when Kerouac, obsessed with identity, tried to trace his glorious Breton and Cornish ancestry: Jean-Louis Lebris de Kerouac. The novel is perhaps a classic example of a French-Canadian immigrant's son unsuccessfully claiming the grandeur of the conqueror and not the inferiority of the vanquished. Kerouac seems to be aware of such a motive, for he presents himself amid both the self-flattering formality of high French culture as well as the diluted substance left over in the wake of grandeur. As for the latter, Kerouac does not mince words about the nature of his descent:

> This cowardly Breton (Me) watered down by two centuries in Canada and America, . . . this Kerouac who would be laughed at in Prince of Wales Land because he cant even hunt, or fish, or fight a beef for his fathers, this boastful, this prune, this rage and rake and rack of lacks, "this trunk of humours" as Shakespeare said of Falstaff, this false staff not even a prophet let alone a knight, this fear of death tumor, . . . this runaway slave of football fields, this strikeout artist and base thief, this yeller in Paris salons and mum in Breton fogs, this farceur jokester at art galleries in New York and whimperer at police stations and over longdistance telephones, this prude, this yellowbellied aide-de-campe with portfolio full of port and folios, . . . this ham, this tester of men's patience and ladies' panties, this boneyard of decay. . . . This, in short, scared and humbled dumbhead loudmouth with-the-shits descendant of man. (*SIP,* 78–79)

Despite this self-loathing, something is accomplished by the trip and the novel—a series of modest, commonplace satoris occur along the way, and the last line brings these sudden insights into the folds of a Western mystery. The novel, which begins and ends with Kerouac and the industrious Parisian taxi driver Raymond Baillet, concludes with an adieu and a final gesture of consolation: "When God says 'I Am Lived,' we'll have forgotten what all the parting was about" (118).

While the spare novel *Satori in Paris* leaves the reader with some lift at the end, some beautifying way to reconcile the otherwise bad news contained therein, *Vanity of Duluoz,* which looks back to the late 1930s and early 1940s (high school years at Lowell, football at Columbia, merchant marine adventures, and the early beat scene in New York City), flatly registers Kerouac's bitter disappointment in waking up from the dream of life. And though Kerouac's skeptical tone dominates the novel, he still manages at times to evoke a different hierarchy of value (a legacy of the Augustinian-Jansenist tradition he can't seem to shake), referring to Pascal's sense of "'OUR UNWORTHYNESS,'" and to our "'imperfections'—our decay and going down, all of us" (*VOD*, 177). In general, this novel is an eloquent example of the loss of mystic consciousness—the will to transcend dying within. By taking in the whole of his late period, one can see Kerouac's characteristic motif (i.e, emerging from misery and mortification to realize an affirmative tone and beatific vision) thinning out along the way, from book two of *Desolation Angels* to *Big Sur* to *Satori in Paris* and *Vanity of Duluoz*. In this last novel, Kerouac gives proof to this process by poking holes in two of his former religious heroes—Jesus and Buddha. With respect to the former, Kerouac feels that one is bound to frustration and defeat by the sheer impossibility of following "His example"; and, concerning the latter figure, the author wonders how the essential spirit of a person can ever escape the enslavement of flesh to a real and ghastly world. "How can you be redeemed," Kerouac complained, "when you have to pass food in and out of your body's bag day in day out, how can you be 'saved' in a situation so sottish and flesh-hagged as that? . . ."

> Birth is the direct cause of all pain and death, and a Buddha dying of dysentery at the age of eighty-three had only to say, finally, "Be ye lamps unto thyselves"—last words—"work out thy salvation with diligence," heck of a thing to have to say as he lay there in an awful pool of dysentery. Spring is the laugh of a maniac, I say. . . . What SIN is there, but the sin of birth? Why doesnt Billy Graham admit it? How can a sacrificial Lamb of birth itself be considered a sinner? . . . Who's going to come out and say that the mind of nature is intrinsically insane and vicious forever? (VOD, 275–76)

This is the way it ends, not with a bang but a disclaimer: "No generation is 'new.' There's 'nothing new under the sun. All is vanity.'" By negating the Beat Generation as a Dionysian happening of mid-twentieth-century American civilization, Kerouac refutes a myth that he himself helped to create; he simply turns his back on it and wanders home, this time returning all the way to Ecclesiastes—to the very origin of Western belief in Hebraic culture. The final image of the novel, which complements the Old Testament, refers to a chalice filled with wine, but this time we know that the contents are now drunk to numb the senses, not open them to joy and the spirit of regeneration.

In his *Confession,* Tolstoy provides a very basic, life-and-death definition of belief: "Faith is a knowledge of the meaning of human life, the consequence of which is that man does not kill himself but lives."[13] Kerouac's own "knowledge" throughout the 1960s was one of compromise, choosing a middle ground between suicide and clinging to suffering life. According to Tolstoy, there are four ways to escape the despair of nothingness, the meaningless absurdity of life: (1) ignorance (not an option for Kerouac); (2) Epicureanism, which Kerouac accepted and rejected in *On the Road* (he was too knowing to take solace in pleasure as a way of life); (3) suicide, which demands great strength of character (Tolstoy did not have the stomach for it, and neither did Kerouac); and (4) hanging on to life, waiting it out despite its futility (Tolstoy opted for this mode of response, hoping that something would happen in the meantime). In drinking himself to death, Kerouac constructed a half-way house between the third and fourth options; hence, the "partial self murder." Evidently, he lost faith in his knowledge of human life so that he found existence impossible to bear. As foretold in 1953, drinking heavily became his concrete mean—"my alternative to suicide, & all that's left."[14] Or, in Ginsberg's words, while en route to Kerouac's funeral: "'So he drank himself to death, . . . which is only another way of living, of handling the pain and foolishness of knowing that it's all a dream, a great, baffling, silly emptiness, after all.'"[15]

During his late period, Kerouac's Tolstoyan compromise manifested itself in an obsession with external religious form, a complete turnaround from the inner mystical experience that had animated his spiritual quest up until the sixties. Hierarchic and triumphalistic forms of Catholic orthodoxy pictured his immersion in crusty Catholicism and became more important than the holy essence underlying the mystery of belief itself. As James Fisher so rightly concluded, "the Cross remained primarily a sign of contradiction for Kerouac, a personal cross he shouldered in the depths of loneliness and alcoholic despair. It did not really provide him with a way back into the world. He continued to reflexively associate Catholicism with sadness, withdrawal, and resignation to suffering."[16] Kerouac's ideological drift to the Roman right made him less sympathetic to the holy outcast and the saintly downtrodden—formerly tried and true vehicles for his idealistic expression of compassionate love. But again, even in the depths of alcoholic desolation, Kerouac had not abandoned all hope—not yet. His passion, eccentricity, and sense of character still shone through in wondrous ways, as when on the back of a letter to Hugo Weber (13 August 1962), he drew a sketch of Christ on the Cross. What makes this sketch so unique is that, compared, for instance, to Grüne- wald's "Crucifixion," which portrays the pain and humiliation of the suffering Savior impaled to the wood, his fingers grasping at the void, Kerouac displays a pumped-up Jesus flexing his biceps in a bril- liant show of empowerment, as if to say, "Your damn right, I am the way and the truth and the life and I don't need three whole days to prove it!"[17]

Though Kerouac claimed (in a drunken letter he wrote to Robert Giroux in 1962) that God is "The Essence of What We Love,"[18] his consciousness became more and more consumed by just the opposite, that is, by fits of dissociation, paranoia, and reaction as the decade wore on. In a grumpy letter written to Nanda Pivano (13 April 1964), an Italian translator of American literature who wanted to publish a beat anthology of poetry, Kerouac griped about being associated with other beat writers. He wanted to cut all ties, and argued the case for being regarded as an independent writer:

> The large body of sustained work that I have created, all that poetry turned into narrative drama, bears no relation to the haphazard scat- tered poems of these others, no relation either technically or spiritu- ally. . . . Especially there is no relation between my purely literary motives and their really political motives. . . . I don't want to appear in any more anthologies among other writers whose opinions I don't share, whose opinions nauseate me & others like myself. If you want to publish me, publish me by myself. This is the same courtesy you would have extended to Victor Hugo or Honore de Balzac a hundred years ago.
>
> Remove me from the anthology altogether. Translate "Visions of Gerard" into Italian for Mondadori, or have it translated, and write a preface & quote what I've said here. You'll find that "Visions of Gerard" is truly honest because it minds its own business and doesnt try to sell insurrection & discontent in our streets, but only reverts to what I finally believe in, peaceful sorrow at home.[19]

Politically, Kerouac claimed to be a "bippie in the middle" during the heyday of the late sixties, but, as gleaned from his letter to Pivano, it's obvious that he grew increasingly conservative. In a letter he wrote to Philip Whalen less than a year before his death, a very crotchety Kerouac revealed his stance vis-à-vis the far left: "I did my part to put Nixon in and times are a-gonna change." This was followed by a statement of dissociation with the counterculture moment, in which Kerouac likened himself to Rousseau, who also had no "reasonable connection" to those who came after him (meaning Voltaire and Robespierre). In the same letter, Kerouac also complained about the demise of literature and poetry—"the lovely era we tried to initiate in the 1950's has become a crock of horsewater, a methodological assessment which might be labeled, or whose proponents might want to tack on your shirt the statement, 'You're putting me on.'"[20]

In the end, Kerouac was consumed by alcoholism and its symptoms—an insidious condition that had its roots in his sensitivity to the burden of time, the guilt and death immersion of the survivor, and a soul sickness that heaved up the immense woe of the world. This soul sickness, in particular, was an inherent part of Kerouac's Roman Catholic heritage and the indelible Augustinian-Jansenistic mark upon it. If the "sickness" conferred spiritual depth and intensity to Kerouac's work—a distinct and lasting religious feeling, then it also shaped and reinforced a penitential will to suffering in the face of hopeless human corruption. This ambivalent inheritance may very well be the taproot of Kerouac's spiritual crisis: although he tried desperately to escape and liberate himself from the pessimistic assumptions underlying the mystical tradition of Catholicism, it surely snared him in the end—for all must fall into the trap of original sin. Perhaps this explains Kerouac's remark, "We're all disillusioned and ashamed." Ironically, in the end we come around. Recall the argument between the two brothers at the conclusion of *The Town and the City*: in a reference to that "'original slap in the face that everyone got,'" Peter questions Francis for using this as an excuse. "'Is that why *you* give up?'" By the end of *Vanity of Duluoz*, Kerouac becomes the "poor fish" in the tank—"doomed for certain suffering." *Fons et origo.* The lasting quarrel Kerouac had with himself (that gave such life and vitality to narrative form) ended in the loss of hope in God's mercy, which is one definition of despair. He gave up on the dream of transcendence, and the lingering murmurs of the quarrel were silenced when the lifelong vultures of alcoholism finally caught and devoured the diminished man, ripping his abdomen apart. And yet the fact that Kerouac yielded after such a long and passionate engagement with various forms of belief—amid a post-Nietzschean world spun out of divine orbit—suggests the range and intensity of his devotion for conceptions of the sacred in human life. In this sense, his late period may be seen as an example of vicarious atonement for a whole pre-Vatican II era of American immigrant Catholics swept away into the metaphysical void of contemporary life.

The fact that Kerouac's late period (the sputtering out of the quest) occurred just as the counterculture of the sixties was burgeoning lends a tragic irony to the decline of this "King of the Beats." His unquenchable thirst for mortification made it clear that his kingdom was not of this world. While the hedonistic and amorphous counterculture looked for a new promised land here and now, sowing dissension and rebellion and freedom in the streets, Kerouac hid away, hankering after salvation. If "Woodstock sprang from his pages," as Burroughs claims, then they must have been the sifted leaves of *On the Road,* which became a bible for the movement's sense of cultural liberation. No doubt, *Road* provided an ethos for the youth of the sixties, giving the counterculture not only a Bacchanalian flavor but also a spontaneous feeling of spiritual restlessness that helped to redefine the era's pursuit of happiness. Of course, such renewal of democracy led to the rise of antiestablishment protest against materialism, oppression (based on race, gender or class), institutionalized violence both at home and abroad, and environmental degradation. Kerouac's antiauthoritarian temperament, independent search for personal meaning, and affirmative vision opened "a new crack in the [postwar] consciousness," as Ginsberg once put it, and inspired the spirit of the sixties to force that crack into a great divide. Be that as it may, as early as 1960, Kerouac had renounced the politicization of his "original idea of Beatific Joy."[21] Clearly, he wanted to keep the "idea" floating in the lofty heights of spiritual-intellectual beauty where he had envisioned it. Moreover, the beatniks and counterculture never truly felt the strong undertow of Kerouac's *Road* and other writings. They mostly bobbed along on the surface and rode the ecstatic waves of his oceanic sentiments. This interest in externals kept hipsters and hippies alike from being engulfed in the depths of Kerouac's soul sickness and tugged away from the safe shore of their own respective *zeitgeists.*

When seen as a writer, or prose artist, and not as "King of the Beats," Kerouac fully emerges as one of the most soulful, inventive, idiosyncratic, and misunderstood literary figures in American letters. Kerouac's own assessment of the changing tastes and styles in literature reveals both his earnest Catholic sensibility and his apprehension about the onset of what would be later called postmodernism. In a letter to his agent Sterling Lord (August 1965), Kerouac's tone is elegiac as he conveys his growing disappointment. It stems from a

> general new distaste in the culture since 1960 for works of realistic sentimentality . . . and a trend towards the Ian Fleming type of sadistic facetiousness and "sickjoke" grisliness about human affairs, a grotesque hatred for the humble and the suffering heart, an admiration for the mechanistic smoothy *killer of sincerity,* a new infernal mockery sniggering down the alleys of the earth (not to mention down the cornrows outside the Drive-In movies.) I just felt that nobody is going to care any more about my vow to write the truth only as I see it, and with sympathetic intention, "thru the keyhole of my eye," . . . arriving at the universal from the subjective point of view just like Proust and Joyce and Celine rather than from the objective point of view, . . . I just felt nobody cared any more whether I or anybody like me lived or died anyway let alone write. But I remember my father's tearful blue eyes and honest Breton face, and I am mindful of what my mother just said: that my way and my philosophy will come back, some great catastrophe is going to make people wake up again, my works and my fellow ham human beings who work in the same spirit, will outlast the sneerers, the uncooperative and unmannerly divisionists, the bloody Godless forever.[22]

Were Kerouac with us today he would remain discouraged, for "the bloody Godless" trends of irony and cynicism he discerned early on have become symptomatic of our era. No doubt he would bemoan the blank parody that merely plays off the glut of cultural infotainment with no clear boundaries or hierarchies. Lost along the wayside in this transition has been the very consciousness of being beat, that is, of sharing in the plight of others. If Kerouac taught us anything, even in his darkest hour, it was this: the notion of sympathy engenders compassion. This is how we should take to the road—"with sympathy, says Whitman. Sympathy. . . . Feeling with. Feel with them as they feel with themselves. Catching the vibration of their soul and flesh as we pass."[23] Kerouac's wager as a prose artist was this: the sincere expression of a sensitive mind and a passionate heart comprises the necessary link of truth. Though scattered about the fragments and juxtapositions of our own time, the links still remain; and, in sorting things out, one might discover that Kerouac was indeed part of that great chain.

I bend my ear to it again and this time hear clearly the coherent song of the brook in *Big Sur*. No more babble—only rest, beyond the river. Yet the mystery still bubbles up. Now it's time to raise a toast—in memory, in tribute, in collaboration. From the close of Kerouac's broadcast interview with Ben Hecht:

> Do you think God is
> Working in us Jack?
> Who do you love Jack?
> Thank-you Jack.

NOTES
BIBLIOGRAPHY
INDEX

Notes

Preface

1. Merton, "Boris Pasternak," p. 21.
2. For Kerouac's comments on writing, see Berrigan's interview, pp. 65–66.
3. Holmes, "The Great Rememberer," p. 125.
4. Charters, *Kerouac: A Biography,* pp. 66–67.
5. Holmes, "The Great Rememberer," p. 130.
6. Allen Ginsberg foreword, in Charters, *Kerouac: A Biography,* p. 9.
7. Berrigan, pp. 84–85.
8. Evidently, leading the simple life in a hut was an idea that captivated Kerouac. In a letter to Ginsberg (14 July 1955), he wrote the following: "Turns out that all my final favorite writers (Dickinson, Blake, Thoreau) ended up their lives in little hermitages . . . Emily in her cottage, Blake in his, with wife; and Thoreau his hut. . . . This I think will be my truly final move . . . tho I don't know where yet. It depends on how much money I can get. If I had all the money in the world, I would still prefer a humble hut. I guess in Mexico. Al Sublette once said what I wanted was a thatched hut in Lowell" (*SL,* 497).
9. Hill, "Kerouac at the End of the Road," *New York Times Book Review,* 29 May 1988, p. 11.
10. Quoted in Millstein, "Books of the Times," L 27. In this *New York Times* review, Millstein also quotes John Clellon Holmes, whose remark about the Beat Generation's "'perfect craving to believe'" I apply, in particular, to Kerouac as the main embodiment of the beats.
11. My understanding and use of IT builds upon the work of previous scholars. According to Lee Bartlett, IT is associated with the visionary search for and spontaneous expression of Dionysian ecstasy. Split into the Appolonian-Dionysian dichotomy by Nietzsche and adopted as archetypal disposition by Jung, the realization of the Dionysian ideal is related to Wilhelm Reich's notion of "orgastic potency": "the ultimate Dionysian transportation out of the ego, into the id" (121). See Bartlett's "The Dionysian Vision of Jack Kerouac," in *The Beats: Essays in Criticism,* pp. 115–26.

Tim Hunt perceives IT as a liminal phase that flourishes in those moments of transition that occur between sequential stages of norm-governed existence. As such,

IT reflects an ecstatic escape from the routine ordering of everyday life. True to the Dionysian double-edged sword, Hunt discerns the ambiguity of IT: the unsettling duality of joyous frenzy and chaotic exhaustion. See Hunt, *Kerouac's Crooked Road*, pp. 33, 40–48, 64–71.

For Gregory Stephenson, IT exceeds the pursuit and goads the hero onward. The heroic quest for IT thus entails continuous activity that culminates in a visionary moment of all-encompassing knowledge, a restored sense of bliss, and recovery of the lost father (and one's true self). As long as IT remains unfulfilled, the legend lives on to chronicle the gains and losses commensurate with its pursuit. See Stephenson's *The Daybreak Boys*, pp. 17–49.

John Tytell views IT as a mounting form of energy with positive and negative valences—"a combination of the opposite tensions that reveal the crucible of creativity: Yin and Yang, Nirvana and Samsara, Eros and Thanatos" (162). See Tytell's *Naked Angels*, pp. 140–211.

And, finally, Regina Weinreich extends Tytell's notion of opposites by examining the antithetical images or tropes of collapse and rebirth inherent in IT, including the way this juxtaposition is inscribed in the linguistic pattern of Kerouac's fiction. According to Weinreich, "'IT' represents the greatest high and the ultimate low simultaneously" (55). See Weinreich, *The Spontaneous Poetics of Jack Kerouac*, pp. 52–56.

Astonishing how one pronoun can activate so much scholarly discourse. If one thing is clear, it's this: Kerouac's use of IT ultimately exceeds our ability to fully explain the reality it embodies. Perhaps this is why Kerouac chose to represent the ineffable and fluid combination of mystical, spiritual, and creative/decreative experience by such a simple utterance. IT is nothing less than a protean god-term for the transcendental impulse in human affairs. Out of the very stuff of IT a legend was born, sustained, and confounded. I am indebted to Daniel F. Kirk for initially drawing my attention to IT and guiding me through the crags and voids of its various manifestations.

12. In his composition notebook for *Satori in Paris*, Kerouac wrote between the lines: "(definition handed to me by Hal Chase of Denver)" There is no such attribution in the published version of the novel. See the first holograph notebook for *Satori in Paris*, Henry W. and Albert A. Berg Collection of English and American Literature, New York Public Library, Astor, Lenox, and Tilden Foundations, New York, New York.

13. In a brief column, the staff writer quotes from a character in Hanif Kureishi's novel, *The Buddha of Suburbia*. See *New Yorker*, 17 November 1997, p. 30.

Introduction: The Sorrows of Young Kerouac

1. Kerouac dedicated *The Town and the City* "to R. G. Friend and Editor." In imitation of Thomas Wolfe's dedication of *Look Homeward, Angel* to editor Maxwell Perkins, Kerouac had originally prepared a more elaborate measure of praise for R. G. (who was mentioned by name, Robert Giroux). However, the policy of

Harcourt, Brace forbade such a tribute for one of its editors; the company approved only of the simple mention with use of initials.

2. One likely model for the Martin children was the Greek-American Sampas family that Kerouac grew up with in Lowell, Massachusetts. Sebastian Sampas, critically wounded on the Anzio beachhead during World War II, was Jack's cherished friend and literary companion; Kerouac's third wife was Stella Sampas, whom he married in 1966.

The huge sense of humanity that inspires *The Town and the City* is conveyed in a letter from Kerouac to Sebastian Sampas (21 March 1943). As a sort of epigraph to the letter, Kerouac writes: "I am drunk— / Thus, truthful." He continues:

> Ah, Sam, what a lonely place my home tonight! . . . I shall confess something to you—for the first time since childhood, tonight I *wept*. . . . It was Saturday night. I lit up a cigarette and walked around the house. Empty! I lay on the bed. I suddenly thought of my mother, and of all other mothers, and suddenly I *understand* humanity, I saw it in a clear light, HUMANITY! . . . The whole poignant legend of young lovers who marry, their families, all the sorrow and joy, etc. I saw Humanity as that which nothing can destroy, a family of lovers.

See Kerouac's correspondence with Sebastian Sampas, Berg Collection, New York Public Library.

3. Holmes, "The Great Rememberer," p. 124.

4. Pascal, p. 115.

5. Merton, *Seeds of Contemplation,* pp. 84–85.

6. Merton, *Seeds of Contemplation,* p. 79.

1. What IT Is?

1. Kerouac's correspondence with his mother (24 July 1947), Berg Collection, New York Public Library.

2. Cowley's acceptance report to Viking Press, dated 8 April 1957, is contained within the Cowley-Kerouac File, the Malcolm Cowley papers, Newberry Library, Chicago, Illinois. On the inside of one manila folder in the file, in Cowley's own hand, is written "Kerouac looked like Gregory Peck."

In the first draft of the report, Cowley hedged on the merit of the novel: "It isn't a great or even a likable book, but it is real, honest, fascinating, everything for kicks, the voice of a new generation." In the final version, the negative judgment is deleted so that the sentence simply reads: "It is real, honest, fascinating," etc. In the final report Cowley also added the praise for Kerouac's style: "The writing at its best is deeply felt, poetic, and extremely moving."

In retrospect, this acceptance report stands as the first official attempt to codify Kerouac as the King of the Beats and to characterize the Beat Generation as wild and reckless; Cowley amplifies the novel's nervous energy and devotion to sensory indulgence, but nowhere does he mention the attempt to affirm anything spiritual in the process. For example: "The characters are always on wheels. They buy cars and wreck them, steal cars and leave them standing in fields, undertake to drive cars from one city to another, sharing the gas; then for variety they go hitch-hiking or sometimes ride a bus. In cities they go on wild parties or sit in joints listening to hot trumpets. They seem a little like machines themselves, machines gone haywire, always wound to the last pitch. . . ."

3. Lawrence, pp. 255–56. In one of his many sketch notebooks (no. 9), Kerouac copied a long quote from Lawrence's *Studies in Classic American Literature* prior to composing *On the Road*. The quote is from the essay on Whitman and shows his impact on Kerouac, especially with respect to the importance of sympathy, which was Kerouac's definition of "beat" given on *The Steve Allen Show* in 1958 (i.e., "sympathetic"), followed by a reference to Whitman's *Specimen Days*. In addition, the quote reaffirms Whitman's democratic and transient location of the soul as well as his identification with the oppressed. What follows are excerpts from Lawrence's quote:

> Stay in the dark limbs of negroes. Stay in the body of the prostitute. Stay in the sick flesh of the syphilitic. Stay in the marsh where the calamus grows. Stay there, soul, where you belong.
>
> The Open Road. The great home of the Soul is the open road. Not heaven, not paradise. Not "above." Not even "within." The soul is neither "above" nor "within." It is a wayfarer down the open road. . . .
>
> Having no direction, even. Only the soul remaining true to herself in her going.
>
> Meeting all the other wayfarers along the road. And how? How meet them, and how pass? With sympathy, says Whitman. Sympathy. . . . Feeling with. Feel with them as they feel with themselves. Catching the vibration of their soul and flesh as we pass.
>
> It is a new great doctrine. A doctrine of life. A new great morality. A morality of actually living, not of salvation. . . . The soul living her life along the incarnate mystery of the open road.

See Kerouac's holograph sketch notebooks ("SK means SKETCHINGS"), Berg Collection, New York Public Library.

4. Suzuki, *Essays in Zen Buddhism*, p. 63.

5. Northrop, p. 354. In distinguishing between transitory and nontransitory factors in the nature of existence, Northrop argues the following: "The Buddhist merely reminds one of the . . . immediately apprehended fact that the self and all things are not merely the many distinguishable and different transitory differentiations, but also the all-embracing, indeterminate aesthetic continuum of which the transitory factors are the temporary differentiations. This . . . indeterminate aesthetic manifold, since it contains the temporal, arrow-like sequence of transitory differentiations within itself, instead of being itself within this arrow-like passage of time, is timeless and hence immortal; or put more exactly, it is outside the death-delivering 'ravages' of time and hence escapes its consequences. It embraces time as one of its determinate differentiations, instead of time embracing it."

6. Only several months before writing the roll manuscript of *On the Road,* Kerouac conveyed his "Strange Dickensian Vision on Market Street . . . in San Francisco in the month of February 1949" to Neal Cassady. In a letter dated 8 January 1951, Kerouac gives Cassady a detailed account of the "little fish-n'-chips joint" and the proprietress he takes to be his English mother in a former lifetime. Although this reads like a first draft of the novel in part two, section 10, there is no mention at all of a Buddhist sense of ecstasy. All of the terms, images, and references in the letter to Cassady are limited to the "Strange Dickensian Vision." Furthermore, the reincarnation that is felt in Kerouac's account is simply not extended to a Buddhist vision of innumerable reincarnations. In the letter, he never takes that "complete step across chronological time into timeless shadows" as he does in the published version of *On the Road.* This suggests that the Buddhist sense of IT was added to this section and passage of the novel sometime after the roll manuscript was written. An inspection of the roll manuscript and various states of the manuscript thereafter (right up to publication) would be necessary to verify such a claim. In closing his letter to Cassady, Kerouac clarifies matters in his own way concerning the fate of the vision—its "glimpse of possible reincarnation" and "presence of God": "It's all in the air and is still there for me to grasp another day, and I hope to, I want to, I know I will" (*SL,* 275–81).

7. Lloyd, *Being in Time,* p. 84.

8. The eight episodes of the biography, which appeared in *Tricycle: A Buddhist Review,* were also given the heading—"Shakyamuni Buddha: A Life Retold." The biography ran consecutively from summer 1993 to spring 1995. Kerouac relied heavily upon Asvaghosha's *Buddha-Charita* and Narasu's *Life of the Historic Buddha* to complete the biography. His other important sources included the following: the *Surangama Sutra,* the *Lankavatara Scripture,* the *Dhammapada,* the *Anguttara Nikaya,* the *Itivuttaka,* the *Digha Nikaya,* the *Majjhima Nikaya,* the *Theragatha,* the *Vinaya Pitaka,* the *Prajna-Paramita-Hridaya Sutra,* the *Samyutta Nikaya,* along with the *Tao-te-Ching,* the *Life of Milarepa,* and the *Mahayana Samgraha.*

9. Northrop, p. 339.

10. Quoted from *The Diamond Sutra and the Sutra of Hui Neng,* p. 74.

2. Tearing Time Up

1. Although Kerouac's discovery of spontaneous prose came to him suddenly on 25 October 1951, the two primary influences were jazz (esp. bop, as played by such musicians as Charlie Parker, Dizzy Gillespie, Lenny Tristano, Thelonius Monk, and Lee Konitz) and Neal Cassady's long, rambling "Joan Anderson" letter, which Kerouac had read in late December 1950. In Kerouac's spontaneous prose, the heated improvisational technique of bop blends with "the style of loose narrative Joan Anderson." As Kerouac wrote to Cassady in 1955, the latter "combine[s] the looseness of invention with natural perfect rhythm—and perfect natural speech" (*SL,* 472–73).

2. Fisher, pp. 236 and 246.

3. In this 11 June 1952 letter, Ginsberg prefaced his criticisms regarding mixed-up chronology, surrealism, and plain "hangup," with praise for Kerouac's erratic genius: "The language is great, the blowing is mostly great, the inventions have fullblown ecstatic style. . . . Where you are writing steadily and well, the sketches, the exposition, it's the best that is written in America, I do believe." In an acerbic letter to Ginsberg (8 October 1952), Kerouac responded to the critique by venting his frustrations and anger (see *SL*, pp. 377–80).

4. Gifford, *As Ever*, p. 130. In this letter (3 July 1952), Ginsberg begins with an obligatory compliment and then, without mincing words, lashes out at what he perceives to be Kerouac's solipsism that suffuses *Visions of Cody*: "It's great allright but he did everything he could to fuck it up with a log of meaningless bullshit I think, page after page of surrealist free association that don't make sense to anybody except someone who has blown Jack. I don't think it can be published anywhere in its present state. . . . He was not experimenting . . . in new deep form, he was purposely just screwing around as if anything he did . . . was O.K. no bones attached. Not purposely, I guess, just drug out and driven to it and in a hole in his own head—but he was in a hole."

3. The Revelation to Ti Jean

1. Quoted in Pelikan, p. 115.
2. Pascal, p. 319.
3. Pascal, p. 330.
4. Kerouac's holograph sketch notebook (no. 3), entry for 31 October 1952, Berg Collection, New York Public Library.

4. The Track of Glory

1. The actual setting for *The Subterraneans* was the East Village of New York City. Kerouac changed the location to San Francisco to avoid any possible libel suits. In real life, the woman was Alene Lee, an African American (*SL*, 497n and 590).
2. Euripides, *The Bakkhai*, pp. 19–20.
3. Beatrice's accusations directed at Dante, in *Purgatorio*, canto 30, 144–45, p. 285.
4. This theme of receiving a mother's angelic love, especially when feeling lost and beaten down by life, was a recurrent one for Kerouac. For instance, an excerpt from "Benzedrine Vision—Mexico Thieves Market—Memoirs of a Bebopper," reads as follows:

> I got tired. I felt like crying. Here I was, in baggy pants, at the end of the road, the down dark road down to further dark road, down there, below all of it friendless—like a streetlight in the fog at dawn in Bayshore Frisco, friendless. Not very inviting. The world. I flew along like a bat and suddenly I began to speak with my mother and to hear her voice counselling, berating, & as always, consoling me in the end, the throat choking and when you want more of salvation & eternity then you were made to carry, but you want to cry

because Tho you're lost you still love love. . . . "Men will understand what's good about you & how that goodness is better than meanness."

See Kerouac's holograph sketch notebook for 1952, Berg Collection, New York Public Library.

5. The final verse of Dante's *Paradiso, The Divine Comedy,* canto 33, 145, p. 303.

6. Euripides, p. 32. In a letter to Neal Cassady (8 January 1951), Kerouac confessed his "secret ambition to be a tremendous life-changing prophetic artist" (*SL,* 274). The secular and sacred rails of Kerouac's track of glory were more clearly expressed to Stella Sampas (who would become his third wife) in a letter posted from Mexico City (10 December 1952): "I am going to be famous, and the greatest writer of my generation, like Dostoevsky, and someday they'll [the literary establishment] see this and the emptiness of their lives spent chasing after fashions & glittering Italian islands—when the soul of man is weeping in the wilderness, and little children hold out their hands for the love of Christ—" (*SL,* 390).

5. Gone Beyond

1. Kerouac's holograph sketch notebook for 1952–1953 (no. 2), Berg Collection, New York Public Library.

2. Goddard's *A Buddhist Bible,* originally published in 1938, is a comprehensive anthology of selections from Pali, Sanskrit, Chinese, and Tibetan sources. Translations of the primary sutras are included, namely *The Diamond Sutra, The Surangama Sutra, The Lankavatara Scripture,* and the *Sutra Spoken by the Sixth [Chinese] Patriarch [Hui-Neng].* Goddard reorganized *The Diamond Sutra* according to the Six Paramitas (spiritual ideals) in order to give this discourse a heightened sense of coherence. The ideals are as follows: charity, kindness, humility and patience, zeal and perseverance, tranquillity, and wisdom. For a while Kerouac was reading this sutra weekly, concentrating on one section and its corresponding ideal per day. Since these Six Paramitas correspond with the first six (of ten) Bodhisattva Stages, this may account, in part, for Kerouac's inability to get beyond the sixth stage to the "turning about" that results in "highest perfect wisdom." See Goddard, pp. 87–107, and 653–55.

The other Buddhist sources in the bibliography Kerouac sent to Ginsberg contain the following: Asvaghosha's *Life of Buddha,* or *Buddha Charita*; Paul Carus's *The Gospel of Buddha*; E. W. Burlingame's *Buddhist Legends*; *The Dialogs of the Buddha, Digha-Nikaya*; Buddhaghosha's *Visuddhi Magga*; and *The Sacred Books and Early Literature of the East.*

3. Neruda, p. 105.

4. The Eightfold Noble Path is the way that leads to the extinction of suffering, which is the promise of the Fourth Noble Truth. The path includes the following: Right Understanding, Right Mindedness, Right Speech, Right Action, Right Living, Right Effort, Right Attentiveness, and Right Concentration. For a concise explanation of each stage, see Goddard, pp. 646–53.

5. Quoted from *The Diamond Sutra and the Sutra of Hui Neng,* p. 24. In

Goddard's and Bhikshu Wai-tao's 1935 translation of the former sutra, the phrase "Highest Perfect Wisdom" is used instead of the more grandiose "Consummation of Incomparable Enlightenment." See Goddard, pp. 87–88.

6. Kerouac's holograph sketch notebook for 1952 (o-c), Berg Collection, New York Public Library.

7. Kerouac's letter to Ginsberg, 18 January 1955 (*SL,* 461). In the same letter, Kerouac referred to *The Diamond Sutra,* also known as the Diamond Cutter, as the "first and highest and final teaching" (*SL,* 463). *The Diamond Sutra* is considered the jewel of transcendental wisdom. It belongs to the *Maha-Prajna-Paramita,* or the perfection of transcendental wisdom, which consists of over a hundred volumes of primary Sanskrit Buddhist material.

8. See *SOD,* "Brooklyn Bridge Blues," pp. 385–87, and Kerouac's two samadhis (intuitive realizations of Essential Mind), pp. 408–17.

9. Fields, p. 216.

6. Icon for the Void

1. Kerouac's holograph notebook for 1952, Berg Collection, New York Public Library.

2. Kerouac's holograph notebooks, respectively, 1955 (MC1) and 1955[?] ("Book of Visions," V1). With respect to the former, the context for the quoted lines was a two-stanza poem, which, along with an opening stanza, comprised the 59th chorus of *Mexico City Blues*:

> Have to buy a couple needles
> tomorrow, feels like
> Shovin a nail in me
>
> Just like shovin a nail in me
> Goddamn—(Cough)—
>
> For the first time in my life
> I pinched the skin
> And pushed the needle in
> And the skin pinched together
> And the needle stuck right out
> And I shot in and out,
> Goofed half my whole shot
> On the floor——
> Took another one—
> Nothin a junkey likes better
> Than sittin quietly with a new shot
> And knows tomorrow's plenty more

3. While Kerouac was working on *Mexico City Blues* and part one of *Tristessa,* he made the following entry in his Dharma journal: "Literature giggles—literature has to do with the mutilation of beasts and living beings. Perfect Ecstasy is possible

at any time, for any length of time, within this burning house of existence. I can educate more along those lines, and point the way to the perfect Absence of Bane, but stories calculated to divert readers from the truth of their present personal horror are no longer in my line." See *SOD*, p. 338.

4. Conversation with John Sampas, literary representative, the estate of Jack Kerouac, Lowell, Massachusetts, 30 September 1998. Also see Amburn, pp. 215–16.

In fact, Kerouac did have sex once with Esperanza. In a *Paris Review* interview, he recounts the following: "All I did was suffer with that poor girl. . . . Absolute beauty. She had bones, man, just bones, skin and bones. And I didn't write in the book how I finally nailed her. You know? I did. I finally nailed her. She said, 'Shhhhhhhhhh! Don't let the landlord hear.' She said, 'Remember, I'm very weak and sick.' I said, 'I know, I've been writing a book about how you're weak and sick.'" See Berrigan, pp. 90–91.

5. Thich Nhat Hanh, p. 91.

6. Kerouac's equalization of divine and earthly realms is a radical, humanistic adaptation of John's first letter, 4:7–21. In particular, the following verses are most relevant: "No one has ever seen God; if we love one another, God lives in us, and his love is perfected in us. By this we know that we abide in him and he in us, because he has given us of his spirit. . . . God is love, and those who abide in love abide in God, and God abides in them." Kerouac's vision is not simply that of a divine halfway house whereby man abides in God (and vice versa) through the mediating practice of brotherly love; rather, it is a matter of identification: oneness with Being itself, "him which is us." For the quoted verses from John's first letter, see the *Holy Bible: New Revised Standard Version,* chap. 4:12–16.

7. Ethereal Flower

1. Titian's *Tribute Money,* painted about 1568, features an intense and menacing pharisee who shows Jesus a coin bearing the portrait of Caesar. The painting is owned by the London National Gallery.

Kerouac's sense of survivor guilt was magnified by Gerard's status as a little saint, whose illness added the dimension of martyrhood. The mythology that surrounded Gerard became a great burden for Jack. After Gerard's death, Kerouac felt a keen sense of guilt because of his own failure to live up to the impossible moral peak set by his brother. Both Jack and his parents internalized the role of Gerard as personal critic and familial standard, respectively. See Nicosia, pp. 25–26.

For Kerouac's self-analysis of this survivor guilt, and the "subconscious will to failure, a sort of death-wish" that resulted, see the letter to his sister Nin (Caroline Blake), 14 March 1945, *SL,* pp. 85–90. esp. p. 87.

2. Kerouac opened his 16 January 1956 letter to Snyder with the following: "Feel good, just finished writing a full-length novel, or should I say, full-length book of sorrows, VISIONS OF GERARD—I'd really like to call it ST. GERARD THE CHILD" (*SL,* 540).

3. "The wheel of the quivering meat / conception" is the opening line from the 211th chorus of Kerouac's *Mexico City Blues.*

The opening and closing lines of "The Great Dharani" that end the *Surangama Sutra* can be viewed in Goddard's *A Buddhist Bible*, pp. 272–73. For *Visions of Gerard*, Kerouac takes a piece from the very heart of this Dharani. The entire heart of "The Great Dharani," taken word for word, comprises the 192nd chorus of *Mexico City Blues*.

Kerouac's own verses that surround the excerpt from "The Great Dharani" in *Visions of Gerard* can be traced back to a month before his completion of the novel. At this time (17 December 1955), he had written the following prayer in his notebook: "I Bless all living and dying things in the endless past; I Bless all living and dying things in the endless present; I Bless all living and dying things in the endless future." A variation of this prayer also appears in *The Dharma Bums* (see p. 123); it was made up just before Christmas 1955 in a river bottom in Riverside, California, during Kerouac's first night camping out with full rucksack. The prayer was related to an unpublished nonfiction work in progress, which consisted of the following Buddhistic essays: "The Happy Truth," "The Blessedness Surely to be Believed," "Ecstasy of Life and Death" (or "Ecstasy For All"), "The Nature of Reality," and "Why is There Life and Death"? See Kerouac's holograph notebooks for 1955, Berg Collection, New York Public Library.

Finally, Kerouac's repeated use of ethereal flower as a Buddhist metaphor for the world may be derived from *The Lankavatara Scripture*. See Goddard, p. 278.

4. The seed for this particular scene on pp. 129–30 of the novel was planted in one of those long confessional letters to Neal Cassady (28 December 1950). In this letter, Kerouac recounted several significant incidents that occurred right after Gerard's death, which left him mystified. At first, Ti Jean thought this was an occasion for joy. "The day he died I saw my big father come up the street from work. He had no news whatever of the death of Gerard. Knowing this I ran to him eagerly with the news. 'Gerard is dead! Gerard is dead!' I sang this in the street. It was something new. Now things would change. Rumours of exciting preparations were in the air." Awaiting some transformation—some good thing to come out of all the pain and sorrow of Gerard's sickness—the child waited merrily for his brother's return. "It was only when I saw his body (I knew it to be inside the box) lowered in the earth and dirt thrown over that my face fell." From that day on, Ti Jean, also called Ti Pousse, "or Little Thumb, for roundness and pinkness," changed "from pink to pale"—"into a sallow weary child; washed-out thin." For the many seeds of *Visions of Gerard*, see *SL*, pp. 251–61; quoted from pp. 259–61.

5. The Pure Land School was founded as the White Lotus Sect in China by Hui-Yuan (circa A.D. 400). It was introduced into Japan by Honen (1133–1211) and became known there as the Jodo Sect. In Mahayana Buddhism, there are many pure lands. They are each dependent on the intercession of a given buddha. Once again, faith alone—not one's karma—is the decisive factor in gaining entry into such a transcendent paradise. Also, the pure lands are not the final stage of ultimate spiritual attainment but the stage immediately preceding nirvana. However—and this is the key to those vastly improved conditions—when one is reborn in a

pure-land, retrogression of one's karma—being degraded to a lower domain of existence—is no longer possible; rather, one is endowed with miraculous powers and assured the attainment of enlightenment.

6. Quoted from one of the most popular descriptions of Amitabha's Pure Land. See Burtt, pp. 208–11.

8. Kindred Spirits

1. The letter was written on 9 December 1957, two days after Kerouac completed *The Dharma Bums*. Cowley-Kerouac File, the Malcolm Cowley papers, Newberry Library, Chicago, Illinois.

2. Ginsberg's comment about *The Dharma Bums* is quoted from his introduction to Kerouac's *Visions of Cody*, x.

3. Letter from Snyder to Kerouac (12 October 1958), in *A Jack Kerouac ROMnibus*, 1995.

4. Emerson, "Nature," in the *The Works of Ralph Waldo Emerson*, p. 552.

5. Kerouac puts this more harshly in *Desolation Angels* when he writes that "for every little sweet lump of baby born that women croon over, is one vast rotten meat burning slow worms in graves of this earth" (268).

The saying—"'pretty girls make graves'"—alludes to the elaborate Buddhist Chain of Causation, also known as the Nirdana Chain Links. Kerouac summarizes the links of the chain in his biographical account of the Buddha:

> Destroy birth, thus death will cease; destroy deeds then will birth cease; destroy attachment then will deeds cease; destroy desire then will attachment end; destroy perception then will desire end; destroy sensation then ends perception; destroy contact of the six sense organs then ends sensation; the six entrances of the sense organs all destroyed, from this, moreover, individuality and the picking out of different related notions will cease. Consciousness destroyed, then consciousness'perishes; consciousness ended, the dream-energy of Karma has no hold and handle; Karma done, ignorance of dreaming ends; ignorance destroyed, then the constituents of individual life will die: the great Rishi was thus perfected in wisdom. (*Wake Up*, episode three, 22–23)

Moving from sacred to profane, Kerouac also reveals a misogynistic motive behind his codification of the Nirdana Links into the popular saying. In a letter to Ginsberg (14 July 1955), just before the time frame for *The Dharma Bums*, Kerouac, bolstering his resolve to remain chaste, remarks: "As for a woman, what kind of man sells his soul for a gash? A fucking veritable GASH—a great slit between the legs lookin more like murder than anything else—" (*SL*, 499).

6. At this time, while living with Ginsberg in his cottage at 1624 Milvia Street, Berkeley, Kerouac had a bodhisattva dream that he wrote down, intending to include it in his ongoing *Book of Dreams*. The dream occurred on 21 September 1955 and amplifies unconsciously the difficulty Kerouac encountered in preaching enlightenment to his cohorts. It runs as follows:

"*Kerouac has swallowed that Buddhism stuff hook line & sinker.*"—It's like we were all in jail and I've received instructions on how to escape. However I'm the only one now who realizes we're all in jail. The others don't know it yet. As I continually talk now of escape, the others think I'm crazy. I escape from jail but (Mahayana) come back to teach the others how. They laugh at me, I get mad & yell at them "Don't you realize you're in jail & that this is the way to escape?" They think I'm crazy because I get mad. "We're bored with that escape talk of yours, we've got work to do." They manufacture iron bars which are used to keep them imprisoned all the more securely. I pray for them & ask my Lord (who gave me escape instructions) to help them realize what they're doing. I wake up from the dream filled with compassion.

See Kerouac's holograph notebook for 1955 (M34), Berg Collection, New York Public Library.

7. Kamo no Chomei, "An Account of My Hut," in Keene, *Anthology of Japanese Literature,* p. 205.

8. *The Heart Sutra,* trans. Edward Conze, p. 81.

9. Goddard, p. 654. Kerouac's satori ("everything is empty but awake") and transcendental vision of Dipankara Buddha are documented in *SOD,* pp. 408–9 and 417, respectively. Other sources for the novel that are contained in *SOD* can be found on the following pages: 239–40; 279; 346; 375–76; 388; 406–7; and 419.

10. Kakuan's *Ten Cow-Herding Pictures* are reprinted in D. T. Suzuki's *Essays in Zen Buddhism.* For background discussion and explanation, see pp. 363–76.

Stages one to three ("Looking for the Cow," "Seeing the Traces of the Cow," and "Seeing the Cow") are rendered implicitly in the first 133 pages of *DB*.

11. Lao Tzu, p. 115. Kerouac must have been conscious of this hubris from his daily reading of *The Diamond Sutra* in Goddard's *Buddhist Bible,* especially the section on "The Practice of Humility and Patience" (the Kshanti Paramita), in which Subhuti, an honored disciple, remarks to the Buddha: "Should a disciple who has attained such a degree of enlightenment, cherish within his mind such an arbitrary conception as, 'I have become an Arahat [fully enlightened one],' he would soon be grasping after such things as his own selfhood, other selves, living beings and a universal self. O Blessed Lord! . . . If I had cherished within my mind the thought, 'I am an Arahat free from all desire'! my Lord could not have declared that Subhuti delights himself in the practice of silence and tranquility." See Goddard, p. 93.

Kerouac's sense of parody, or caricature, during the premature awakening episode of the novel, which I believe is slight and light-handed, is more strongly stated in William Blackburn's reading of *DB*. See Blackburn, pp. 15–17.

12. See Watts, "Beat Zen, Square Zen, and Zen," p. 11. Watts thought that beat Zen, as represented by Ginsberg, Kerouac, and Snyder, was "always a shade too self-conscious, too subjective, and too strident to have the flavor of Zen" (8). In his attempt to make hard-and-fast distinctions among various forms of Zen, Watts proves that he is too strident as well. Moreover, he misreads Kerouac's lines of nonassertion as hostility and underestimates the discipline and rigor that actually did go into his

Buddhism as well as his writing. "Beat Zen" is, in fact, a misnomer; for Ginsberg, Kerouac, and Snyder it never was simply a matter of "anything goes." Perhaps the best way to refute this charge—the "underlying protestant lawlessness of beat Zen"—is to recall the craftsmanship and endurance reflected in the process of writing *Mountains and Rivers Without End,* a collection of poetry Gary Snyder began in 1956 (mentioned in *DB*) and finally completed and published in 1996.

In a revised and expanded version of the essay, Watts attributes the self-consciousness, stridency, and subjectivity of beat Zen to Kerouac in particular. Despite the criticism, however, Watts does acknowledge the following: "There is something endearing about Kerouac's personality as a writer, something which comes out in the warmth of his admiration for Gary [in *DB*], and in the lusty, generous enthusiasm for life which wells up at every point in his colorful and undisciplined prose." Also, in separating the shadow from the substance regarding the beat "spiritual and cultural movement," Watts clearly places Kerouac amid the latter. See Watts, *This Is It,* pp. 79–110; esp. pp. 92 and 99–102.

13. Kamo no Chomei, in Keene, *Anthology of Japanese Literature,* p. 211.

14. Snyder, *Riprap & Cold Mountain Poems,* p. 44. The selected verses translated from Han Shan also appear in Kerouac's *DB,* p. 20.

9. Downsizing

1. See Goddard, pp. 653–55; quoted from p. 654.

2. Thich Nhat Hanh, pp. 190–91.

3. *The Diamond Sutra and the Sutra of Hui Neng,* (Price's and Mou-Lam's translation), p. 37. For Goddard's and Wai-tao's translation of the same passage, see *A Buddhist Bible,* p. 90 (14 C).

4. Saigyo, p. 165. Purified at a pilgrimage site, Saigyo writes:

Heaped on my body,
sins of words too
are washed away,
my mind made spotless
by the Three-Tiered Waterfall.

5. In contrast to the "roars of me," one of Kerouac's most successful poems of nonattainment is "Skid Row Wine," in *Pomes All Sizes,* pp. 109–10. The poem starts off: "I coulda done a lot worse than sit / in Skid Row drinkin wine."

6. For a complete philosophical discussion of each continuum, see Northrop, pp. 322–58; quoted from pp. 337 and 339, respectively.

7. Kerouac's paraphrase of the passage only slightly alters the original, which reads as follows: "The Bodhisattva-Mahasattvas, in teaching the Dharma to others, should first be free themselves from all the craving thoughts awakened by beautiful sights, pleasant sounds, sweet tastes, fragrance, soft tangibles, and seductive thoughts. In their practice of charity, they should not be influenced by any of these seductive phenomena." See Goddard, p. 88.

8. Vroom, p. 40.

9. Kerouac's holograph notebook for 1961 (A), Berg Collection, New York Public Library.

10. From an interview with Holmes in the documentary film *What Happened to Kerouac?* dir. Richard Lerner and Lewis McAdams, Vidmark Entertainment, 1985.

11. Kerouac's letter to Stella Sampas (17 November 1962), Berg Collection, New York Public Library.

12. See the first epigraph to Snyder's *Mountains and Rivers Without End.* Jetsun Milarepa (1052–1135) was a great Tibetan Buddhist saint who belonged to the Kargyutpa Apostolic Succession. Living as a hermit in the Tibetan Himalayas, he led a vigorously ascetic form of Buddhist spirituality.

13. For this significant change in identity, see the introduction to Kerouac's *Lonesome Traveller,* p. 9.

14. Augustine's *City of God,* p. 46, and Buddha's *Lankavatara Scripture,* in Goddard, p. 352, respectively.

15. Berrigan, p. 103.

10. The Old Rugged Cross

1. Notebook entry for 18 April 1960, in *A Jack Kerouac ROMnibus.*

2. Tolstoy, *A Confession,* p. 31.

3. For Kerouac's views on "the cruel nature of bestial creation" and original sin, see *Vanity of Duluoz,* pp. 273–77.

4. For a sampling of Kerouac's journal entries from 1948 to 1950, see the *New Yorker,* 22 and 29 June 1998, pp. 46–59; quoted from p. 56.

5. John Ciardi, "Epitaph for the Dead Beats," in *Kerouac and Friends,* ed. Fred W. McDarrah, p. 257. (Ciardi's essay appeared originally in *Saturday Review,* 6 February 1960.) For other examples of highbrow critical views on Kerouac, Ginsberg, Burroughs, Corso, Orlovsky, and the beats in general, see Diana Trilling's mannerly essay, "The Other Night at Columbia: A Report from the Academy," and Norman Podhoretz's dismissive article—"Where Is the Beat Generation Going?"

6. Kerouac's holograph notebook for 1961 (A), Berg Collection, New York Public Library. The earnest plea for spiritual consolation is confirmed by a related entry, which records both a testimonial to Christian mercy and a premonition of the manner in which Kerouac died: "When I threw up blood the other day, & thought I must be hemorrhaging to death, quietly there in bed, I realized I loved only Heaven. . . . And not with a big grassy desire, just any old heaven and—the Golden Eternity doesn't really care if I spend a whole lifetime forgetting it! On Jung's door, the sign:— 'Called or not called, God is here.' Pray or don't pray for heaven, you'll see it."

7. For Kerouac's sense of himself as a "literary monk" and "old time French farceur," see his letters to Stella Sampas (9 February 1962 and 22 April 1964, respectively), Berg Collection, New York Public Library. Both identities appear right at home with Kerouac's resigned attitude of "a peaceful sorrow."

8. William Wiegand's review of *Big Sur* in the *New York Times Books,* 16 September 1962. Weigand accurately goes on to write: "Partly because of its coherence,

the novel does become an argument at the end, and it is clearly an argument against manifestos, against doing any thing according to a program even the beat program. Happily, the argument is advanced with Kerouac's usual superb sense of idiom and with his usual personal eccentricity."

9. See Holmes's insightful essay on Kerouac, "The Great Rememberer," pp. 113–35; quoted from p. 132. As early as 1966, Holmes perceptively addressed the misrecognition and the critical disregard of Kerouac's writings. The passage is worth quoting in full:

> Though he has already created a larger body of work than any of his contemporaries, to most people his name summons up the image of a carefree do-nothing sensation-hunter. Though that body of work creates a dense, personal world that is as richly detailed as any such American literary world since Faulkner, he is continually thought to be nothing but the poet of the pads and the bard of bebop. And though he is a prose innovator in the tradition of Joyce, whose stylistic experiments will bear comparison with any but the most radical avant-gardists of the century, he is constantly ticketed as some slangy, hitchhiking Jack London, bringing a whiff of marijuana and truck exhaust into the lending libraries. In short, the kind of writer that only America could produce, and that only America could so willfully misunderstand. One has only to remember Melville "the writer of boys' sea stories" and Whitman "the author of 'O Captain My Captain'" to recognize what legacy of national neglect Kerouac has fallen heir to. For ours is a benevolent society. Not for us to doom our Mark Twains to a garret. No, instead we praise them as vaudevillians. And later wonder why they gnashed their teeth. (113–14)

10. Quoted in Dante, *Purgatorio, The Divine Comedy,* canto 16, 82–84, p. 149. The excerpt is from Marco Lombardo's speech to Dante and Virgil on free will while the latter two figures traverse the third terrace of the wrathful.

11. James, p. 508. Kerouac was familiar with William James's seminal study on religion *(Varieties of Religious Experience)*, and he was particularly engaged by the chapters on "Saintliness" and "The Value of Saintliness."

12. For an early distinction Kerouac makes between "ruthless and indifferent" nature and the "warmth and love and cheer" of culture, see his diary entry for 30 July 1942, while en route to Arctic Greenland as a merchant marine aboard the *S.S. Dorchester (VOD,* 135–36).

13. Tolstoy, *A Confession,* p. 33.

14. Tolstoy, *A Confession,* p. 65. Compare the following passage from Tolstoy to the ending of *Big Sur* and the conviction expressed by Kerouac in the middle of his sound-poem, "Sea":

> But then [after the desire to commit suicide] I stopped and looked at myself and at what was going on inside me. I recalled the hundreds of occasions when life had died within me only to be reborn. I remembered that I only lived during those times when I believed in God. Then, as now, I said to myself: I have only to believe in God in order to live. I have only to disbelieve in Him, or to

forget Him, in order to die. What are these deaths and rebirths? It is clear that I do not live when I lose belief in God's existence, and I should have killed myself long ago, were it not for a dim hope of finding Him. I live truly only when I am conscious of Him and seek Him. What then is it you are seeking? a voice exclaimed inside me. There He is! He, without whom it is impossible to live. To know God and to live are one and the same thing. God is life.

Afterword

1. Kerouac's holograph notebook for 1953, Berg Collection, New York Public Library.

2. Quoted from Ginsberg's *Howl and Other Poems,* p. 16.

3. Kerouac's notebook entry for 8 August–25 November 1951, in *A Jack Kerouac ROMnibus.*

4. For details of this "sudden vision," see Kerouac's holograph notebook for 1962, Berg Collection, New York Public Library.

5. Ginsberg, "Kerouac's Ethic," in Anctil et al., *Un Homme Grand,* p. 56.

6. Kerouac's notebook entry for 5 September 1945, in *A Jack Kerouac ROMnibus.*

7. Holmes, "The Great Rememberer," p. 133.

8. James, p. 387.

9. In his journal, Holmes describes several of Kerouac's visits to see him in Old Saybrook, Connecticut, in the 1960s. The entries made for the September 1962 visit, when Jack was forty years old, show Kerouac close-up during a week-long binge:

> His genius is exhausting, unique, volcanic, and is fed somehow by booze. I've been spacing myself & feel goodish. But his strange amalgam of spurious ideas, verbal illumination, cornball politics, dead certain aesthetic feeling, huge relish for life, fatalistic physical strength—all that I knew so well once, has come back to me in a rush. . . . Anyway, I'm enjoying these wasteful, abusive days of literally hours & hours of frantic, drunken talk. . . . Jack sits in torn blue pajama bottoms, a rank tee shirt, grimy socks and Japanese slippers, unshaven in nearly a week, his hair never combed till 5:00, growing headier & headier in the armpits, smoking his little Camels, fixing his brandies & soda, padding around with stiff, faltering old man's steps, talking in torrential gusts. . . . He drinks a fifth of Courvoisier everyday, plus rations of scotch, beer & wine to fill it out—all told considerably more than a quart of hard booze in every 24 hours. He sleeps 8 hours and drinks the other 16. . . . Sweet & tentative when sober, he becomes truculent, paranoiac, garrulous, stiff-jointed, wild-eyed, exhaustless, and amnesiac when drunk. Booze alone can seem to produce in him the "ecstasy" he needs to get thru time. . . . He is a phenomenon, and those who knew him 10 years ago would be shocked & saddened now, to see him so recklessly burning himself up. . . . Way deep down, I think, he wants to die, and no amount of self-abuse, disaster or sadness can expunge the feeling of loss & estrangement which has always scarred him, dogged him, driven him. . . . Sodden, a-stink, bent on

oblivion, he still has more eccentric genius than anyone I've known. (From *Visitor: Jack Kerouac in Old Saybrook,* 13 and 16 September, 1962)

10. Berg Collection, New York Public Library.

11. Kerouac's holograph notebook for 1966, Berg Collection, New York Public Library.

12. James, p. 143. I am indebted to William James for broadening my understanding of the "sobering process."

13. Tolstoy, *A Confession,* p. 54. For the "four methods of escape from the dreadful situation in which we all find ourselves," see pp. 45–46.

14. Kerouac's holograph notebook for 1953, Berg Collection, New York Public Library.

15. Quoted in Holmes's account, *Gone in October,* p. 41. Ginsberg's comments were made during a question-and-answer session that followed a reading of Kerouac's poetry as well as his own at Yale University just prior to attending Jack's funeral in Lowell, Mass.

In his account of the funeral, Holmes attempts to explain Kerouac's excessive drinking. Ultimately, the well-reasoned insights Holmes offers give way to a sense of mystery and a social critique:

> Why did he drink like that? I think it was because his was a deeply traditional nature, so sensitive to social and familial cohesions, and their breakdown in the modern world, that he intuited more about the contemporary human mood in his nerves and mind than anyone I had ever known. . . . He drank, as well, because he had no gift for even a saving cynicism, and couldn't act out the simplest role (much less the infinitely complex role of "spokesman" or "prophet"), and because, though he was the most insatiably gregarious man when tipsy, he was not easily sociable when sober, and increasingly, as he got older, was occupied with the enigma of his own identity. . . . And finally he drank because I don't think he wanted to live anymore if there was no place to direct his kind of creative drive, except inward. But I don't really know. All I know for sure is that it has pained *this* head for years to imagine the waste to him of those thousand barroom nights, and that something must be awry in an America where a man of such human richness, and such extraordinary gifts, would be most appropriately mourned in a hundred saloons because he felt he had no other place to go—the fraternal warmth for which his whole soul longed having been exiled to the outer edges of life in the America of his time. (51–52)

16. Fisher, p. 242.

17. Berg Collection, New York Public Library. For a depiction of Matthias Grunewald's "The Crucifixion," first position, center, of his *Isenheim Altar,* 1512–1515, see Harpham, pp. 147–63 (figures 7, 10, and 11).

18. The letter written to Giroux was never mailed. Berg Collection, New York Public Library.

19. Berg Collection, New York Public Library. For related details expressed in further correspondence with Pivano, see "In the Kerouac Archive," p. 51.

20. The letter from Kerouac to Whalen was dated 4 December 1968, Berg Collection, New York Public Library.

21. Kerouac's notebook entry for 11 November 1960, in *A Jack Kerouac ROMnibus.*

22. "In the Kerouac Archive," p. 76.

23. Kerouac's holograph sketch notebook (no. 9), Berg Collection, New York Public Library. Kerouac copied down this quote from D. H. Lawrence's essay on Whitman, pp. 255–56.

Bibliography

Amburn, Ellis. *Subterranean Kerouac: The Hidden Life of Jack Kerouac.* New York: St. Martin's Press, 1998.

Anctil, Pierre, et al., eds. *Un Homme Grand: Jack Kerouac at the Crossroads of Many Cultures.* Ottawa: Carleton University Press, 1990.

Anderson, Terry H. *The Movement and the Sixties: Protest in America from Greensboro to Wounded Knee.* New York: Oxford University Press, 1995.

Aronowitz, Al. "The Beat Papers: Part 2: Chapter Two: Interview with Jack Kerouac, 1958." Blacklisted Journalist—http://www.bigmagic.com/pages/blackj/ (see column 22, 1 June 1997).

Augustine, Saint. *The City of God.* Trans. Gerald G. Walsh, S. J., et al. Garden City, N.Y.: Image Books, 1958.

———. *Confessions.* Oxford: Oxford University Press, 1991.

Baltimore Catechism, no. 2, 19th ed. N.p., 1911.

Baltimore Catechism, no. 2. Buffalo: Rauch and Stoeckel Printing Co., 1929 and 1933.

Bartlett, Lee. *The Beats: Essays in Criticism.* Jefferson, N.C.: McFarland, 1981.

Baumer, Franklin L. *Modern European Thought: Continuity and Change in Ideas, 1600–1950.* New York: Macmillan, 1977.

Beal, Samuel, trans. *Texts from the Buddhist Cannon, Commonly Known as Dhammapada.* Series no. 58. San Francisco: Chinese Materials Center, 1977.

Berrigan, Ted. "The Art of Fiction XLI: Jack Kerouac." *Paris Review* 11.43 (summer 1968): 60–105.

Blackburn, William. "Han Shan Gets Drunk with the Butchers: Kerouac's Buddhism in *On the Road, The Dharma Bums,* and *Desolation Angels.*" *Literature East and West* 21 (January–December 1977): 9–22.

Burroughs, William S. *Junky.* New York: Penguin Books, 1977.

———. *Naked Lunch.* New York: Grove Press, 1959.

Burtt, E. A., ed. *The Teachings of the Compassionate Buddha.* New York: Mentor/Penguin Books, 1982.

Carus, Paul. *The Gospel of Buddha.* Chicago: Open Court, 1895.

Cassady, Carolyn. *Off the Road: My Years with Cassady, Kerouac, and Ginsberg.* New York: William Morrow, 1990.

Cassady, Neal. *The First Third: A Partial Autobiography and Other Writings.* San Francisco: City Lights Books, 1981.

Challis, Chris. *Quest for Kerouac.* London: Faber and Faber, 1984.

Charters, Ann. *Kerouac: A Biography.* San Francisco: Straight Arrow Books, 1973.

———, ed. *The Portable Beat Reader.* New York: Penguin Books, 1992.

———, ed. *The Portable Jack Kerouac Reader.* New York: Viking, 1995.

Clark, Tom. *Jack Kerouac.* San Diego: Harcourt Brace Jovanovich, 1984.

Cowley, Malcolm. *The Literary Situation.* New York: Viking Press, 1954.

Dante. *Inferno. The Divine Comedy of Dante Alighieri.* Trans. Allen Mandelbaum. New York: Bantam Books, 1980.

———. *Paradiso. The Divine Comedy of Dante Alighieri.* Trans. Allen Mandelbaum. New York: Bantam Books, 1984.

———. *Purgatorio. The Divine Comedy of Dante Alighieri.* Trans. Allen Mandelbaum. New York: Bantam Books, 1982.

The Diamond Sutra and the Heart Sutra. Trans. Edward Conze. London: George Allen and Unwin, 1958.

The Diamond Sutra and the Sutra of Hui Neng. Trans. A. F. Price and Wong Mou-Lam. Berkeley: Shambala, 1969.

Dickstein, Morris. *Gates of Eden: American Culture in the Sixties.* New York: Basic Books, 1977.

Dolan, Jay P. *The American Catholic Experience: A History from Colonial Times to the Present.* Garden City, N.Y.: Doubleday, 1985.

Dorfner, John J. *Kerouac: Visions of Rocky Mount.* Raleigh, N.C.: Cooper Street Publications, 1991.

Ellmann, Richard. *Four Dubliners: Wilde, Yeats, Joyce, and Beckett.* New York: G. Braziller, 1987.

Emerson, Ralph Waldo. *The Works of Ralph Waldo Emerson.* New York: Walter J. Black, Inc., n. d.

Euripides. *The Bakkhai.* Trans. Robert Bagg. Amherst: University of Massachusetts Press, 1978.

Feied, Frederick. *No Pie in the Sky: The Hobo as American Cultural Hero in the Works of Jack London, John Dos Passos, and Jack Kerouac.* New York: Citadel Press, 1964.

Ferlinghetti, Lawrence. *The Canticle of Jack Kerouac.* Boise, Idaho: Limberlost Press, 1993.

Fields, Rick. *How the Swans Came to the Lake: A Narrative History of Buddhism in America.* Boston: Shambhala, 1986.

Fisher, James Terence. *The Catholic Counterculture in America, 1933–1962.* Chapel Hill: University of North Carolina Press, 1989.

Foster, Edward Halsey. *Understanding the Beats.* Columbia: University of South Carolina Press, 1992.

Four Huts: Asian Writings on the Simple Life. Trans. Burton Watson. Boston: Shambhala, 1994.

French, Warren. *Jack Kerouac.* Boston: Twayne Publishers, 1986.

Gifford, Barry. *Kerouac's Town.* Berkeley: Creative Arts, 1977.

————, ed. *As Ever: The Collected Correspondence of Allen Ginsberg and Neal Cassady.* Berkeley: Creative Arts, 1977.

Gifford, Barry, and Lawrence Lee. *Jack's Book: An Oral Biography of Jack Kerouac.* New York: St. Martin's Press, 1978.

Gilmore, Thomas B. *Equivocal Spirits: Alcoholism and Drinking in Twentieth-Century Literature.* Chapel Hill: University of North Carolina Press, 1987.

Ginsberg, Allen. *Howl and Other Poems.* San Francisco: City Lights Books, 1959.

————. *The Visions of the Great Rememberer.* Amherst, Mass.: Mulch Press, 1974.

Goddard, Dwight, ed. *A Buddhist Bible.* Boston: Beacon Press, 1938, 1966.

Goethe, Johann Wolfgang von. *Faust.* Trans. Walter Kaufmann. Garden City, N.Y.: Doubleday, 1961.

Han-Shan. *Cold Mountain: 101 Chinese Poems.* Trans. Burton Watson. Boston: Shambhala, 1992.

Harpham, Geoffrey Galt. *The Ascetic Imperative in Culture and Criticism.* Chicago: University of Chicago Press, 1987.

Hipkiss, Robert A. *Jack Kerouac: Prophet of the New Romanticism.* Lawrence: Regents Press of Kansas, 1976.

Holmes, John Clellon. *Go.* New York: Thunder's Mouth Press, 1988.

————. *Gone in October: Last Reflections on Jack Kerouac.* Hailey, Idaho: Limberlost Press, 1985.

————. "The Great Rememberer." In *Representative Men: The Biographical Essays.* Fayetteville: University of Arkansas Press, 1988.

————. *Visitor: Jack Kerouac in Old Saybrook.* California, Pa.: A. and K. Knight, 1981.

Hunt, Tim. *Kerouac's Crooked Road: Development of a Fiction.* Hamden, Conn.: Archon Books, 1981.

A Jack Kerouac ROMnibus. Ed. Ralph Lombreglia and Kate Bernhardt. New York: Penguin Electronic USA, 1995. CD-ROM.

Jackson, Carl. "The Counterculture Looks East: Beat Writers and Asian Religion." *American Studies* 29.2 (spring 1988): 51–70.

James, William. *The Varieties of Religious Experience: A Study in Human Nature.* New Hyde Park, N.Y.: University Books, 1963.

Jarvis, Charles E. *Visions of Kerouac.* Lowell, Mass.: Ithaca Press, 1974.

Jones, James T. *A Map of Mexico City Blues: Jack Kerouac as Poet.* Carbondale: Southern Illinois University Press, 1992.

Keene, Donald, ed. *Anthology of Japanese Literature.* Rutland, Vt.: Charles E. Tuttle, 1955.

Kerouac, Jack. *Big Sur.* New York: Farrar, Straus and Cudahy, 1962.

————. *Book of Blues.* New York: Penguin Poets, 1995. Selected blues poems, 1953–61.

————. *Book of Dreams.* San Francisco: City Lights Books, 1961. Written 1952–60.

————. *Desolation Angels.* New York: Perigree Books, 1965. Written in 1956 and 1961.

———. *The Dharma Bums.* 1958. New York: Penguin Books, 1986.

———. *Doctor Sax: Faust Part Three.* New York: Grove Press, 1959. Written in 1952.

———. *Good Blonde & Others.* Ed. Donald Allen. San Francisco: Grey Fox Press, 1993. Compiled and written 1957–69.

———. *Heaven and Other Poems.* Bolinas: Grey Fox Press, 1977.

———. *Jack Kerouac: Selected Letters, 1940–1956.* Ed. Ann Charters. New York: Viking Press, 1995.

———. *Lonesome Traveller.* London: Panther Books, 1960.

———. *Maggie Cassidy.* New York: Avon Books, 1959. Written in 1953.

———. *Mexico City Blues.* New York: Grove Press, 1959. Written in 1955.

———. *Old Angel Midnight.* Ed. Donald Allen. San Francisco: Grey Fox Press, 1993. Written 1956–59.

———. *On the Road.* New York: Penguin Books, 1957. Written in 1951.

———. *Pic.* New York: Grove Press, 1971.

———. *Pomes All Sizes.* Introduction by Allen Ginsberg. San Francisco: City Lights Books, 1992. Written in 1960s.

———. *Pull My Daisy.* New York: Grove Press, 1961.

———. *Satori in Paris.* New York: Grove Press, 1966.

———. *Scattered Poems.* San Francisco: City Lights Books, 1971. Selected poems, 1945–67.

———. *The Scripture of the Golden Eternity.* 1960. San Francisco: City Lights Books, 1994. Written in 1956.

———. *Some of the Dharma.* New York: Viking Press, 1997. Written 1953–56.

———. *The Subterraneans.* New York: Grove Press, 1958. Written in 1953.

———. *Tristessa.* New York: Penguin Books, 1960. Written in 1955 and 1956.

———. *Vanity of Duluoz: An Adventurous Education, 1935–46.* New York: Coward-McCann, 1968.

———. *Visions of Cody.* Introduction by Allen Ginsberg. New York: McGraw-Hill, 1972. Written in 1951–52.

———. *Visions of Gerard.* New York: Farrar, Straus, 1963. Written in 1956.

———. "Wake Up" ("Shakyamuni Buddha: A Life Retold"). Eight episodes in *Tricycle: The Buddhist Review* from summer 1993 to spring 1995.

Kerouac, John. *The Town and the City.* New York: Harcourt, Brace, 1950. Written 1946–48.

Knight, B., ed. *Women of the Beat Generation.* Berkeley: Conari Press, 1996.

Kolakowski, Leszek. *God Owes Us Nothing: A Brief Remark on Pascal's Religion and on the Spirit of Jansenism.* Chicago: University of Chicago Press, 1995.

Lao Tzu. *Tao Teh Ching.* Trans. John C. H. Wu. Boston: Shambhala, 1961.

Lawrence, D. H. *Studies in Classic American Literature.* New York: Thomas Seltzer, 1923.

Lee, Robert A., ed. *The Beat Generation Writers.* London: Pluto Press, 1996.

Levy-Beaulieu, Victor. *Jack Kerouac: A Chicken Essay.* Trans. Sheila Fischman. Toronto: Coach House Quebec Translations, 1975.

Lloyd, Genevieve. *Being in Time: Selves and Narrators in Philosophy and Literature.* London: Routledge, 1993.

Marlowe, Christopher. *Doctor Faustus.* Cambridge: Harvard University Press, 1962.

McDarrah, Fred W. *Kerouac and Friends: A Beat Generation Album.* New York: William Morrow, 1985.

McDarrah, Fred W., and Gloria S. McDarrah. *Beat Generation: Glory Days in Greenwich Village.* New York: Schirmer Books, 1996.

McNally, Dennis. *Desolation Angel: Jack Kerouac, the Beat Generation, and America.* New York: Random House, 1979.

Merton, Thomas. "Boris Pasternak and the People with Watch Chains." *Jubilee* (July 1959): 17–31.

———. *Seeds of Contemplation.* Norfolk, Conn.: New Directions, 1949.

Miles, Barry. *Jack Kerouac, King of the Beats: A Portrait.* New York: Henry Holt, 1998.

Montgomery, John. *Jack Kerouac: A memoir in which is revealed secret lives & West Coast whispers, being the confessions of Henry Morley, Alex Fairbrother, & John Montgomery, triune madman of the Dharma bums, Desolation angels, & other trips.* Fresno, Calif.: Giligia Press, 1970.

———, comp. *Kerouac at the "Wild Boar" & Other Skirmishes.* San Anselmo, Calif.: Fels and Firn Press, 1986.

Moore, Thomas. *The Soul of Sex: Cultivating Life as an Act of Love.* New York: Harper Collins, 1998.

Motier, Donald. *Gerard: The Influence of Jack Kerouac's Brother on His Life and Writing.* Harrisburg, Pa.: Beaulieu Street Press, 1991.

Neruda, Pablo. *One Hundred Love Sonnets.* Trans. Stephen Tapscott. Austin: University of Texas Press, 1986.

Nhat, Hanh Thich. *Living Buddha, Living Christ.* New York: Riverhead Books, 1995.

Nicosia, Gerald. *Memory Babe: A Critical Biography of Jack Kerouac.* New York: Grove Press, 1983.

Northrop, F. S. C. *The Meeting of East and West: An Inquiry Concerning World Understanding.* New York: Macmillan, 1946.

Parkinson, Thomas, ed. *A Casebook on the Beat.* New York: Thomas Y. Crowell, 1961.

Pascal, Blaise. *Pensées.* Trans. Martin Turnell. New York: Harper and Brothers, 1962.

Pelikan, Jaroslav. *The Christian Tradition: A History of the Development of Doctrine.* Vol. 5, *Christian Doctrine and Modern Culture Since 1700.* Chicago: University of Chicago Press, 1989.

Philips, Lisa, ed. *Beat Culture and the New America, 1950–1965.* New York: Whitney Museum of Art, 1995.

Rahula, Walpola. *What the Buddha Taught.* New York: Grove Press, 1974.

———. *Zen and the Taming of the Bull: Towards the Definition of Buddhist Thought.* London: Gordon Fraser, 1978.

Ross, Nancy Wilson, ed. *The World of Zen: An East-West Anthology.* New York: Vintage Books, 1960.

Saigyo. *Poems of a Mountain Home.* Trans. Burton Watson. New York: Columbia University Press, 1991.

Sedgwick, Alexander. *Jansenism in Seventeenth-Century France: Voices from the Wilderness.* Charlottesville: University Press of Virginia, 1977.

Snyder, Gary. *Mountains and Rivers Without End.* Washington, D.C.: Counterpoint, 1996.

———. *Riprap & Cold Mountain Poems.* San Francisco: Four Seasons Foundation, 1958.

Stephenson, Gregory. *The Daybreak Boys: Essays on the Literature of the Beat Generation.* Carbondale: Southern Illinois University Press, 1990.

Suzuki, D. T. *Essays in Zen Buddhism.* First series. New York: Grove Weidenfeld, 1961.

———. *Manual of Zen Buddhism.* New York: Grove Press, 1960.

———. *Zen and Japanese Culture.* Rutland, Vt.: Charles E. Tuttle, 1959.

Thundy, Zacharias. *Buddha and Christ: Nativity Stories and Indian Traditions.* Leiden, N.Y.: E. J. Brill, 1993.

Tolstoy, Leo. *A Confession and Other Religious Writings.* Trans. Jane Kentish. New York: Penguin Books, 1987.

———. *The Kingdom of God is Within You.* Trans. Constance Garnett. Lincoln: University of Nebraska Press, 1984.

Tonkinson, Carole, ed. *Big Sky Mind: Buddhism and the Beat Generation.* New York: Riverhead Books, 1995.

Turner, Steve. *Angelheaded Hipster: A Life of Jack Kerouac.* New York: Viking Penguin, 1996.

Tytell, John. *Naked Angels: The Lives & Literature of the Beat Generation.* New York: McGraw-Hill, 1976.

Vroom, Hendrik. *No Other Gods: Christian Belief in Dialogue with Buddhism, Hinduism, and Islam.* Trans. Lucy Jansen. Grand Rapids, Mich.: William B. Eerdmans, 1996.

Warner, Nicholas O. *Spirits of America: Intoxication in Nineteenth-Century American Literature.* Norman: University of Oklahoma Press, 1997.

Warren, Henry Clarke, comp. and trans. *Buddhism in Translation.* New York: Atheneum, 1982.

Watson, Steve. *The Birth of the Beat Generation: Visionaries, Rebels, and Hipsters, 1944–1960.* New York: Pantheon Books, 1995.

Watts, Alan W. "Beat Zen, Square Zen, and Zen." *Chicago Review* 12.2 (summer 1958): 3–11.

———. *The Spirit of Zen: A Way of Life, Work, and Art in the Far East.* New York: Grove Weidenfeld, 1958.

———. *This Is It, and Other Essays on Zen and Spiritual Experience.* New York: Pantheon Books, 1960.

Weinreich, Regina. *The Spontaneous Poetics of Jack Kerouac: A Study of the Fiction.* Carbondale: Southern Illinois University Press, 1987.

What Happened to Kerouac? Directed by Richard Lerner and Lewis McAdams. 96 min. Vidmark Entertainment, 1985. Videorecording.

Wolfe, Thomas. *Look Homeward, Angel, a Story of the Buried Life.* New York: C. Scribner's Sons, 1929.

———. *Of Time and the River, a Legend of Man's Hunger in His Youth.* New York: C. Scribner's Sons, 1935.

———. *You Can't Go Home Again.* New York: Harper and Brothers, 1940.

Wolfe, Tom. *The Electric Kool-Aid Acid Test.* New York: Bantam Books, 1968.

Index

"Account of My Hut, An" (Chomei), 136
"Aftermath: The Philosophy of the Beat Generation" (Kerouac), 178
alcohol: in *Big Sur,* xii, 181–82, 189, 190; death from, 179–80, 198–202, 205, 207–8; despair and, 167, 175–76, 179–80, 187–88, 204; Holmes on, 228n. 9, 229n. 15; renunciation of, xvii, 75, 80, 81; spirituality and, xviii, 74, 80, 177, 200; in *The Subterraneans,* 74, 75, 78. *See also* drugs
Amburn, Ellis, 101
America: literature in, 227n. 9; lost souls in, 6–7, 47–48, 52; materialism in, 8, 137–39, 185–86; visions of, 41, 42, 132, 190
asceticism: hedonism *vs.,* xvii, 21, 80, 92, 201; renunciation and, 8, 92–93, 94, 136, 169. *See also* attachment; solitude
attachment: Buddhism and, 92–94, 136, 158, 164; enlightened, 158–59, 164, 173; to mind, 153, 154; to mother, 171; to sensation, 154–55, 167; to sexuality, 101, 102–3, 106–7, 108, 135; suffering and, 89–90, 111, 120, 127, 178. *See also* asceticism; ego; suffering
Augustine, Saint: on original sin, 54, 177, 195, 204, 207; on suffering, 170

Baillet, Raymond (*Satori in Paris*), 203
Bakkhai, The (Euripides), 76, 82
Balzac, Honoré de, 92, 166, 206
Bartlett, Lee, 213n. 11
Baso, George (*Big Sur*), 190
Baudelaire, Charles-Pierre, 81
Beal, Samuel, 87

beat culture: clique of, 27, 169; conceptual roots of, 33, 196–97; generation gap and, 8–10, 215n. 2 (chap. 1); Kerouac's disavowals of, 70–71, 204, 206–7; Kerouac's fame and, xviii, 176, 179–81, 187–88; in literature, 19–20, 22–23, 70–71, 132; rise of, 170, 208; spirituality and, 137–38, 179, 181, 213n. 10, 224n. 12; suffering and, 80; sympathy in, xiii, 209–10, 216n. 3; in urban America, 69, 160, 165, 186, 203
Beckett, Samuel, 160
"Benzedrine Vision—Mexico Thieves Market—Memoirs of a Bebopper" (Kerouac), 99, 100
Berlin, Isaiah, 98
Bible: John in, 112, 129, 221n. 6; power of God in, xv; Revelation, 61, 64, 65, 66, 68, 129; suffering and, 13–14, 140, 141, 204
Big Sur (Kerouac), 176–95, 196, 201, 204, 226n. 8 (chap. 10); alcohol in, 199–200; brook imagery in, xi, 210; Buddhism in, 180, 191, 193, 194; Christianity in, 180, 182, 192–93, 195, 198; sadness in, xii–xiii, 178, 181–82, 184, 189; sexuality in, 187, 188–90, 192, 193, 194
Billie (*Big Sur*), 188–90, 191, 192, 194
Blackburn, William, 224n. 11
Blake, Ron (*Big Sur*), 187–88
Blake, William, 92, 213n. 8
bodhisattva: detachment and, 154, 225n. 7; Kerouac's desire to be, xvii, xviii, 94, 223–24n. 6; stages of, 142, 144, 145, 151, 169, 219n. 2
bohemian. *See* beat culture

BEN GIAMO was born in Cleveland, Ohio, and attended Baldwin-Wallace College, the New School for Social Research, and Emory University. He is an associate professor and the chair of the Department of American Studies at the University of Notre Dame. His books include *On the Bowery: Confronting Homelessness in American Society* and *The Homeless of* Ironweed: *Blossoms on the Crag.*